BALLOTS, BULLETS, AND BARGAINS

AMERICAN FOREIGN POLICY AND PRESIDENTIAL ELECTIONS

MICHAEL H. ARMACOST

COLUMBIA UNIVERSITY PRESS NEW YORK

COLUMBIA UNIVERSITY PRESS

PUBLISHERS SINCE 1893

NEW YORK   CHICHESTER, WEST SUSSEX

cup.columbia.edu

Library of Congress Cataloging-in-Publication Data

Armacost, Michael H.

 Ballots, bullets, and bargains : American foreign policy and presidential elections / Michael H. Armacost.

      pages   cm

 Includes bibliographical references and index.

 ISBN 978-0-231-16992-9 (cloth : alk. paper)

 ISBN 978-0-231-53913-5 (e-book)

 1. Presidents—United States—Election—History.   2. United States—Foreign relations—1945–1989.   3. United States—Foreign relations—1989–   I. Title.

 E183.A68 2015

 324.973—dc23   2014049266

Columbia University Press books are printed on permanent and durable acid-free paper.

This book is printed on paper with recycled content.

Printed in the United States of America

c 10 9 8 7 6 5 4 3 2 1

COVER IMAGE: © ALEX MAJOLI/MAGNUM PHOTOS

COVER DESIGN: CHANG JAE LEE

CONTENTS

ACKNOWLEDGMENTS

I AM GRATEFUL TO MANY FOR THEIR HELP IN PREPARING THIS manuscript. A number of colleagues at Stanford University encouraged or indulged my commitment to work on this subject. They include Professor Gi-Wook Shin, director of the Walter H. Shorenstein Asia-Pacific Research Center; Daniel Sneider, associate director for research at the Asia-Pacific Research Center; Professor Dave Brady, deputy director of the Hoover Institution; Professor David Kennedy, emeritus professor of history; and Professor Coit Blacker, senior fellow and former director of the Freeman Spogli Institute for International Studies.

Longtime friend and Foreign Service colleague Don Keyser read much of the manuscript in draft and offered a host of helpful comments. Any errors that remain, are, of course, my responsibility alone.

I have also benefited from conversations on this subject with other colleagues, including Dr. Donald Emmerson, Dr. Thomas Fingar, and Professor Henry Rowen.

Debbie Warren and Irene Bryant have provided immeasurably valuable assistance in typing the manuscript and adapting it to the stylistic requirements of Columbia University Press.

I am deeply indebted to Anne Routon, senior editor, and Irene Pavitt, senior manuscript editor, both at Columbia University Press, and to copy editor Mary Sutherland. They professionally and cheerfully guided me through the publication process.

Last but surely not least, I am grateful for the patience and encouragement of my loving wife, Bonny, to whom the book is dedicated.

BALLOTS, BULLETS, AND BARGAINS

INTRODUCTION

FOREIGN POLICY PERIODICALLY EXERTS A DECISIVE INFLUENCE ON presidential elections in the United States. Conversely, our presidential election system—that is, the process through which we select party nominees, choose among them in a general election, and manage a transition for the victor from the rigors of a campaign to the practicalities of governance—exercises a substantial influence on the conduct and content of American foreign policy. The interplay between our election system and the substance of foreign policy is the subject of this book.

In one respect, of course, the assertion that our presidential election system influences foreign policy merely affirms the obvious. Presidents are ultimately responsible for making foreign policy; hence elections, which determine who will occupy the Oval Office, fundamentally shape the policies that the United States pursues beyond its shores.

But the process through which we select our presidents exerts its own impact on policy. So does the manner in which our Constitution and political traditions inform the way victorious candidates get their administrations up and running. This is intuitively evident to foreign policy professionals every time a presidential election looms.

During my twenty-four years in government, I served in the State Department, Defense Department, National Security Council staff, and American embassies in Manila and Tokyo. During that time, I witnessed six presidential sweepstakes. It was always clear when an election loomed. Foreign policy issues that appealed to powerful domestic constituencies moved up on the agenda. Negotiations requiring distasteful accommodations with foreigners tended to get kicked down the road. If the United States was involved in armed conflict, presidents sought more urgently to find a formula for winning or settling. Defense budgets usually soared. Major exporters of manufactured goods and services enjoyed easier access to subsidies or protection from foreign competitors. Politically powerful ethnic groups—whether Jews, African Americans, Hispanics, Taiwanese, Greeks, Cubans, Armenians, or others—attracted special attention. The White House search for diplomatic successes intensified. So did the "spinning" to rationalize foreign policy setbacks or obfuscate failures.

There is nothing particularly surprising about this. Politics does not invariably trump strategy during presidential election campaigns. But elections place foreign policy choices in a context in which their domestic political consequences acquire greater weight. In that sense, foreign policy is an extension of domestic politics.

I share with many foreign policy professionals a certain disquiet about some of the effects of our electoral system on policy—for example, the simplification of complex diplomatic issues into bumper-sticker-size campaign slogans, the enhanced influence of political advisers more concerned with the appeal of foreign policy initiatives at home than their efficacy abroad, and the prolonged "time outs" or lulls that campaigns generally impose on the conduct of diplomacy.

Yet, throughout my career in government, I generally welcomed elections as action-forcing events—occasions that could have a salutary effect on our foreign policy. After all, they bring fresh blood and new ideas into the policy-making circuit. They may persuade an incumbent belatedly to tackle with urgency some issues that have been long neglected. When the country is on the wrong track, elections encourage and facilitate course corrections. When the gap between foreign policy aims and the resources devoted to their achievement becomes too wide, elections may spur efforts to find a more sustainable balance between ends and means. They can provide practical incentives to accelerate the implementation of promising projects and to wrap up or wind down policy endeavors that are costly yet ineffectual. In short, elections establish regular deadlines for revisiting campaign promises, assessing results, enforcing accountability, and selecting new management.

While serving overseas, I was reminded that our presidential elections unfold in a gigantic echo chamber. Candidates generally speak to domestic constituencies as if outsiders were not listening in. Rhetoric directed at American voters can have an unfortunate—even toxic—impact abroad as contenders pander to local prejudices, express disdain for foreign leaders, and volunteer gratuitous and often uncharitable judgments about the institutions and policies of particular foreign countries.

No country's elections are observed by foreigners with more attentiveness and nervousness than ours. For countries that enjoy the support of powerful voting blocs in the United States, our elections offer golden opportunities to entice new commitments or solicit new subventions from Washington. For adversaries like the Soviet Union during the Cold War, or Iran now, presidential campaigns provoke predictable expressions of animosity, muscular threats, and occasional hints of a readiness to talk. Commercial rivals like Japan in the 1980s and China today associate our campaigns with demands for fair trade, embroidered with threats of retaliatory measures. Other countries attract attention for local political reasons. For decades, Republican candidates growled at Fidel Castro to rally Cuban American voters in Florida; Democratic candidates snarled at Turkey to harvest Armenian American votes in California. And contenders from both parties made the obligatory campaign swing through Israel, Ireland, and Italy.

Our presidential election system is, to be sure, unique in many respects, particularly when compared with a parliamentary democracy like Great Britain's. In the Westminster-style system, the leader exercises considerable discretion in determining the timing of elections. Campaigns are normally limited by law to a relatively short duration. Candidates for the job of prime minister almost always possess substantial experience in the field of foreign policy due to lengthy tenure in the legislature, perhaps including ministerial service touching on external matters. Leaders of the Opposition have generally served in "shadow cabinets" and, in the course of those duties, learned to articulate or defend the party's approach to national security issues. Policy discontinuities are constrained even when party control of the legislature changes hands due to sharp limits to patronage in the foreign policy bureaucracy. Transitions from one party's control to another's take place normally in a matter of hours or days.

All these features of Britain's parliamentary system are in sharp contrast with American practices. Our presidents have fixed terms, which are limited in duration and number. They frequently enter the Oval Office with scant experience in national government, let alone foreign policy. Presidential campaigns are extremely long, inordinately expensive, and physically grueling. They demand that the candidates first court a major party to secure its endorsement and nomination, and then cultivate a diverse electorate in a federal system to win the highest office. The requirements of successful campaigning are only tangentially related to the demands of governance. The popular vote may not be decisive, but the verdict of the Electoral College is. Election Day is separated from the inauguration of the winner by a transitional period of ten weeks. And the start of a new administration is accompanied by the replacement of virtually the entire upper echelon of senior policy makers in the executive branch.

These attributes of our presidential election system inevitably have policy consequences both for Americans and for those beyond our legal jurisdiction and territorial domain. The latter may regard the results of a particular election with relief, resignation, or disquiet. They rarely exhibit indifference toward the outcome. Little wonder; the uncertainties can be unsettling. Former Pakistani president Zia al Haq put the matter succinctly and poignantly: "Being a friend of the United States is like living on the banks of a great river; the soil is wonderfully fertile, but every four or eight years, the river, flooded by storms that are too far away to be seen, changes its course, and you are left in a desert all alone."[1]

At home, this system imposes a certain trajectory on the experience of many presidencies. Former National Security Adviser Zbigniew Brzezinski captured its essence in his memoir.[2] A new administration, he wrote, "tends to expend an enormous amount of energy coping with the unintended, untoward consequences of its initial, sometimes excessive, impulses to innovate, to redeem promises, and to harbor illusions. In time, preconceptions give way to reality, disjointedness to intellectual coherence, and vision to pragmatism. But by the time that happens, the presidential cycle is usually coming to an end." With an air of resignation, he concluded that "the four-year election process has a pernicious influence on foreign policy," but he "doubted that much could be done to eliminate or alter the structural handicap."[3] The effects of this cycle are only somewhat mitigated by the fact that most presidents get two terms in office. In my experience, Brzezinski's commentary proved to be an apt characterization of the learning curve of many, though not all, administrations.

In the end, of course, we live with the policy consequences of our system. We celebrate our democracy despite its shortcomings because no other system could so consistently safeguard our freedom. But it is important to recognize the potential effects that each feature of our election system—the struggle for the nomination, the general election campaign, the transition period between Election Day and the inauguration of the victor, and the start-up phase of a new administration—may have on the substance of foreign policy, above all because suggestions for adjusting or reforming that system regularly surface.

When I left the Brookings Institution to return to teaching in 2002, I surveyed available books and articles that examined the relationship among presidential elections, politics, and the conduct of foreign policy. I concluded that the subject had attracted less systematic study than it deserved.

There are indeed many thoughtful studies of one or another facet of the subject. Among the books that touch on the subject, I found a number that are particularly informative. Kenneth Waltz's *Foreign Policy and Democratic Politics: The American and British Experience* is a durable and detailed comparative study of the relative virtues of British and American institutional capabilities for making foreign policy.[4] William Quandt's *Camp David: Peacemaking and Politics* offers a thoughtful reminder that a president determined to tackle highly complex and controversial foreign policy challenges may best concentrate his efforts on the second and third years of his first term, since the first and fourth will be heavily preoccupied with getting a new administration up and running, and mounting a bid for reelection.[5]

Difficult Transitions: Foreign Policy Troubles at the Outset of Presidential Power by Kurt Campbell and James Steinberg provides a wealth of practical guidance to newly elected presidents for managing the shift from campaigning to governance.[6] And among the many volumes offering incoming presidents advice on how best to exercise their influence over the policymaking process, Richard Neustadt's *Presidential Power: The Politics of Leadership* still stands out, not least because John F. Kennedy regarded it so highly and took its admonitions so seriously.[7]

Beyond this, academic research on political campaigns is rich and extensive. Journalistic accounts of them are numerous, and some are provoc-
ative. The memoirs of presidents and their principal foreign policy and
political advisers are abundant, and many are candidly revealing. And the
interplay between elections and foreign policy is a subject of endless fasci-
nation to pundits and commentators. These are the materials on which I
have drawn.

The arc of the analysis follows the sequence of the electoral process. As a
point of departure, chapter 1 offers a brief primer on the U.S. presidential
election system—its constitutionally defined rules, its informal customs and
conventions, and the party competition that provides its political infrastructure and helps inform its results.

Chapter 2 investigates the ways in which struggles for the nomination
influences policy by pushing candidates initially to the right or left, respectively, to court "party regulars." The results of this are most visible when
incumbent presidents are challenged by members of their own party. It
also looks at the casual manner in which vice presidential nominees are
chosen.

Chapter 3 examines general election campaigns, where the objective of
politics normally shifts to courting "swing voters" and "strays" from the
other party. It looks at the ways in which an election deadline may spur
White House incumbents actively to burnish their foreign policy legacy,
defer tough problems for later, or herald significant course adjustments. It
examines the methods by which incumbents can utilize foreign policy instruments for electoral advantage. It asks how the diversions of a lengthy
campaign can affect U.S. diplomacy for good or ill. It inquires into how the
political imperatives of a campaign may affect the management of international crises or shape the contours of negotiating tactics.

Chapter 4 focuses on the election campaigns of nonincumbent challengers, and how their case for change may shape either timely or imprudent
foreign policy commitments. It explores how campaigns may test that
challenger's foreign policy credentials or expose an incumbent's record to
critical scrutiny. It looks into how general election campaigns may provide
an opportunity to modify pledges made in quest of the party's nomination. It examines how, why, and with what consequences Democratic contenders often seek to "outflank" GOP rivals from the right on national

security, while Republican contenders often resort to "anything but . . ." tactics on foreign policy in their campaigns.

Chapter 5 looks at the peculiar foreign policy challenges of the transition period—that awkward interval between Election Day and Inauguration Day. In particular, this chapter examines the problems encountered by incumbents seeking to burnish their foreign policy record as the clock runs out on their tenure in office. And it looks into the incentives and disincentives for collaboration or competition over foreign policy issues between outgoing and incoming presidents.

Chapter 6 is devoted to the start-up phase of a new president's tenure. It asks why new incumbents so often experience diplomatic stumbles as they seek to manage the transition from campaigning to governing. It examines the insistent pressures on new presidents to get out of the blocks quickly, and the factors that complicate their effective launch of complicated, controversial initiatives abroad. And it explores why some presidents manage, despite all the usual obstacles, to get off to a smooth start in foreign policy.

The conclusion explores the virtues and the liabilities of our presidential electoral system for the conduct of statecraft. It also takes a look at proposals that have been offered to enhance its strengths and ameliorate its weaknesses.

These, then, are the issues this volume will explore. I have written this book essentially for students. When I left the Brookings Institution in 2002 to take up duties at the Shorenstein Asia Pacific Research Center at Stanford University, I realized that many young people—particularly the foreign students in my classes—were familiar with neither the details of our election system nor their impact on the content and conduct of our diplomacy. This volume represents my effort to provide an accessible explanation of both.

In the research undertaken for this book, I focused on those elections that have taken place since 1948. That includes virtually the entire period in which America has exercised global leadership. It not only embraces all the presidential elections I can personally remember but also provides a broad and representative set of cases to examine.

1 ELECTIONS, PARTIES, AND POLITICS

BEFORE ADDRESSING THE IMPACT OF THE AMERICAN PRESIDENTIAL election system on the conduct of foreign policy, it is necessary to review some of the central features of that system. Its fundamental contours, set by the Constitution, are stable and rarely change. But the customs and conventions of political life, and the party competition that drives our elections, are constantly in flux. Hence, this primer on where things stand in the wake of the 2012 election.

CONSTITUTIONAL RULES

Since passage of the Twelfth Amendment in 1804, candidates for president, along with their vice presidential selection, run on a single party ticket. They are the only political leaders whose electoral fate depends on a national constituency and who can legitimately claim a national political mandate. They may not be residents of the same state.[1]

We elect our presidents for a fixed term. Presidential elections are held on the first Tuesday in November every fourth year. No provision in the Constitution allows for holding a presidential election early, or for delaying it in the face of, say, a national or international crisis. Despite the bitter contention over the Florida outcome in the 2000 election, no do-over was possible because the election date is fixed by the Constitution. Hence, the courts addressed only whether and how to manage recounts.

Candidates for the presidency must be natural-born citizens. Thus California's Austrian-born former governor, Arnold Schwarzenegger, is ineligible, as are all naturalized citizens. But individuals born abroad may be eligible to become a candidate if at least one parent had met U.S. residency requirements.

None can be younger than thirty-five, a provision that is much less restrictive today than in the days of our Founding Fathers, when life expectancy was much shorter.

Since passage of the Twenty-second Amendment in 1951, no president is permitted to serve for more than two terms. If a vice president (or someone else in the established line of presidential succession) inherits the office as a result of the death, infirmity, resignation, or impeachment of an incumbent during the last two years of his term, he may run twice for reelection.

The outcome of U.S. elections is determined not by the popular vote but by a poll of electors selected by each state to cast ballots in the Electoral College. These state electors, whose number is equivalent to the total of each state's members of the Senate and House of Representatives plus three for the District of Columbia—538 in all—cast their ballots in accordance with a "winner-takes-all" standard in most states, and convey their votes to Washington, D.C.[2] They are counted on January 6 of the year following the election at 1:00 P.M. at a joint session of Congress. If the Electoral College vote does not yield a majority to any candidate, the House of Representatives chooses the president; each state casts but a single vote. The winner requires a majority of all states.

While presidential elections are held in early November, the president-elect is not inaugurated until January 20, leaving a ten-week interval in which the incumbent retains the formal prerogatives of the office, albeit with much diminished political influence, while the newly elected chief executive possesses a powerful mandate but performs no official duties.[3]

In the Constitution of the United States, the authority to make American foreign policy is distributed rather ambiguously between the executive and legislative branches. The distinguished scholar Edwin Corwin described this allocation of responsibilities between separate branches as "a standing invitation to struggle." Since the White House and Congress are frequently controlled by different parties, these institutional struggles betray at times a highly partisan character. Still, the branches are inherently unequal, for the president commands the troops, manages negotiations, and possesses the "bully pulpit."

These provisions, set by the Constitution, are difficult, though not impossible, to change. They provide the ground rules for our presidential electoral politics.

CHANGING POLITICAL CUSTOMS AND CONVENTIONS

The constitutional framework for presidential elections is supplemented by a host of political customs and conventions. Many of the rules that shape the nomination of presidential candidates are party rules. Moreover, the laws that regulate the management of presidential elections are for the most part state rather than federal laws. They have evolved over time, and the aggregate changes that have emerged since the first post–World War II election in 1948 have been quite dramatic.

The Constitution makes no reference to political parties, yet candidates for the presidency and vice presidency are by tradition selected by party conventions. While contests for the presidency are open to contenders from all parties, for more than one hundred years only those selected by either the Republicans or the Democrats have had any realistic chance of being elected.

Thus third-party candidates have been confined to the role of "spoilers." They occasionally exert a decisive influence on the outcome of a presidential election without having any chance of winning. John Anderson in 1980, Ross Perot in 1992, and Ralph Nader in 2000 were among recent third-party candidates who arguably exerted a consequential influence on the outcome. George Wallace was the only third-party candidate who managed to win any Electoral College votes, receiving a total of forty-six in the 1968 election.

Presidential candidates face a dual challenge. They must first secure the nomination of a major party. This demands a successful cultivation of the party's base—the key constituencies that faithfully provide it with energy, ideas, funds, and votes. Then, they must persuade at least a strong plurality of the general electorate to give them their vote. As Larry O'Brien, a former director of the Democratic National Committee (DNC), once noted, "While an aspiring candidate can be nominated as the leader of a faction, he cannot be elected unless [he] present[s himself] as the party's national leader."[4]

The time-tested formula for winning elections in the United States is consequently twofold: first, one must tend the base and mobilize party regulars to secure the nomination, and second, add enough independent swing votes plus "strays" from the other party to amass a majority in the Electoral College or, failing that, in the House of Representatives.

Party nominees for the presidency enjoy unusual power and discretion in the selection of their running mates.[5] Until the Franklin D. Roosevelt administration, selection of vice presidential nominees was left to the parties. According to the Twenty-fifth Amendment to the Constitution, passed in 1967, if a vice president dies or resigns, the president could appoint a successor, subject to approval by a majority of the House and the Senate. In 1973, Gerald Ford was the first vice president chosen in accordance with this provision.

Over the past sixty years, the vice presidency has become a powerful springboard into the Oval Office. Yet, there are no established arrangements for selecting a running mate, and in practice the decisions are essentially left to the presidential candidates after their nominations are locked up. To say that these procedures are casual would be an understatement. In 2008, Sarah Palin was not well known, even by John McCain when he selected her as his running mate.

In nominating candidates for the presidency, the influence of professional politicians (i.e., party leaders) has gradually diminished; the power of primary party voters has grown dramatically. State caucuses and conventions have given way to state primaries as the decisive means of selecting a candidate. Indeed, Hubert Humphrey was the last presidential contender chosen by prominent politicians at a party convention; in 1968, he became the Democratic nominee without having competed in a single primary or caucus.

Thereafter, the party leaders lost control, and the nomination process became more democratic and more chaotic. As Joe Klein observed, "Presidential politics was now a matter of self-promotion rather than smoke-filled selection by political experts."[6] Arguably, the growing power of "party regulars" in the selection of candidates increases the sensitivity of those candidates to the policy reflexes and ideological prejudices of the rank-and-file party activists. This tends to push Democratic candidates to the left, and Republicans to the right, at least until the struggle for the nomination is resolved. Mitt Romney's desperate effort to demonstrate his conservative credentials during the 2012 GOP primary season is but the most recent illustration of this phenomenon.

Many recall those earlier "smoke-filled rooms" with nostalgia. Now "candidates emerge based on their own judgment of their overwhelming talents and virtues, rather than those of their political peers."[7]

Campaigns have become progressively longer and more exhausting both for the candidates and the public. In the early post–World War II decades, the fight for the nomination essentially unfolded in the late winter and spring of an election year, while the general election commenced in earnest with the party conventions in midsummer and moved into high gear on Labor Day. Now, one campaign is scarcely over before presidential wannabes begin to test the waters for the next election. In 1947, political advisers urged Harry Truman to avoid partisan political activity until after the July 1948 convention on grounds that he was president of all the people, not merely the leader of a party. In 2011, President Obama headlined more than two hundred fund-raisers in the year before he sought reelection.

The primary calendar is in constant flux. Generally it has become more heavily "front-loaded," as states have sought to augment the influence of their voters over the selection of the party's nominee by scheduling primaries earlier. The primary season once kicked off in March and continued into June; it now commences in January. In 2004, John Kerry's nomination was essentially sealed by mid-March when a host of "Super Tuesday" primaries were held. In 2008, more than 100 million voters went to the polls for primaries scheduled on February 5. Yet, predictions to the contrary notwithstanding, neither Barack Obama nor Hillary Clinton delivered an early knock-out punch in 2008; they continued to slug it out in state primaries and caucuses until early June, even though Senator Obama had long since staked out what seemed an irreversible lead in "selected delegates."[8]

In 2012, the number of primaries held on Super Tuesday surprisingly dropped from twenty-four to nine. California moved its primary back from February to June, and New York from February to April, calculating that repositioning themselves in the primary queue would enhance the states' influence over the nomination. Washington State decided to forgo a primary altogether in order to save funds.

A campaign for the presidency has become a grueling test of endurance. Seemingly endless campaigning tries the resilience of the candidates and the patience of voters. The prospect of relentless public scrutiny and scurrilous political attacks may discourage potential candidates, even those with estimable records of public service, from seriously contemplating a run for the presidency. As Daniel Henninger has noted, "Any flaw or past stumble is metastasized into a public nightmare for spouses and children."[9]

But the demands of a lengthy and arduous campaign also expose the candidates to the diversity of the nation's voters, the full range of public concerns, and the constant pressure of the media. This provides a stern and visible measure of the candidates' competence and character as well as their physical stamina. It permits strong candidates to recover from early miscues, and it wears down contenders with less staying power.

Despite efforts to regulate election expenditures, they continue to rise exponentially as campaigns grow longer and rely more heavily on media advertising and sophisticated "get out the vote" drives. The total amount spent on behalf of the two major party tickets in 1948 has been estimated at somewhere between $25 million and $30 million.[10] Until 1972, there were no serious limits in place on the money presidential candidates could raise and spend. The 1970s saw a rash of new laws to regulate such expenditures. The amount that individuals could contribute to a candidate was limited. Voluntary public financing of presidential nomination and general election campaigns was introduced, and public disclosure of contributions thus increased. The cost of campaigns grew, but only modestly, from 1976 to 1996.

Since then, costs have skyrocketed. Spending by both parties for the 1996 election exceeded $448 million. It reached $1 billion in 2004 and surpassed $2 billion in 2012. Much of this money is now raised through Political Action Committees (PACs), whose donors are not publicly revealed. And public funds for campaigns have been recently spurned by candidates eager to escape spending limits.

Fund-raising imperatives imposed by the high cost of television advertising and sophisticated get-out-the-vote schemes do not inhibit candidates of modest means from seeking the presidency. Harry Truman, Dwight Eisenhower, Lyndon Johnson, Richard Nixon, Bill Clinton, and Barack Obama all came from families of modest means. Nonetheless, they surely enhance the influence of "special interests," augment the power of money within each of the major parties, and increase the burden of fund-raising on the candidates.

Campaigns have also become a lot less personal and much more professionalized. In 1948, Harry Truman and Thomas Dewey barnstormed around the country, accompanied by a small coterie of friends and political advisers. They spoke directly to voters from the backs of their trains. When Barack Obama and Mitt Romney dashed hither and yon across the country raising funds and "pressing the flesh" in 2012, most of the events were carefully choreographed, and the scope for spontaneous exchanges was limited.

They communicated with voters primarily through the national media. They were trailed by gaggles of consultants, pollsters, fund-raisers, and spinmeisters, whose connections to them were more professional than personal. Marketing and branding have become more and more critical, and elections have become contests in packaging and advertising. Politics has been substantially drained of spontaneity. And many campaign advisers are now essentially free agents, full of calculated enthusiasm but lacking in principled conviction.

Party conventions no longer select the nominees; they showcase the candidates who prevailed in the primaries and caucuses. With the drama and relevance of the conventions much diminished, they claim less time from the television networks and have been reduced essentially to highly scripted "infomercials" designed to connect the nominees to the electorate and kick off the fall campaign.

Campaigns have also become more focused. Candidates once regularly promised to make an appearance in all fifty states. Now the number of swing states in which the major party candidates seriously compete has dramatically declined. Those that remain—a dozen or so—get the lion's share of the candidates' attention and advertising budgets.

The length and strenuousness of campaigns means that presidential contenders now come to office having spent the bulk of their time for several years with people better equipped to get them elected than to help them govern. The transition from campaigning to governing—most particularly in the field of foreign policy—is consequently fraught with greater uncertainties. As campaigns have become more prolonged and professionalized, they may indeed contaminate the process of governance itself, by bringing with it a focus on short-term opinion polling rather than a concern for longer-term policy results.

Voter turnout in presidential elections, which over the past half century exceeded 60 percent only four times (from 1956 through 1968), consistently declined in the late twentieth century but has picked up since 2004. Arguably, this has further reinforced the role of party regulars at the expense of

the general electorate—a significant proportion of whom continue to identify themselves as "independents."

Perhaps, as some political scientists maintain, low voter turnout is a signal that the electorate is generally content. In that case, the fact that voting
rates have increased in the last couple of elections may reflect a higher level
of anxiety within the electorate. In each of the last three elections, the
winner amassed a modest, though clear, majority. The 2008 results also
produced the first black president, the first Roman Catholic vice president,
and the first presidential contest between two sitting senators in many
generations.

Since 1976, major party candidates have with increasing frequency
run for the presidency as self-proclaimed outsiders, promising, as ever, to
"clean up the mess in Washington." In such campaigns, longtime Washington "hands" tend to be given shorter shrift, and the hardy band of close
advisers that subsequently accompany the winners to the White House
include fewer people with substantial foreign policy experience.

In this context, it should be no surprise that four of our last six presidents—
Jimmy Carter, Ronald Reagan, Bill Clinton, and George W. Bush—came
from the ranks of governors. They were largely bereft of experience in government service at the federal level. This by no means consigned them to
certain failure in the White House. To the contrary. But it did mean that
early in their tenure, each had a steep learning curve in the field of diplomacy and national security policy.

The results of the 2008 election notwithstanding, sitting senators have
proven generally to be less successful candidates for the presidency. Prior
to Barack Obama, only two managed to get elected during the previous one
hundred years—Warren Harding and John F. Kennedy. Perhaps this was
because senators were perceived as lacking executive experience, and found
it difficult to explain and defend to increasingly partisan constituencies the
compromises that inevitably dotted their voting records.

Senator Ted Kennedy urged Barack Obama to throw his hat in the ring
in 2008 rather than waiting to accumulate wider political experience. "The
votes you're going to have to cast," he told Obama, "whether it's guns or
whether it's abortions, or whether it's any one of the hot-button items, fin-
ishes you as a national political leader in this country."[11] Senator Harry Reid
also saw Obama's inexperience in the Senate as an electoral asset, for it allowed him "to cast himself as a figure uncorrupted and unco-opted by Evil

Washington, without the burdens of countless Senate votes and floor speeches."[12]

Presidential politics has become more polarized and policy differences between the candidates, including overseas issues, have multiplied and intensified. There are a variety of reasons for this.

- Ideological differences *within* the major parties have sharply diminished as the voters over several decades sorted themselves out geographically.[13] Meanwhile, policy differences *between* the parties have intensified. The so-called red states (Republican) have gotten redder, and the blue states (Democratic) have gotten bluer. According to exit polls in 2012, President Obama won the votes of only 6 percent of Republicans; Romney earned the votes of only 7 percent of Democrats. The number of swing states—in which there were closely contested presidential races— were down to nine; in 1960 there were twenty. As Gerald Seib observed, "Democrats are talking to Democrats, and Republicans are talking to Republicans, but fewer people [are] trying to talk to one another across [the] partisan divide."[14]

- Since the 1970s, activist special interest groups have proliferated. They have their own policy agendas, which they pursue relentlessly with large stashes of cash. Some have accumulated formidable power on foreign policy initiatives of concern to their clients. Most have clearly identifiable affiliations with one major party or another. And this tends to reinforce other sources of political polarization.

- The news media exacerbate these tendencies. The Old Media— network news, the major metropolitan daily newspapers, national news magazines—encouraged moderation, restraint, and a sense of decorum in normal debates over policy. They are being supplanted by New Media—radio talk shows; cable television; and social media sites like Twitter, YouTube, Facebook, and the "blogosphere." The last make little effort to conceal their partisan loyalties and often manifest contempt for their political opponents.[15] The New Media also blur the lines between news and entertainment, while amplifying the differences between parties and candidates, reducing the civility of political discourse, and accelerating the news cycle.

- New technologies altered the dynamics of the 2012 campaign. Barack Obama accumulated 33 million fans on Facebook. Between them, they were "friends" with 98 percent of the total Facebook population in the United

States. This provided the president's campaign a capacity to reach most eligible voters swiftly and efficiently. Four years earlier in the 2008 election cycle, neither Facebook, nor Twitter, nor *Politico*, nor the iPhone was a significant factor in the campaign. Even now, these technologies are utilized mainly in the service of somewhat traditional goals like organizing grassroots neighborhoods and getting out the vote. But the impact is increasingly dramatic.

• As divisions within the electorate became increasingly sharp and voters seemingly sorted themselves into red and blue states, in 2000, 2004, and 2012 the major parties concentrated more on mobilizing their base, than moving toward the center during general election campaigns. But Karl Rove, the architect of George W. Bush's campaigns in 2000 and 2004, indulged no illusions that either party could win simply by mobilizing their base. "It isn't big enough," he noted, "and what one does to mobilize them may alienate other voters one needs." The test of electoral arithmetic, he emphasized, is this: "Can you realistically hope to win by cobbling together a coalition of nearly predictable hard-core partisans; some newly energized supporters; a reasonable number of swing voters; modest defections from the opposition party; and some newly registered voters? If so, where are these people and what will it take to get them to cast a vote for your candidates? And if one slice of this group can't be reached, how do you make up the difference?"[16] In 2008 and 2012, Barack Obama's team proved to be more skillful than John McCain's and Mitt Romney's in finding answers to those queries.

Election outcomes appear to have been getting closer; strong mandates, more elusive. To be sure, there have been occasional landslide elections. Dwight Eisenhower managed to win two, as did Ronald Reagan. Lyndon Johnson and Richard Nixon secured one each. But it has been more than thirty years since the last one. In four of the last six elections, the winner did not even attract a majority of the votes, and in 2000 the winner in the Electoral College lost the popular vote.

The Constitution says very little about transitions. At one point, they consisted of little more than handing over the keys to the White House. As recently as 1952, the transition was managed largely through communications between two men—Clark Clifford, representing President Truman, and General Wilfred Perkins, representing President-elect Dwight Eisenhower. They had no staff, no budget, and no formal process to support their activities. To the extent that money was required, it was obtained from leftover campaign funds or private donations. Over the years, the process has become much more institutionalized and a lot more expensive.

Some transitions work more or less seamlessly; some don't. Congressional statutes now provide for public funds to be used to facilitate orderly transitions. But otherwise, custom largely prevails. Some collaboration between the incumbent and his successor is essential (e.g., in providing briefing materials and help in expediting security clearances for potential appointees). But the interests of outgoing and incoming presidents do not necessarily converge, and when party control of the White House changes hands, transitions are uncertain and not infrequently unruly affairs.

The United States is virtually the only major country that essentially sweeps out several senior layers of policy makers every time a new administration takes office. Under our spoils system, which sanctions the practice of rewarding campaign workers and financial supporters with senior positions in the executive branch, all new administrations are staffed with substantial numbers of political appointees with limited knowledge and operational experience encumbering positions of potential importance to national security.

A new president is responsible for filling positions down to the fifth layer of the bureaucracy. Officials in four of these layers—secretaries, deputy secretaries, undersecretaries, and assistant secretaries—require Senate confirmation, a process that has become increasingly contentious and time-consuming. Thus identifying, appointing, and assembling a competent and more or less unified national security "team" is no simple matter, and it takes more and more time. This complicates the early months of every new administration and arguably increases the risk of early foreign policy miscues.

In the course of my twenty-four years in the Foreign Service, I was confirmed by the Senate three times. On each occasion, the confirmation process became more prolonged, more intrusive, less confidential, and a lot less fun. When I was nominated to serve as the U.S. ambassador to Japan in 1989, a junior senator put a hold on my nomination for several weeks. The maneuver had little, if anything, to do with me; he was merely using the nomination as a bargaining chip to secure an executive-branch appointment for a member of his own staff.

Thus getting elected president now takes longer, costs more, requires the assistance of a large retinue of specialists, invites candidates to run for the

White House as "outsiders," and only rarely yields landslide victories or clear political mandates. All these features of our campaigns naturally have their effects on the way the parties position themselves for presidential contests, on the methods incumbents use in conducting their campaigns, and the manner in which victors approach their foreign policy responsibilities once they are safely ensconced in the White House.

A further word about the political parties is necessary, for they provide the infrastructure of the American political system. The management of our presidential elections would be unimaginable without them.

PARTY COMPETITION FOR THE WHITE HOUSE

In our presidential elections, the parties select the nominees, provide the campaign workers, solicit for funds, and define, articulate, and reflect the philosophic differences that give shape to campaigns. The two major parties—the Democrats and Republicans—possess distinctive sets of foreign policy reflexes, which shape the conduct of those who emerge triumphant in our presidential sweepstakes. To be sure, any attempt to characterize the policy DNA of the major parties requires acknowledgment of several caveats.

Both the Democratic and Republican parties remain large, relatively fluid coalitions. They provide "big tents" under which a variety of constituencies huddle. Neither party is marked by "group think," and divergent foreign policy "camps" exist in both. But dominant tendencies are discernible. And these are buttressed by the growing ideological, cultural, and geographic cohesion that each coalition has acquired in recent decades.

Within the contemporary Republican Party, moderate realists, neoconservatives, and neoisolationists are all alive and well. The end of the Cold War and the shift in the GOP's base to the South and West particularly energized the neoconservative, populist/nationalist, and quasi-isolationist elements of the party. A few years back, Henry Kissinger even noted wistfully that the term "realist" was becoming a derogatory label among a number of Republicans.

In the scramble for the 2012 GOP nomination, Ron Paul was the most prominent proponent of a semi-isolationist approach to foreign policy. Rick Santorum expressed the populist nationalism of the Tea Party movement, exhibiting little tolerance for multilateral organizations and reflecting what James Kitfield described as a "don't tread on me" pugnacity.[17] Newt

Gingrich embraced a neoconservative agenda—disdain for talking with autocratic adversaries, scorn for the United Nations, assiduous support for Israel, and an instinctive reliance on U.S. military strength to promote American values abroad. Jon Huntsman articulated a moderate realism recalling the foreign policy tenets of George H. W. Bush.

Mitt Romney's views on foreign policy remained somewhat obscure and ambivalent throughout the 2012 campaign. He clearly expected domestic issues to be decisive; he picked Paul Ryan, a House expert on the budget, as his vice presidential nominee; and he failed to differentiate his foreign policy priorities clearly from those of President Obama during their debate on foreign policy.

Within the Democratic Party, the main ideological tension is between liberal internationalists and pacifist anti-imperialists. Among them one finds, as in the GOP, alternating patterns of coexistence and animosity. The latter camp—the antiwar wing of the party—is robust, pugnacious, outspoken, formidable at fund-raising, and influential with the elite press. It tends to exercise its greatest influence during the primary season, particularly when the United States is involved in unpopular foreign conflicts.

Mindful of the party's reputation for "softness" on national security issues, Democratic presidential candidates are generally careful to position themselves as "tough" defenders of national interests, especially during general election campaigns. Consistent with these electoral necessities, in his 2008 campaign Barack Obama highlighted principled opposition to the Iraq invasion during the primaries: a readiness to increase troop levels to Afghanistan and authorize drone attacks against terrorist camps in Pakistan during the general election campaign. By 2012, a successful covert operation to kill Osama bin Laden; extensive use of drones to combat al-Qaeda in Yemen, Somalia, and West Africa; and a widely advertised "pivot" to Asia positioned him favorably with the voters on national security issues.

Each of the major parties is, of course, constantly evolving. Each has experienced wrenching transformations in recent decades. The Democrats, the dominant party from the early 1930s to the late 1960s, charted the course for America's postwar foreign policy. The so-called liberal anti-totalitarianism that marked the ideology of Harry Truman, Jack Kennedy, and Lyndon Johnson opposed tyranny from both the Left and the Right. These liberal internationalist presidents spawned the Truman Doctrine, the Marshall Plan, NATO, the Bretton Woods financial institutions, the

Point Four Program, the General Agreement on Tariffs and Trade (GATT), the Alliance for Progress, and the Peace Corps. Without embarrassment and with only modest intraparty opposition, they pursued a favorable balance of power; collected allies in Europe, Asia, and the Middle East; and used force when they felt it necessary.[18]

The tough-minded Democratic foreign policy tradition fractured over the Vietnam War and transformed liberalism "from an aggressive anti-communist, internationalist movement into a more pacifist, anti-imperialist, neo-isolationist cause."[19] George McGovern united the Left behind opposition to the Vietnam War in 1972, but in the process he suffered a crushing electoral defeat, hastened the defection of neoconservatives and blue collar "Reagan Democrats" to the GOP, and turned the party's national security reputation into damaged goods.

Meanwhile, the erosion of productivity and stagnation of wages in the 1970s and 1980s encouraged the out-migration of people from Democratic Party strongholds in the Rust Belt, and reinforced the disposition of the labor unions toward a protectionist trade policy. It is noteworthy that until 2008, the Democrats who occupied the White House after 1964 were all southerners—Lyndon Johnson, Jimmy Carter, and Bill Clinton—who consciously distanced themselves from the party's left wing.

With the end of the Cold War, Bill Clinton sought to find a new foreign policy synthesis, which emphasized a readiness to use American power in the service of American values. Humanitarian interventions in Somalia, Haiti, Bosnia, and Kosovo were its most striking expressions.

Meanwhile, the GOP, a distinct minority party in the early post–World War II decades, experienced a different yet parallel transformation. "Taft Republicans," the party's dominant faction in the 1940s, favored laissez-faire economics at home and isolationism abroad. But these were discredited by depression and war. From 1940 until 1960, the GOP's eastern establishment controlled presidential nominations, elected governors in the biggest states, controlled the major media outlets, and through respected public figures like Senator Arthur Vandenberg and John Foster Dulles, facilitated bipartisan support for many Democratic foreign policy initiatives. Thus during the 1940s and 1950s, conservatism was in recess even within Republican ranks.

In the 1960s, liberal anti-totalitarianism and its domestic analogue, the New Deal and Great Society, provoked a backlash among conservatives who regained grassroots control of the GOP party machinery. Barry Goldwater,

Friedrik von Hayek, Milton Friedman, and William Buckley redefined the GOP's ideology, while Ronald Reagan captured its heart and galvanized new grassroots support in the South, West, and Rocky Mountain states.

But radicalization of some of the Democratic Party's leadership during that turbulent decade offended many of that party's working-class voters. And its sponsorship of far-reaching civil rights legislation alienated its southern base. The GOP subsequently drew even with the Democrats in its number of registered voters. After 1968, it controlled the White House for twenty-eight of the next forty years and consistently employed national security issues in election campaigns the way the Democrats had traditionally used the Depression and Social Security against the GOP. By 2008, however, long, costly, and inconclusive nation-building ventures in Iraq and Afghanistan had deeply tarnished the GOP foreign policy brand.

The changing outlook of both parties on foreign as well as domestic policy reflects, in turn, powerful demographic changes in America. The relentless movement of people from the Eastern Seaboard and Upper Midwest to the South and West underpinned the growth of conservative strength in the GOP. It produced a new breed of libertarians, who wanted less government and more freedom, and a new breed of "social conservatives"—evangelical Christians who wanted to enlist the federal government in "doing the Lord's work" (e.g., abolishing abortion at home and stamping out religious persecution and promoting democracy abroad).

Dominant in the red states, the GOP's core constituencies fall inside what Ron Brownstein has described as "the picket fence"—a party of tradition honoring "marriage, kids, Sunday morning in the pews." Their voters are primarily located in rural, suburban, or exurban communities composed of small businessmen, farmers, and Protestant evangelicals.[20] The party's geographic base in the South, the border states, and the Rocky Mountains area is reflected in its strong support for the military, its occasionally jingoistic rhetoric, and its heightened sensitivity to the views of churchgoing Christians.

Meanwhile, the Democrats have flourished particularly in the Northeast, the West Coast, and parts of the old Midwest Rust Belt. They have become a party of urban dwellers, union members, professionals, academics, and those comfortable with racial and cultural diversity. The principal Democratic constituencies tend to cluster in metropolitan centers and reflect a more secular outlook. The blue-state Democrats retain a richer set of intellectual links to Europe; stronger emotional bonds with Africa, Latin America, and Asia; and greater doubts about the benefits of free trade than their GOP counterparts.

Since 1948, the Democrats have prevailed in eight presidential contests, the Republicans in nine. From the 1940s through the 1960s, it appeared that the GOP could win only when their standard bearer was a national hero like Dwight Eisenhower, or when the Democrats messed up on foreign policy in a major-league way (e.g., in Korea and Indochina). Between the Vietnam War, which left the Democrats hopelessly divided, and 2008, they appeared capable of winning presidential elections only when foreign policy concerns receded, as they did in the mid-1970s after the Watergate scandal and the defeat in Vietnam, and again in the early 1990s when the Cold War ended and the Soviet Union disintegrated.

The shifting fortunes of the major parties has both reflected and shaped the contours of American diplomacy and the public debate about it. The intensity of partisanship on foreign policy issues has waxed and waned. From 1948 until 1968, Democrats and Republicans embraced a broad consensus that the Cold War was the nation's overriding external challenge, and containment was the appropriate strategy for combating it. The Vietnam War shattered that consensus, and partisanship increased during the Carter and Reagan presidencies. With the end of the Cold War, it receded temporarily but returned with a vengeance when the Iraq War turned sour.

In their persistent political competition, each party reveals a set of recurring policy reflexes that characterize their philosophic attitudes as well as their operational instincts for conducting foreign policy. These general inclinations are more distinctive among committed party regulars than more casual voters.

Until recently, Democrats appeared more comfortable when domestic issues enjoyed priority. They at times have regarded foreign policy as a distraction, diverting attention away from "their" issues and draining resources away from "their" spending priorities at home. Republicans, by contrast, were more disposed until the 2012 campaign, to nationalize elections in order to play the national security card, which they had long considered "their" strong suit.

Democrats and Republicans have a somewhat different take on the linkage between foreign and domestic policy. Democrats persistently pursue "renewal at home in the service of freedom abroad."[21] They tend to argue that America's standing in the community of nations requires us to be an exemplar of rectitude and justice in our domestic arrangements. Republicans are more likely to tailor foreign policy priorities to their hopes for lower taxes and diminished regulation at home, the promotion of entrepreneurial capitalism abroad, and the projection of U.S. power around the world.

Republicans are inclined to believe that "what is good for the United States is good for the world," while Democrats are likelier to maintain that "what is good for the world is good for the United States."[22]

Democratic foreign policy reflexes are powerfully shaped by reflections on Vietnam and Iraq, and the risks of drifting into quagmires. Republicans are more likely to dwell still on the lessons of the 1930s—the risks of appeasement and the dangers of protectionism.

Democrats are attracted to collective security as a methodology for promoting peace. They regard international cooperation as essential to the pursuit and maintenance of peace, and hope that Americans will take the lead in organizing it. Republicans are more inclined to consider peace a by-product of American strength, wielded energetically, and when necessary unilaterally, and even in some cases preemptively. They are more hawkish, and if the country is engaged in armed struggle, the GOP is likeliest to demand victory as the objective, while resisting limits on the means and methods of combat.

Democrats tend to be more idealistic and reflexively Wilsonian. They are intrigued by geoeconomics, reformist in their approach to the world, and zealous in the pursuit of American values overseas. Republicans generally take more pride in their realism, and their foreign policy reflexes are more akin to those of Teddy Roosevelt. They are more fascinated by geopolitics, more comfortable with the accumulation of national power, and more eager to use it in pursuit of American interests.

Democrats need to believe in America's virtue but want to assure themselves that the United States is worthy of that belief. They are more skeptical about the purity of U.S motives, and more apprehensive about American hubris. Among Republicans, by contrast, confidence in America's virtues is deeply ingrained—a matter of smug self-satisfaction, accompanied by a "certain indifference to what fancy-pants East Coasters, let alone Europeans, think about it."[23] Conservatives revered Reagan for calling the Soviet Union an "evil empire," admonishing Gorbachev to "tear down that Wall," and denying the moral equivalence between East and West; Liberals considered such rhetoric as ill-informed, ill-advised, and undiplomatic.

Democrats seek to restrain or discipline American power by embracing multilateral institutions and cultivating respect for international law, treaties, and conventions. It has promoted UN peacekeeping, International

Monetary Fund (IMF) bailouts, and the punishment of war criminals by turning them over to the International Criminal Court. Republicans are more prone to unleash American power and resist constraints on American sovereignty. While acknowledging the value of certain international institutions, they prefer to keep them on a shorter leash and tighter budget than do Democrats. The GOP practices à la carte multilateralism and frequently exhibits discomfort with, if not scorn for, international conventions or rules that constrain U.S. diplomatic maneuverability.

Democrats are generally more risk averse in brandishing threats or using force abroad. In the post–Cold War world, they have been prepared to intervene with military force, but principally on behalf of humanitarian causes in which U.S. strategic interests were modest and the risks of casualties low. The GOP is more favorably disposed to use military force to advance U.S. interests, but has less enthusiasm about utilizing it for humanitarian purposes.

Republicans are inclined to focus national security policy on geopolitical concerns and military threats. Democrats are more likely to expand the scope of national security concerns to include global warming, international pandemics, and the outsourcing of jobs.

Democrats exhibit greater trust in the benign force of nationalism and greater tolerance for the neutralism of other states. Republicans prefer policies reflecting a clear sense of moral clarity and, on matters of consequence to Washington, are more disposed to insist that others declare whether they are "with us or against us."

Democrats are more hopeful that economic interdependence will attenuate threats to the peace yet more fearful that it will result in the outsourcing of American jobs. They appear more confident in the utility of economic sanctions and are more likely to employ them against Rightist governments, particularly military regimes. They are more eager to deploy economic assistance to alleviate poverty and address basic human needs.

Republicans are more attentive to the diplomatic leverage that economic interdependence may supply, somewhat more skeptical about the efficacy of economic sanctions (though they are quite prepared to apply them against Communists, nuclear proliferators, or those engaged in religious persecution), and more disposed to employ economic aid to supply security assistance to allies or create incentives for market reforms.

Democrats, with their strong connections to universities, relish vigorous engagement in the international "battle of ideas," and they consistently encourage an expansion of cultural and educational exchanges. Republicans, with their deeper roots on Madison Avenue, more enthusiastically embrace the notion that public diplomacy can be improved by applying the methods of the advertising industry.

Both parties are committed to arresting nuclear proliferation. The Democrats, however, are more likely to pursue this aim through multilateral mechanisms and are more willing to buy out potential proliferators with economic and other concessions. Republicans are more partial to counter-proliferation, more reluctant to reward bad behavior by making deals with proliferators, and more tempted to contemplate regime change as a means of coping with this threat.

Democrats push harder for international cooperation to reduce environmental degradation and are less attentive to the economic cost of such measures. Republicans are more skeptical about the scientific case for environmental regulation and more reluctant to implement measures, which pose significant risks to national development or favored corporate interests.

Democrats seemed more confident until recently that Americans can plant the seeds of democracy in foreign soil, and appeared more willing to tackle the vexing tasks of nation-building. Republicans traditionally exhibited greater skepticism about the efficacy of democracy promotion abroad. While neoconservatives are often inclined to intervene abroad to foster democracy—and George W. Bush was its most enthusiastic presidential proponent—Republicans tend to proceed operationally from the sanguine presumption that democratization can be accomplished simply and cheaply by merely taking down oppressive regimes, an outcome scarcely confirmed by recent U.S. experiences in Iraq, Afghanistan, and Libya.

Thus voters choose in presidential contests between candidates representing two broad foreign policy traditions. The competencies, experiences, policy reflexes, and intellectual biases of the major parties exert political appeal, which tends to ebb and flow in response to changing circumstances. And voters must measure the capabilities and promises of rival candidates against the fluctuating demands of events.

The latter are often decisive. A former British prime minister was once asked after winning a parliamentary election what would determine the foreign policy of his administration. Without hesitation he answered, "Events, dear boy, events."

His comment remains apt. Events exert a powerful influence on the outcome of presidential elections. They may play to an incumbent president's strength or weaknesses, and alternatively give him an edge or compromise his prospects for reelection. A challenger can respond to events with words and promises, but only the president can act—for good or ill. That gives him a noteworthy advantage while also putting him squarely on the spot. Our interest in the chapters that follow will be less in what candidates say during campaigns than what presidents do, both during and after elections are over.

2 QUEST FOR THE NOMINATION

Appealing to the Base

THE FIRST CHALLENGE FOR THOSE SEEKING THE PRESIDENCY IS TO secure the nomination of one of the major parties. The Republican Party "regulars" are more conservative and the Democratic Party "faithful" are more liberal than the general electorate. Candidates who win tend relentlessly to cultivate and protect their base. They cannot prevail if they abandon it. The trick is to capture the loyalty and commitment of one's party's key constituencies without alienating moderate or independent voters, whose support will be needed when the general election rolls around. This chapter examines the foreign policy consequences of "playing to the base."

These consequences are most visible when an incumbent president, unable satisfactorily to resolve pressing foreign policy problems, is impelled to abandon hopes of securing his party's nomination for another term in office. Harry Truman and Lyndon Johnson experienced that disappointment. They were not defeated for the nomination by other challengers; they dropped out after deciding that a campaign for renomination was not worth the fight.

There are also potentially serious foreign policy implications when an incumbent in the White House is challenged seriously for the nomination by a member of his own party. Gerald Ford faced such a challenge from

Ronald Reagan in 1976, Jimmy Carter from Ted Kennedy in 1980, and George H. W. Bush from Pat Buchanan in 1992.[1] Such campaigns expose the incumbents to the foreign policy DNA of their own base in a more intense way for a more sustained period prior to the general election contest.

The elections of 1952 and 2008 presented a choice between two major party candidates, neither of whom had held national elective office. These contests were not ostensibly referenda on an incumbent's record. Nevertheless, Dwight Eisenhower devoted much of his campaign to maligning President Truman's policies, and Barack Obama spent more time trashing George W. Bush than attacking John McCain, Obama's rival.

Since Eisenhower and Obama had no record to defend, the foreign policy views they articulated in their campaigns would, of course, have to be implemented, modified, or jettisoned, only if they were elected.

Finally, since the vice presidency has become a powerful launchpad for presidential candidacies, it would appear appropriate to briefly examine the extraordinarily informal, even casual, procedures through which running mates are chosen.

DECIDING THE NOMINATION IS NOT WORTH THE FIGHT

Foreign policy mishaps forced Harry Truman and Lyndon Johnson reluctantly to relinquish their hopes for a second full term. Both presided over costly, protracted, limited wars, which they appeared able neither to win militarily nor to end diplomatically. This failure eviscerated their support at home—above all, within their own party.

There were striking similarities between the circumstances that Truman and Johnson confronted. Each inherited the White House as a result of the death of a president. Both served out their predecessor's term, won reelection once, and were eager to run again. Public frustration with inconclusive Asian wars dramatically weakened their standing at home, and adverse results in New Hampshire primaries in 1952 and 1968, respectively—primaries, incidentally, in which neither actively campaigned—persuaded them that the Democratic nomination was not worth the fight.

As these elections loomed, both Truman and Johnson understood that the voters were eager to see progress toward resolving their respective conflicts in Korea and Vietnam. Each was bedeviled by roughly the same unattractive options. In search of victory they could escalate the fighting, but only at the risk of a wider conflict. Alternatively, they could push for a negotiated settlement, recognizing, however, that an agreement required the cooperation of adversaries (who displayed little sense of urgency to settle), and that American voters might regard the achievable terms with distaste. The default option was to stay the course in a stalemated conflict that was rapidly losing public support.

In Korea, by early 1951 the goals that Americans had considered appropriate when the nation went to war—"total enemy defeat, total destruction of the enemy's armed forces, his unconditional surrender, the complete occupation of his territory, the removal of the existing government, and its replacement by a regime that would respond to our concepts of 'democratization'"—were clearly beyond reach.[2] Another effort to reunify the Korean Peninsula by force was indeed a "bridge too far." That had been tried in the fall of 1950 and had provoked China's entry into the war and America's hasty and disorderly retreat well south of the thirty-eighth parallel.

A substantial escalation of the war now would exacerbate the political outcry at home while offering no assurance of military victory. In any event, the Truman administration regarded Western Europe as the most significant strategic prize, believed that it would be foolhardy to dissipate American resources indefinitely in a peripheral Cold War theater, and considered a wider conflict with China "the wrong war in the wrong place at the wrong time against the wrong enemy."[3]

China's intervention in Korea in November 1950 took a toll on American public support for the war, on Douglas MacArthur's reputation for generalship, and on public enthusiasm for unifying the peninsula by force. By the spring of 1951, stabilizing a military control line across the middle of Korea proved to be feasible militarily, and this laid the groundwork for negotiating an armistice agreement.

Truce talks among the United States, China, and North Korea commenced in July 1951. Secretary of State Dean Acheson, among others, anticipated that the negotiation of an armistice agreement would be relatively simple and quick. It was anything but. The Chinese and North Koreans, egged on by Stalin, who had recommended pursuit of a long-drawn-out war in Korea, displayed no eagerness to reach an agreement. They quibbled over the most trivial issues, while seeking to bolster their military position on the battlefield.

Establishing agreement on a military control line was the first challenge in the bargaining at Panmunjom. The UN commander, General Matthew

Ridgway, was reluctant to relieve the application of military force to push the Chinese and North Koreans farther north for fear of losing leverage with which to speed the resolution of other issues. But fighting to generate pressure in negotiations was not a natural reflex in America's diplomatic tradition, and the Joint Chiefs of Staff (JCS) opposed Ridgway's view on grounds that casualties were running high, the battle lines they controlled provided good natural defenses, and holding and fortifying them was readily achievable.

Meanwhile, public opinion in America had turned sharply against the war. Korea was increasingly regarded as a conflict that was "neither noble nor necessary." A poll conducted in October 1951 revealed that two-thirds of Americans considered the war "utterly useless." Senator Robert Taft, a possible GOP presidential nominee in 1952, was eager to curtail U.S. casualties, which were running at two thousand a week, rather than continue a war "that can't accomplish anything."[4] Truman's public approval rating had dropped to 22 percent. The British and other allies were pushing for swift progress in the truce talks, and it was in this context that Truman agreed in late November 1951 to restore the status quo ante at the existing military control line—that is, close to the thirty-eighth parallel.

By early spring 1952, differences on other significant issues had been largely resolved. But the negotiations deadlocked over how to treat prisoners of war. In previous American wars, all POWs had been exchanged swiftly and involuntarily. Indeed, the Geneva Convention on Prisoners of War, which the United States had signed but not ratified, treated such a general exchange of all POWs as the norm. Securing the earliest possible return of UN prisoners seemed a logical and politically attractive objective, and it initially enjoyed substantial bureaucratic support within the Truman administration. The JCS were among its early and vocal proponents, as was Secretary of State Acheson.

However, some key officials—General Robert McClure was one, Ambassador "Chip" Bohlen another—recalled with horror the fate of many Russian prisoners returned to the Soviet Union following World War II. And the concept of forcible, involuntary repatriation of POWs caused others deep political misgivings in the context of the East–West ideological struggle.

The issue was bucked to the president for a decision in February 1952. Without apparent hesitation, Truman opposed a forced all-for-all repatriation. He regarded it as an "inequitable" deal, since the UN Command held substantially more POWs than the Communist forces did, and many of the

POWs held by the Communists were South Koreans and Nationalist Chinese whom the North Koreans and Chinese had forced into the military against their will.

Truman also found the voluntary repatriation principle appealing, because "he [did] not wish to send back those prisoners who surrendered and have cooperated with us, because he believes they will be immediately done away with."[5] Acheson fell in behind the president, and America's decision to give POWs a choice as to whether to return to their homeland was firmly maintained throughout the 1952 election campaign, even though it appeared the major impediment to an armistice agreement.

Initially the Communists, who ardently opposed voluntary repatriation, hinted that there was some give in their position. But UN screenings taken in April 1952 revealed that some 70,000 of the roughly 120,000 Communist POWs feared that their lives would be at risk if they returned home. This hardened Chinese and North Korean opposition to voluntary repatriation and derailed the truce talks.

The screening results were not in fact as surprising as they seemed. Few in Washington realized that U.S. personnel provided lax oversight on the prison camps, and that this had permitted Taiwanese nationalists and South Korean anti-Communists to use a variety of dubious methods—some coercive—to dissuade prisoners from electing to return home.[6]

Those in Washington who were aware of these methods did not, however, press for a reconsideration of the policy. Truman evidently was uninformed about such details, and the deadlock in the talks persisted through the end of his administration.

The net result was dubious. More and more people asked why Americans had to "die for a tie." Critics wondered why negotiations continued to break down over esoteric issues like the neutrality of the conference site or the principle of voluntary repatriation. The war thus provoked increasingly bitter partisanship at home.

The administration policy on POWs was highly principled but not terribly effective. Many lives were sacrificed while the POW drama was played out. After the truce talks began, there were 124,000 UN casualties, including 9,000 American dead, many of them sustained after the POW issue became the principal stumbling block to an agreement.

Whether a more flexible stance on this issue would have led to an earlier conclusion of the armistice, and possibly some impact on the 1952 presidential election, is not clear. There is no doubt that the North Koreans and Chinese were war weary by mid-1952. But Joseph Stalin was still happy to see the United States pour scarce resources into an inconclusive struggle in a remote area. He pressed Pyongyang and Beijing hard to soldier on. It was perhaps no coincidence that the armistice was not concluded until after March 1953, when Stalin died.

Alexis Johnson, the State Department's senior action officer on armistice-related issues, later contended that a truce agreement might have been worked out before the 1952 elections had the president demonstrated greater flexibility on the POW issue.[7] But Johnson also maintained that Truman did what he thought was right despite the risk of adverse political consequences for himself and his party.

In the end, Truman's actions proved inconclusive militarily and unsuccessful diplomatically. The war ground on, and it was increasingly evident that he and his party would pay the political price for the stalemate.

Truman informed his staff in the fall of 1951 that he did not expect to run for reelection. But he continued to keep the option alive, largely, it appears, because of his low estimate of the other available candidates. He regarded Alben Barkley as too old, Averell Harriman too inexperienced, and Estes Kefauver too untrustworthy. So he kept kicking the decision down the road.

Whatever his hopes that something might turn up, they vanished on March 11 when Estes Kefauver beat him handily in the New Hampshire primary, in which Truman's name was put on the ballot without his permission. On March 29, President Truman took himself out of the race.

Lyndon Johnson confronted an even more acute political dilemma as the 1968 election approached, because the domestic consequences of the war in Vietnam were even more toxic. Like Truman, Johnson presided over a costly, prolonged, and inconclusive war, and he was unable to turn up any politically palatable military options or plausible diplomatic initiatives for breaking out of it.

Widening the war promised to exacerbate unrest at home with no assurance of victory in the field. Augmenting U.S. force levels was domestically risky and morally hazardous; the heavier the burden Washington shouldered for South Vietnam's security, the less responsibility Saigon felt obliged to assume. The political weakness of the South Vietnamese authorities meant that significant American troop withdrawals could trigger their demise. A negotiated settlement of the conflict was the administration's fervent wish. But it required the collaboration of Hanoi, which appeared highly unlikely without major inducements, like an unconditional halt to all bombing of the North—an option strongly resisted by key members of Johnson's national security team.

Johnson told his national security adviser, Walt Rostow, in late 1967 that the most important decision the administration needed was a "strategy for the next 12 months on Vietnam—military, political, negotiating."[8] He recognized that unless they did something quick about Vietnam, "we would lose the election.[9]

But as Johnson pondered whether to embark on another reelection campaign, he faced divided counsel within his national security team over strategy in Vietnam. His field commander, General William Westmoreland, urged escalation—more troops, intensified military operations, attacks on supply routes through Laos and Cambodia, heavier bombing of North Vietnam, and the mining of its harbors.

His secretary of defense, Robert McNamara, however, thoroughly disillusioned by the war, was now at odds with Westmoreland and favored a de-escalation of the fighting and a bid for a negotiated settlement. McNamara dismissed the likelihood that a corner could be turned in the war before the 1968 election.

Each thought the existing policy was failing. Their proposed remedies, however, were at cross-purposes, and each preferred to stick with the existing policy rather than shift to the course recommended by the other. From a domestic political vantage point, widening the war risked greater domestic opposition, and the budgetary costs associated with escalation could put the president's domestic priorities in jeopardy. Yet, de-escalation and the commencement of even modest troop withdrawals heightened the dangers of military setbacks at a time when there was little optimism that a negotiated settlement was within reach.

President Johnson chose to defer a tough strategic choice. As Stephen Sestanovich noted when his key advisers disagreed, "[H]e had no idea what to do. Rather than use discord as a tool for finding a better policy, he ignored it. The opposing recommendations before him canceled each other out."[10]

Hanoi's Tet Offensive, however, forced the need for a decision on the president's agenda. Although the administration portrayed Tet as a last-gasp effort by the enemy, its impact on the American public was devastating. It divided the Washington foreign policy establishment, discredited the military "hawks," and further energized the antiwar movement throughout the United States. It undercut support for Westmoreland's pending request for more than two hundred thousand additional American troops, and increased interest within the administration in trying a partial bombing halt as an incentive for negotiations.

Meanwhile the president's political base was withering. The war was fracturing the country and especially the Democratic Party. By the spring of 1968, Johnson's job-approval ratings had headed south; 64 percent disapproved of his handling of the Vietnam issue. The president could scarcely speak anywhere except military installations without fear of major protests. Significant Democratic Party bosses like Jesse Unruh of California began openly to express their misgivings about Johnson's leadership. The disapproval of the war in the mainstream press was overwhelming.

Even Richard Russell, the dean of southern senators, decided that it was time to get out of Vietnam. Johnson's longtime Texas friend, John Connally, confided to the president his doubts about his reelection chances. It was clear that Bobby Kennedy was organizing his own nascent campaign, and psychologically the war in Vietnam was becoming an "unshakeable burden" on the president and his family.

The crowning blow came in the New Hampshire primary. President Johnson prevailed, but by only a narrow 49 percent to 42 percent margin over Senator Eugene McCarthy. This, in turn, triggered Bobby Kennedy's swift entry into the presidential sweepstakes. Before announcing his candidacy, Kennedy slyly offered to forgo the race if the president would publicly acknowledge the failure of his policy in Vietnam, and establish a presidential commission to look at new policy options. This was an offer of "humiliation" rather than "conciliation," and Johnson promptly rebuffed it.[11] But Johnson also bowed to the inevitable by announcing on March 31 his own decision not to run for reelection.

Neither Truman nor Johnson was particularly enthusiastic about the candidates nominated by their party to succeed them, though each had a large hand in selecting his potential successor. Truman considered Adlai Stevenson weak and indecisive; Johnson endorsed Hubert Humphrey but confided on at least one occasion that he actually preferred a Republican, Nelson Rockefeller.

Stevenson indelicately suggested to Truman that his electoral prospects would be more promising if Secretary of State Acheson were to publicly announce his intention to retire at the end of Truman's term—a recommendation Truman resented and firmly rejected.[12] Humphrey's campaign picked up genuine momentum only after he clearly differentiated his views on Vietnam from the policy of the president he had faithfully served. But it proved to be too little, too late.

The elections of 1952 and 1968 were essentially referenda on the records of Truman and Johnson, respectively. Neither campaign afforded the electorate a particularly thoughtful debate over future strategic choices in Korea or Vietnam. Both, however, produced new leadership and a subsequent adjustment of U.S. strategy in the Far East.

One might then ask: How did George W. Bush manage to adapt his administration's policies in Iraq to avert a comparable rebuff from his party and the electorate in 2004? As his bid for reelection approached, he was presiding over a preventive war against Iraq, whose premise—that Iraq had a robust inventory of weapons of mass destruction—was being exposed as flawed intelligence. Saddam Hussein had been swiftly ousted, but an unanticipated Sunni insurgency appeared to be taking root. The potential political fallout was reflected in the unexpectedly robust antiwar candidacy of Democrat Howard Dean in the run-up to the January 2004 Iowa caucuses.

Both President George W. Bush and his main political adviser, Karl Rove, initially relished the chance to campaign as a wartime president. Security conditions in Iraq deteriorated steadily in late 2003 and 2004, but public opposition to the conflict had yet to crystallize, at least within the Republican Party. The financial costs of the conflict appeared manageable. The country's post–September 11 mood remained deeply patriotic, and the GOP's foreign policy credentials still enjoyed wide respect.

The broad goals that President Bush had articulated in defense of the invasion—ousting Saddam Hussein, disrupting Iraq's nuclear program, and fostering democracy in the Middle East—were broadly appealing objectives. The Bush administration got a bounce out of the capture of Saddam Hussein in late 2003, and within the Republican Party, dissent was muted.

GOP party regulars generally stuck by the president; there was little support for tossing out an incumbent in the still early phase of what the administration described as "a long war" against al-Qaeda and other terrorist groups "with a global reach." And no one challenged George W. Bush for the GOP nomination.[13]

INCUMBENTS CHALLENGED FOR THE NOMINATION

As noted earlier, incumbent presidents are challenged occasionally in the primaries by members of their own party. Gerald Ford, Jimmy Carter, and George H. W. Bush successfully surmounted intraparty challenges for the nomination. The question is: How did those primary season insurrections affect the conduct and content of foreign policy?

Gerald Ford's Challenge from Ronald Reagan

In 1976, I was working on East Asian issues in the Policy Planning Staff at the State Department. Winston Lord was its director, and he enjoyed a close and productive relationship with Secretary Henry Kissinger. The staff was highly talented, its mandate covered the full scope of American foreign policy, and its analytic work was much in demand by senior State Department officials, including the principals on the seventh floor. Yet, by early spring, we found ourselves less and less fully occupied as requests for our work gradually tailed off.

At first this seemed puzzling, but its cause gradually became clear: the president faced a real dogfight for the GOP nomination. Ronald Reagan's challenge on foreign policy was aimed at the heart of the Nixon/Kissinger/Ford approach to East–West issues. It precipitated major adjustments in the president's national security team and in the substance of his foreign policy.

Strategically, "détente" constituted the administration's method of enmeshing the Soviet Union in an array of constraints designed to temper the growth of its power and moderate the conduct of its foreign policy. Governor Reagan dismissed it as a misguided effort grounded in a false supposition: that the United States was not prepared to do what was necessary to compete effectively with Moscow. In the wake of the debacle in Vietnam, moreover, Americans—at least key constituencies within the GOP—were tired of being pushed around. They were in no mood to placate adversaries. Governor Reagan's criticism of "détente" struck a political nerve.

Gerald Ford's bid for reelection was scarcely typical. He had never won a national election; President Nixon appointed him vice president when Spiro Agnew left office in disgrace in late 1973. Ford inherited the Oval Office when the threat of impeachment forced Nixon to resign in August 1974, and Ford's early decision to pardon Nixon left an enduring political scar.

President Ford had limited time to put his personal stamp on the presidency as the 1976 election campaign unfolded under extremely trying circumstances. Nixon was in exile; the GOP split; the Democrats held a huge majority in Congress; Ford's predecessor's domestic policies had alienated many conservatives,[14] and the Nixon/Kissinger/Ford foreign policy legacy was under attack from both Reagan Republicans and so-called Jackson Democrats.[15]

In 1973, a liberal Congress cut off military aid to South Vietnam. In 1975, Saigon was overrun militarily and absorbed by Hanoi. Though Ford bore little responsibility for this outcome, he was the fall guy as far as the political Right was concerned. Beyond this, strategic arms negotiations with Moscow stalled; the defense budget was cut; the intelligence community's prerogatives and capabilities were circumscribed; and Ronald Reagan, who proved to be a formidable challenger, articulated conservative misgivings about the administration's foreign policy record with simplicity and force.

Asked how he defined "détente," Reagan responded, "Isn't that what a farmer has with his turkey—until Thanksgiving?" He maintained that détente sought to freeze the Cold War in place when the point was to win it. And he complained that détente perpetuated Communism and nuclear weapons, both of which he hoped eventually to dismantle."[16]

In combating the insurgency within his own party, Ford moved steadily to the right, in hopes of dissuading Ronald Reagan from running, or, if that failed, defeating him in the primaries. In October 1975, he cleared the decks for the campaign with a major staff and cabinet reshuffle. He announced that Nelson Rockefeller would not be on his ticket in 1976, thinking that this would make it easier to hold off a Reagan challenge at the convention, while giving himself the option of offering the vice presidency to the California governor.

He also replaced the CIA director Bill Colby with George H. W. Bush, and fired Defense Secretary Jim Schlesinger and appointed his chief of staff, Don Rumsfeld, to fill that post. He deprived Secretary Kissinger of his national security adviser title, replacing him at the White House with Brent Scowcroft. These personnel changes were designed to mollify the Right, temper infighting within his national security team, and demonstrate that the president was fully in charge.

The moves only partially succeeded. Conservative circles lamented Jim Schlesinger's departure. And Don Rumsfeld proved to be a very savvy bureaucratic operator, fully capable, as Kissinger later acknowledged, of forestalling State Department hopes of revitalizing strategic arms talks with Moscow.

As the nomination contest with Reagan heated up, the president expunged the term "détente" from his vocabulary, and consigned Henry Kissinger to a somewhat less visible public role. In an off-the-record session with party loyalists in Oklahoma, Ford's campaign chairman, Jim Baker, asserted that Kissinger would not make it into the cabinet of a second Ford administration—an indiscretion that leaked to the press, and for which Baker paid with a White House "correction" and much "groveling" before the Secretary of State.[17]

At the Republican Convention, the foreign policy plank, initially drafted by members of Senator Jesse Helms's staff, attacked the Soviet Union, disparaged "détente," denounced Kissinger's statesmanship, disowned the Panama Canal Treaty negotiations, excoriated the Helsinki Conference on Security and Cooperation in Europe (CSCE) Treaty, dismissed the value of trade with Communist nations, and declared the party's firm support for Taiwan.

Early drafts were watered down in committee, but despite the furious opposition of Kissinger and Scowcroft, the administration ultimately decided not to fight the Right on the platform's wholesale repudiation of its foreign policy record. As Dick Cheney, White House chief of staff, put it, "Principle is okay up to a certain point . . . but principle doesn't do any good if you lose the nomination." He added, "Platforms don't mean anything; they are forgotten the day after the convention."[18] President Ford grudgingly accepted this counsel.

On one issue the president was fully in sync with his conservative critics—that of defense spending, which he enthusiastically increased. The Pentagon's budget had expanded only 6 percent from 1969 to 1975. Now Ford pushed it up 9 percent on top of a 7 percent increase authorized the previous year.

Of greater consequence, from February 1976 on, the administration imposed a virtual hiatus on initiatives toward the Communist world. The Strategic Arms Limitation Talks (SALT negotiations) were put on hold.[19] Nixon's promise to complete normalization with the People's Republic of China by 1976 was quietly buried.[20] A subtle exploration of possibilities for diplomatic openings to Castro's Cuba, initiated in 1974 through unofficial envoys, was shelved. Thoughts of relieving the trade embargo on Vietnam in return for concessions on the POW/MIA issue were abandoned. While the administration did attempt, with conservative approval, to contest

Soviet and Cuban inroads in Africa, Congress stymied these efforts through restrictions on the sale of arms and the provision of training to anti-Communist forces in Angola.

Meanwhile, conservative opposition forced the administration to slow ball negotiations with Panama over the future of the canal. Reagan's frequently repeated assertion: "It's ours! We built it! We paid for it! And we should keep it!" resonated strongly with the public and the Congress.[21] The administration recognized that ratification of a Panama Canal treaty had no chance during an election season. Thirty-seven senators, more than enough to pigeonhole a treaty, went on record during the campaign opposing any handover of sovereignty over the Canal to Panama.

Ellsworth Bunker, the U.S. negotiator, was instructed to engage in a diplomatic shuffle "implying both progress and foot-dragging, without making either too obvious."[22] Secretary of State Kissinger candidly acknowledged the reasoning behind these instructions to Foreign Minister Aquilino Boyd of Panama in mid-June 1975. "We have no discipline now," he observed. "If the Democrats win, they will pursue our policy. If Ford wins, you know what we would do. The thing is to get through the next few months without it becoming an issue."[23]

The president's political weakness also exposed the administration to renewed requests from Taiwan for additional consulates, the appointment to Taipei of a seasoned ambassador of distinction (Leonard Unger was named), and reassurances to the Senate about the continuity of the U.S. defense commitment.[24]

Kissinger sought to limit the fallout from these concessions by trying out new formulas for an accommodation with Beijing. He proposed, for example, to maintain a U.S. liaison office in Taipei while opening an embassy in Beijing, and to schedule troop withdrawals from Taiwan that would gradually remove one half the remaining three thousand Americans from the island by the summer of 1976.

Kissinger informed the Chinese that the United States could negotiate such an agreement only up through the fall of 1975—that is, before the 1976 campaign commenced in earnest. Needless to add, the Chinese did not bite. They were not prepared to toss a lifeline to an administration whose political future was uncertain, at a time when it was abandoning previous commitments to "complete normalization" during its second term.

In short, President Ford's efforts to ward off Reagan's challenge and pin down the GOP nomination produced wholesale foreign policy adjustments.

To be sure, Ford neither withdrew his support for Kissinger nor preemptively capitulated to conservative critics, as his snub of Aleksandr Solzhenitsyn, his trip to Helsinki to sign the CSCE Treaty,[25] his grain sales to the Soviet Union, his substantive defense of the concepts underlying détente, his support for the principle of majority rule in Rhodesia,[26] and his sacking of Defense Secretary James Schlesinger all attest. But he did what he felt he needed to do to survive politically. In the end, he managed to secure the nomination, though not without putting central elements of his foreign policy on hold through the balance of the campaign, and since he lost, through the remainder of his term.

For Gerald Ford, tending his base required major foreign policy adjustments. But his experience was quite rare, in part because few incumbents are directly challenged for the nomination. And the others who have been challenged—Jimmy Carter and George H. W. Bush—confronted intraparty insurrections motivated principally by domestic economic and social concerns.

Jimmy Carter's Challenge from Ted Kennedy

In 1980, Jimmy Carter's foreign policy record was certainly susceptible to criticism from his Democratic base. He had tackled with noteworthy courage several tough issues, which ruffled the feathers of prominent Democratic constituencies. The negotiation and ratification of the Panama Canal Treaty and the administration's zeal for arms control agreements with the Soviet Union offended partisans of "Scoop" Jackson and conservative Democrats in the South. The president's role as the successful mediator of the Camp David agreement provoked opposition from many Jewish voters who perceived Carter as too eager to mollify Israel's Arab neighbors. Party members solicitous of Taiwan's concerns were angered by his normalization of relations with China. In a sense, Carter's major foreign policy achievements, however laudable diplomatically, were all "political losers."[27]

These foreign policy concerns, however, did not propel Ted Kennedy into the race. Whatever his personal motivations may have been, he publicly justified his quest for the nomination by pointing to a weak economy, high unemployment, the urgency of health-care reform, and rising energy prices—that is, the preeminent domestic concerns of the Democratic Party's liberal base.

In the course of the campaign, Kennedy also criticized Carter's response to a variety of foreign policy challenges, including the hostage crisis in Iran, a Russian brigade deployed to Cuba, Fidel Castro's troops in Africa, and the Soviet invasion of Afghanistan. Still, domestic issues lay at the heart of Kennedy's bid for the nomination.

Kennedy presented the president with a deadly serious political challenge; in late 1979, he led Carter by thirty points in the polls. His challenge also inflicted major damage on the president's hopes for reelection by hardening divisions among Democrats, diverting money needed for the general election campaign, and rehearsing negative campaign themes, which the GOP nominee, Ronald Reagan, later appropriated.

Kennedy's bid for the nomination did not significantly alter Carter's foreign policy. Events did. But they pushed the administration in a direction quite different than that proposed by the Massachusetts senator. The liberal wing of the party, which Kennedy represented, was noticeably dovish on external policy. But Tehran's hostage taking and Moscow's decision to put troops into Afghanistan impelled Carter progressively to toughen national security policy.

To the extent Kennedy opposed these policies—for example, by publicly criticizing the shah of Iran rather than the Ayatollah Ruhollah Khomeini, or opposing key sanctions the president proposed vis-à-vis the Soviet Union—he arguably weakened the administration's international bargaining position. But there is no clear evidence that he forced major changes in administration external policies—or, for that matter, fatally undermined them.[28]

On the contrary, in the year preceding the Democratic Convention, the influence of Zbigniew Brzezinski, the most hawkish of Carter's advisers, increased perceptibly at the expense of liberals within the administration's national security team. One of the most salient decisions in the hostage crisis was whether to permit the shah to enter the United States for medical treatment. The president, despite personal misgivings, acceded to pressures from prominent conservatives like Henry Kissinger and David Rockefeller (echoed by Brzezinski), and authorized the shah's entry.

It is true that on the central issue of the Iran crisis—according priority to the safe return of all hostages—Carter agreed with the liberals. But his decision was a matter of personal conviction, not an accommodation to political pressure from Kennedy or the party's liberal base.

Foreign policy issues intruded only marginally on the nomination fight. Carter welcomed opportunities to portray Kennedy as "soft on the Soviet Union," and as too closely aligned with fringe elements on the party's left. For example, against the advice of many of his political counselors, Carter proposed a revitalization of the Selective Service System (military draft), arguing that this would signal to Moscow the seriousness of America's concern about its invasion of Afghanistan. He expected that Kennedy would oppose this, as he had opposed the Olympic boycott against the Soviets, and that this would complicate his bid for the nomination.

Cutting off grain exports to Moscow in response to its invasion of a neighbor posed a particularly delicate political test for Carter. The vice president, Walter Mondale, worried about the support of Midwest farmers, was extremely blunt in his criticism of this proposal. "Mr. President," he noted, "we need to be strong and firm, but that doesn't mean you have to commit political suicide."[29]

But President Carter was primarily concerned about the response of others: "What can I say to Margaret Thatcher or Helmut Schmidt if we fail to exercise the single option that hurts the Russians most?" He doubted that America's allies would act in concert with the United States unless his administration implemented politically tough measures. Kennedy opposed the embargo; Carter, nonetheless carried it out. He also won the Iowa caucus by a 2–1 margin.

Coercive military options were initially considered only in relation to contingencies involving the death or trial of the hostages or spiraling disorder within Iran. Carter was prepared to mine Iranian waters but only in the event the hostages were physically harmed. He was prepared to contemplate a direct military attack on Iran only if the hostages were executed. He eventually authorized a rescue mission but only after the negotiating track had collapsed. All these decisions reflected the policy reflexes of the president and his White House circle rather than pressures from the Kennedy camp.[30]

Failure of the hostage rescue mission, mounted in April 1980, rendered further U.S. military plans moot. In the meanwhile, Moscow's invasion of Afghanistan convinced many Democratic voters that Carter's perceptions of the Soviet Union had been too sanguine. Kennedy scarcely led this charge, though he was among those who sought to exploit the issue for political advantage.

In the wake of the Soviet invasion of Afghanistan, Carter recognized that the SALT II Treaty had no chance of being ratified in the Senate. Accordingly, he asked Senator Robert Byrd not to bring it to the floor for a vote. However, because of his own commitment to the agreement, and perhaps the sensitivities of his party, he left it on the Senate calendar. It remained there, undisturbed, for the balance of his term.

On at least one occasion, Kennedy benefited from an administration diplomatic miscue. On March 1, 1976, the United States voted for a UN resolution calling on Israel to dismantle its settlements in occupied Arab territories and Jerusalem. Bob Straus and Fritz Mondale, recognizing the damage this could do to the president's standing with Jewish voters, persuaded him to retract the vote lest he lose the New York primary on March 25. The president promptly and publicly disavowed the vote, dismissing it as a bureaucratic snafu. Seizing on a technicality, Donald McHenry, the U.S. Permanent Representative to the UN, arranged to have a second vote the next day, and the United States abstained.

But Secretary of State Cyrus Vance, who was requested by the White House to minimize the political damage in congressional testimony on the issue, defended the vote as one that was consistent with long-standing U.S. opposition to settlements, support for international law, and devotion to the Middle East peace process. His explanation was substantively compelling but politically unhelpful, coming as it did just four days before a tough primary. The incident served as a reminder that whatever diplomatic virtue there might be in maintaining even-handedness in the Middle East, it does not play that well in American electoral politics.

In the end, adverse primary results in New York—and Carter's subsequent losses to Kennedy in New Jersey, Pennsylvania, Michigan, and California—were but a minor impediment to Carter's successful march to renomination. Early on, Hamilton Jordan had persuaded the president to start his bid for reelection early. The White House consequently jump-started a major fund-raising effort in 1979, jiggered the primary schedule to the president's advantage, and calculated with considerable prescience how they could roll up the delegates they needed to win.

All in all, the administration's foreign policy dilemmas probably helped Carter wrap up the nomination. Khomeini and Leonid Brezhnev challenged major U.S. national interests during our election season. When the country faces foreign crises, the public generally rallies around the flag. In practice, this means rallying around the president, and so they did. President

Carter sought to maximize that effect by adopting a "Rose Garden" electoral strategy, declaring that he would not leave the capitol to campaign but would remain in Washington to attend to pressing business.

In the end, however, vain efforts to initiate a serious negotiation with Tehran, to persuade allies to join in meaningful sanctions, or to conjure up plausible military or covert options for rescuing the hostages fueled growing frustration among the voters. This underlined America's apparent impotence in the face of a prolonged crisis. The electorate ultimately took out its frustrations on the incumbent. But these frustrations came to a head after the Democratic Convention, in which Carter won his quest for renomination in a breeze.

Patrick Buchanan's Challenge to George H. W. Bush

George H. W. Bush's challenge from Pat Buchanan had an entirely different character. Eighteen months before the 1992 election, the president's reelection seemed a virtual certainty. In 1991, his approval rating was sky-high following the U.S. victory in the first Gulf War. Democratic contenders appeared so persuaded that Bush would be reelected that prominent political figures like Bill Bradley, Dick Gephardt, Sam Nunn, and Mario Cuomo decided to skip their party's nomination fight.

George H. W. Bush had compiled an enviable record as a foreign policy president. He deftly managed the end of the Cold War, helped Germany achieve reunification without leaving the North Atlantic Treaty Organization (NATO), reduced East–West arms levels, ejected Saddam Hussein from Kuwait, dispatched Manuel Noriega from Panama, and launched a promising negotiation of Arab–Israeli issues in the Middle East. His political advisers modeled their plans for the 1992 campaign on Ronald Reagan's triumphant 1984 "Morning in America" romp.

By fall, however, signs of political trouble began to surface. A little known Democrat, Harris Wofford, surged from behind in an early November Senate race to defeat Bush's attorney general, Dick Thornburg. This set off alarm bells in the West Wing. The president and his chief of staff hurriedly called off a planned trip to the Far East scheduled for later that month. It was subsequently put back on the calendar, but its content changed dramatically to reflect growing political anxieties.

The president also confronted signs of domestic trouble. The economy had slowed, and the administration failed to put stimulus measures swiftly into place. Meanwhile, the White House appeared to be losing touch with key elements of the Republican base.

Conservatives recited a litany of complaints. "Reagan," they opined, "cut taxes; Bush increased them. Reagan reduced government regulation; Bush reversed this trend. Reagan won the Cold War; Bush cultivated Communist leaders." And religious conservatives expressed chagrin over the growing secularization of society and what they regarded as the inattentiveness of the administration to their social agenda. These harsh judgments were unfair but firmly held and politically damaging. They suggested that "galvanizing the base" was going to be tough sledding.

It was in this context that Patrick Buchanan surfaced as a challenger for the GOP nomination. He attacked the Bush administration's alleged diffidence toward the "cultural causes" dear to some conservatives, and the president's expansive vision of American foreign policy responsibilities. He derided the president as a "warmed over Jimmy Carter" and an "elitist," out of touch with average Americans.

If Ted Kennedy's challenge to Carter was defined principally by domestic economic concerns, Buchanan's challenge to Bush was shaped principally by anxieties about cultural and social issues. Buchanan mounted a populist campaign, but the brand of populism he promoted—nativist, protectionist, isolationist—was out of step with the convictions of moderate and mainstream Republicans. As Dick Darman, Bush's director of the Office of Management and Budget (OMB) later noted, Buchanan was against government, except when he perceived a need for government "to thwart immigration, stop imports, and impose his own set of values."[31]

The major figures in the George H. W. Bush administration did not regard Buchanan as a serious threat. They dismissed him as a television pundit with a wacky platform, pursuing a vain, self-indulgent, and ineffectual campaign. Winner-take-all primaries and state caucuses made Buchanan's bid for the nomination quixotic in many states, but this did not prevent him from doing harm to the president's reelection prospects.

When President Bush was slow to cultivate his base energetically, some Reagan conservatives and Democrats drifted toward Buchanan. Meanwhile, many suburban independents were attracted to Ross Perot, a maverick third-party candidate who presented no real threat to Bush's renomination, but who siphoned off more than enough votes in the general election to deny him reelection.

How did the challenge, first signaled by Buchanan's manic primary efforts and then by Perot's independent crusade, affect the administration's foreign policy? The basic answer is this: only on the margins.

The suggestion that President Bush was out of touch with voters on domestic matters doubtless impelled him to spend more of his time concentrating on the economy and social issues. Buchanan's criticism of America's expansive and expensive foreign policy efforts may have delayed U.S. aid commitments to Russia and the former Soviet republics as well as reducing their scale. After having cancelled his trip to the Far East in November, the president rescheduled it for early January 1992.

The trip's content also changed. Preparations over many months had concentrated on fleshing out the contours of a global partnership between the United States and Japan. Cabinet level visitors and an advance White House team that had spent three weeks in Tokyo in the fall of 1991 had endorsed those plans. I was serving as ambassador to Tokyo at the time and was invited to Hawaii for an East Asian Chiefs of Mission meeting in early December 1991.

The president was there to speak at the fiftieth anniversary of Japan's attack on Pearl Harbor. I briefed him on plans for his visit to Kyoto and Tokyo, and his comment, "What's in that agenda for me?" revealed the extent to which political circumstances were changing back home. I subsequently suggested to Brent Scowcroft that it would be helpful if someone from the White House would visit Tokyo to be sure that the president's concerns were reflected in plans for the visit.

Bob Zoellick, deputy to James Baker, the White House chief of staff, was consequently dispatched to Japan just before Christmas. When he was invited to outline Washington's priorities for the visit to senior Japanese officials, he observed crisply, "Autos, autos, autos!" This wholesale adjustment of priorities required both the U.S. and Japanese teams in Tokyo to scramble throughout the holiday season to prepare for a visit that commenced on January 4. In the end, a mutually agreed set of understandings were fashioned. But the president's illness at a dinner hosted by Prime Minister Kiichi Miyazawa hogged most of the headlines.[32]

Unrelenting criticism from Buchanan and Perot did not, however, deflect the administration from its foreign policy priorities, including its determination to complete negotiation of a North American Free Trade Agreement (NAFTA) before the Republican Convention.

President Bush was also intrepid in pushing for a settlement in the Middle East. Having evicted Saddam Hussein from Kuwait in 1991, he recognized the need to move forward on the Israeli–Arab issues. The timing for such movement was propitious. Radicals in the Middle East were discredited, moderates were in the ascendant, American prestige was at an all-time high, and the Soviet Union appeared prepared to play a constructive role.

Zbigniew Brzezinski criticized the Bush administration retrospectively for "leav[ing] behind an unexploited opportunity in the Middle East."[33] I believe that judgment was unjustifiably harsh. In the run-up to the 1992 election, no foreign policy issue claimed more of the administration's time and attention. Secretary of State Baker engaged in persistent shuttle diplomacy. He steadfastly sought a diplomatic formula on which an international conference on the Middle East could be convened in Madrid. The conference, which produced direct talks between the leaders of key Arab states, Israel, and the Palestinians, relaunched a serious peace process with UN Resolutions 242 and 338 as the guiding principles.[34]

To his credit, moreover, the president did not duck a risky political fight to preserve his reputation as an honest broker in the region. Israeli Prime Minister Yitzhak Shamir aggressively pressured the administration for $10 billion in housing loan guarantees to assist Israel's absorption of Jewish émigrés from the Soviet Union. Shamir cynically calculated that in a preelection environment he could readily secure huge loan guarantees from Washington even as Israel expanded its settlements in the West Bank or Gaza.

The president and his secretary of state were convinced that even indirect subsidies of additional settlements would kill any chance for Arab participation in a rejuvenated peace process. Although both Israel and America faced elections, and the American Israel Public Affairs Committee (AIPAC), the powerful Jewish lobbying group in Washington, was determined to demonstrate its political muscle, President Bush stonewalled the request for unconditional loan guarantees and mobilized the requisite congressional support to make his decision stick.

This hard-nosed, politically risky stance contributed to the Likud Party's defeat in the Israeli elections in June 1992, and Shamir's replacement by Yitzhak Rabin. The possibilities for peace between Israel and its neighbors temporarily looked up. Dennis Ross, a key adviser to both Bush and Clinton on the Middle East, commented poignantly to a colleague as the Israeli poll results were coming in: "There is good news and bad news. The good news is that we now have an Israeli government that can make peace. The bad news is that we won't be here to be able to help them do it."[35]

A new Israeli government could not be rushed immediately into major negotiations. The president was increasingly preoccupied with his own re-election chances. This priority prompted him to ask Jim Baker to relinquish his duties at the State Department to return to the White House as chief of staff and campaign manager. Baker accepted the assignment with some reluctance but with the recognition that hopes for major breakthroughs in the Middle East would have to await the outcome of the election.

It was not the Buchanan insurgency or the Perot third-party challenge that pushed Middle East diplomacy off the rails. On the contrary, had the president pandered to his base on the right, he would not have been pre-pared to challenge the Israelis as directly as he did. But it did illustrate how the rigors of a campaign often impel an incumbent to kick important dip-lomatic business down the road to concentrate on securing reelection.

CONSEQUENTIAL NOMINATION BATTLES BY NON-INCUMBENTS

In 1952, Dwight Eisenhower and Adlai Stevenson—neither of whom had previously held national office—earned the presidential nominations of their respective parties. The 2008 election pit John McCain against Barack Obama; the first time two sitting senators had faced off in a presidential election in many decades.

Eisenhower's bid for the nomination was especially instructive not only because he won but because in the process of defeating Robert Taft at the GOP Convention, he picked up policy commitments, which seemed at odds with his personal convictions and his fundamental rationale for seeking the presidency.

Barack Obama's quest for the nomination did not perhaps turn decisively on foreign policy issues. But his positions on several national security mat-ters enhanced his political prospects for defeating Hillary Clinton in their battle to head the Democratic ticket.

Dwight Eisenhower's Bid for the Nomination in 1952

Many Republicans believed that Robert Taft was entitled to the GOP nom-ination in 1952. Wendell Wilkie and Thomas Dewey, representatives of the eastern establishment wing of the party, had been trounced by Franklin Roosevelt in 1940, 1944, and 1948. The conservative wing of the party felt it was now its turn to field a candidate. Taft promised what Barry Goldwater later termed "a choice, not an echo." During Truman's tenure, Taft had voted against NATO, opposed the Marshall Plan, and railed against the containment strategy.

Republican moderates were determined to block Taft, to find a candidate devoted to collective security, and the international commitments the United States had shouldered in the late 1940s. From their point of view, Eisenhower was a natural.

Whatever personal ambitions fueled Eisenhower's quest for the White House, he publicly traced his interest in the presidency to his distaste for Truman, his fear of leaving the GOP field open for Douglas MacArthur or Robert Taft, and his resolve to preserve an internationalist foreign policy.

When moderate Republican leaders first sought to enlist Eisenhower as a candidate, he was the NATO commander. As a serving military officer, he was barred from seeking elective office, and he displayed little interest in throwing his hat in the ring. But he did allow the inference that while seeking to remain above the partisan fray, he would be susceptible to a "draft."

Ike had no experience in partisan politics, but he exhibited shrewd political judgment. He recognized that "the seeker is never so popular as the sought," that a diffident stance allowed him to remain aloof from deals with party hacks, that opponents would be loathe to attack him as long as he remained the Supreme Allied Commander in Europe, and that playing coy put off the necessity of debating Robert Taft with all the attendant risks of splitting the Republican Party.

There were clear limits, however, to the patience of his main backers. They understood that the GOP party machinery was effectively in the hands of Taft's supporters, who were actively recruiting delegates. To generate the political momentum essential for a draft, Ike's advisers needed to secure his permission to organize a national campaign, raise the funds needed to wage it, put his name in play in key primaries, and return him to the United States so voters could see him and learn his views.

In time, Eisenhower agreed. But by delaying his return, he managed to escape many of the burdens of an active campaign, such as involvement in preconvention maneuvering and the rigors of fund-raising. He wisely insisted that Citizens for Eisenhower, a powerful support vehicle, be kept independent from the Republican Party so that his candidacy could attract Democratic as well as Independent support from the outset.

For these and other reasons, some questioned the depth and authenticity of Ike's GOP credentials. Throughout most of his career, he had been closer to prominent Democrats than to Republican leaders. He had filled critical jobs in the service of Franklin Roosevelt and Harry Truman. And his views on foreign policy were thoroughly compatible with those of the Democrats who charted America's post-1945 course in international affairs.

The moderate Republicans who advised Eisenhower—Lucius Clay, Henry Cabot Lodge, and John Foster Dulles, among others—were all resolute internationalists. They were practical men who knew that grabbing the nomination would offend the party's "foot soldiers," and that some nod in the direction of the Old Guard would be required to preserve party unity. While Ike's declared motivation for running was to ensure that the nation's security was not left in the hands of isolationists, he acknowledged the political need to arrange some understandings with Taft—particularly on foreign policy, where their differences were substantive and significant.

Accommodations with Robert Taft and his followers would not be easy. They despised Roosevelt, disparaged Truman, and deplored the wartime agreements struck with the Soviet Union. They had little positive empathy for Eisenhower, who had been a major steward of FDR's wartime policy in Europe, had refused to race Soviet general Georgy Zhukov to Berlin as World War II ended, and had been chairman of the JCS when the Communists prevailed in China's civil war. Still, if Ike was to have a united party behind him in the general election campaign, he needed to throw some "red meat" to the party's right wing.

On foreign policy, therefore, Eisenhower "tacked to the right" to cultivate party regulars, facilitate his nomination, and unite the GOP. He selected John Foster Dulles as his chief foreign policy adviser. This gave him a strong and experienced partner and someone who, despite his long association with the establishment wing of the GOP, consistently had been attentive to the party's congressional leadership and was well liked and respected by Robert Taft.

Dewey's decision in 1948 to treat foreign policy as off-limits for partisan criticism was considered a sure recipe for defeat. Hence Ike acquiesced in a Republican platform that was designed to exploit Truman's vulnerability on foreign policy at the same time currying favor with Republican leaders in the Congress. It attacked the agreements struck at Yalta, implied appeasement of the Soviet Union by the Truman administration, promised liberation for enslaved nations in Eastern Europe, repackaged military deterrence in a what was characterized as a cheaper and more efficient form ("massive retaliation at times and in places of our own choosing"), and expressed support for modifications in the treaty-making powers of Congress (the Bricker Amendment). Several of these positions were closer to Taft's sentiments than to Eisenhower's convictions.

While Ike played along with the platform, he did so somewhat cynically. Those were, after all, the days when platforms were designed to rally the party faithful during the campaign, not to drive the agenda of governance after the election was over. The GOP platform attracted much unfavorable attention from the Europeans and prompted Sir Anthony Eden, the British foreign minister, gratuitously to suggest that Eisenhower not pick Dulles as his secretary of state—a recommendation he blithely ignored.[36]

Ike also studiously avoided direct attacks on Senator Joseph McCarthy, from whom he generally remained aloof. This incensed many moderate Republicans, particularly when Ike failed to denounce the Wisconsin senator for his verbal attacks on General George Marshall, and when, on the advice of his political counselors, he deleted anticipated criticism of McCarthy from a major campaign speech.

Rhetorically, Eisenhower attempted to make amends with the Right. In an address in Detroit in the spring of 1952, he declared that he had no personal responsibility for Yalta or Potsdam, and that the decision not to drive U.S. forces to Berlin was a political call made well above his pay grade. In June, he went even farther, denouncing Yalta, blaming the Democrats for the "loss of China," and accusing Truman of "being too soft on corruption at home and Communism abroad."

Finally, he chose Richard Nixon as his vice presidential running mate. This was to some extent a concession to the Right, and Ike's method for inoculating himself on the issue of domestic Communist subversion, though Nixon's selection was also commended by considerations of age and geographic balance.

As a candidate, while Ike was prepared to denounce Yalta, he also sought to minimize expectations that an Eisenhower administration would be prepared militarily to challenge the Soviet Union's sphere of influence in Eastern Europe. He gingerly embraced the "massive retaliation" language favored by conservatives on strategic policy, but he did not intend to pursue a posture of brinksmanship vis-à-vis Moscow. Promises of roll back or liberation stirred the party faithful, but Ike was prepared to pursue this objective in Central Europe only by political means.

Little wonder that following his election, Ike confronted difficulties on foreign policy within his own camp. Securing the nomination impelled him to make commitments to his party base. This, in turn, required some "winking and nodding" during the general election campaign. But Eisenhower self-consciously deferred any major review or debate of America's grand strategy until the election was over in order to prevent its "politicization" amid partisan rancor. During the campaign, though, he took care that he did not box himself in through his language on delicate foreign policy issues. In short, he exhibited a natural understanding of the distinction between campaigning and governing.

Barack Obama's Campaign for the Nomination in 2008

Barack Obama emerged out of the blue in 2007/2008 to grab the Democratic nomination away from Hillary Clinton. Foreign policy was not necessarily the decisive factor, but neither was it an inconsequential feature of their spirited rivalry.

Obama burst onto the national scene as the keynote speaker at the 2004 Democratic Convention. At the time, he articulated Senator John Kerry's pitch on the Iraq War—that is, a poorly executed strategy for a war whose justification was not the prime subject of dispute. His views on foreign policy were not subsequently clarified through his brief service in the U.S. Senate. Though a member of the Foreign Relations Committee, he convened no significant hearings as a subcommittee chairman, undertook no serious foreign travel, nor issued any particularly memorable statements.

Yet when he declared his candidacy for the White House, he possessed one noteworthy foreign policy asset—a speech given as an Illinois state senator in 2002, in which he had expressed uncommonly prescient reservations about a possible U.S. invasion of Iraq.

"I don't oppose all wars," he declared. "What I am opposed to is a dumb war. What I am opposed to is a rash war . . . a war based not on reason but on passion, not on principle, but on politics." He condemned Saddam Hussein but added, "I also know that Saddam poses no imminent and direct threat to the United States or to his neighbors, that the Iraqi economy is in shambles, that the Iraqi military is a fraction of its former strength, and that in concert with the international community he can be contained until, in the way of all petty dictators, he falls away into the dustbin of history."

And he concluded, "I know that even a successful war against Iraq will require a U.S. occupation of undetermined length, at undetermined cost, with undetermined consequences. I know that an invasion of Iraq without a clear rationale and without strong international support will only fan the flames of the Middle East, and encourage the worst, rather than the best impulses of the Arab world, and strengthen the recruitment arm of al-Qaeda."[37]

Prospectively and retrospectively, these remarks provided a cogent, realist critique of the centerpiece of the George W. Bush administration's invasion of Iraq. They sharply differentiated his position on the war from that of his main opponent, Hillary Clinton. It fired up the antiwar Left in the run-up to the Iowa caucuses, and it supplied the premise for his pledge to withdraw American combat troops from Iraq by a date certain—a possibility that was ironically enhanced by the success of Bush's 2007 "surge" of additional troops to Iraq—a policy that Obama strongly opposed.

Howard Dean had demonstrated in 2004 the political advantages that accrued to the antiwar candidate during the Democratic primary season. And while Dean ultimately self-destructed in the Iowa caucuses, he forced John Kerry—the ultimate nominee—noticeably to the left on the Iraq issue. Senator Obama absorbed this lesson and used it shrewdly in his campaign against Hillary Clinton, who had voted in the Senate to authorize the use of force in Iraq and stubbornly resisted any expression of remorse or self-reflection for that decision.

Hillary Clinton sought to counter Obama's challenge by casting doubt on his experience in the field of national security—a field, however, in which her own résumé was at the time a bit thin. Senator Obama worked to neutralize this by emphasizing his multicultural background, his experience of living abroad during his youth, his cadre of experienced foreign policy advisers, and his readiness to encourage Democrats to change the way they thought about national security.

He spoke of foreign policy in a somewhat different vocabulary, but one that had a natural appeal on the Left. He downplayed great power diplomacy. He emphasized the central importance of transnational challenges such as nonproliferation, climate change, and energy security. He condemned the Iraq war as a major mistake rather than a reasonable idea, badly executed. He highlighted the interconnectedness of the world and the necessity of multilateral cooperation.

He extolled the importance of adding new instruments to the U.S. diplomatic tool kit. He promised to talk with the leaders of rogue states—Iran, Syria, Cuba, North Korea, and Venezuela—without preconditions during his first year as president. He portrayed himself as the candidate who understood the profound changes in the world and how American foreign policy needed to be adjusted to cope with them. And he offered such admonitions in language that was compatible with the views of liberal internationalists in the Democratic Party.

On trade, he vied with Hillary Clinton for union support by voicing a rather protectionist agenda. He signaled that he would vigorously enforce existing agreements, urged a time-out on new trade liberalization efforts, and promised that he would insist on renegotiating labor and environmental features of NAFTA. He was the beneficiary of a favor from House Speaker Nancy Pelosi, who set aside the normal ground rules for handling trade agreements negotiated under fast-track procedures, thus sparing him a potentially tough vote to ratify bilateral trade agreements the Bush administration had concluded with Panama, Colombia, and South Korea.

Barack Obama did not ignore the Democratic Party's essential need to demonstrate toughness on national security. He juxtaposed a "war of choice" in Iraq, with a "war of necessity" in Afghanistan. A misguided intervention in Iraq, he argued, had diverted the Bush administration's attention away from the greater dangers posed by al-Qaeda in Afghanistan, where, he observed, the United States was losing ground in a geopolitical theater of greater strategic importance. Extricating the United States from combat in Iraq and devoting greater resources to vanquishing Islamic extremists in South Asia were two sides, he argued, of the same coin.

In short, he positioned himself favorably for the Democratic nomination on the foreign policy front. He changed the conversation on national security issues somewhat, and in the process put Hillary Clinton on the defensive, making her sound like a conventional candidate committed to the same old, same old at a time when young Democratic Party voters were ostensibly yearning for change. More important, he organized a disciplined and surprisingly effective ground game for rounding up delegates, particularly in a host of far-flung, small states. He virtually monopolized the black

vote in battleground states like North Carolina and Georgia, and he punc-
tured Hillary Clinton's "aura of inevitability" by winning big in Iowa and
other early contests.

Both Dwight Eisenhower and Barack Obama demonstrated a knack for cultivating their political base in order to nail down the nomination of their
respective parties while leaving themselves the flexibility to adapt their
policy positions pragmatically to their political needs during the general
election, and the necessities of international politics thereafter.

In the early maneuvering for the 2016 election, one sees a variety of
familiar tactics. Rand Paul initially sought to brand himself as a neo-
isolationist on grounds of fiscal prudence and risk aversion toward humanitarian interventionism and external nation-building missions. But in the
face of emerging geopolitical challenges from Vladimir Putin's Russia,
Xi Jinping's China, and Islamist extremists occupying large swaths of Iraq
and Syria, Paul adapted his foreign policy stance to support air strikes
against the Islamic State, suggest modifications in planned cut to the Pentagon budget, and back a somewhat more active U.S. global role.

By way of contrast, Hillary Clinton, the odds-on early favorite for the
Democratic nomination, felt free to elide pressures from left-wingers in the
party's base, differentiate her foreign policy views from those of an increasingly unpopular president, and position herself for the general election
contest by targeting her message to court centrist and moderate voters.

NOMINATING VICE PRESIDENTS

Picking a vice president is the first presidential decision a candidate for the
White House makes. In this analysis, the selection of a running mate takes
on significance for several reasons.

The duties of the vice president are often a target of derision. Constitutionally, his only assignment is to preside in the Senate, where he has no
voting power except to break infrequent ties. He cannot even speak on the
floor except with the Senate's consent. John Adams called it "the most insignificant office that ever the invention of man contrived or his imagina-
tion conceived." Will Rogers noted, "All he [the vice president] has to do is
get up in the morning and ask, 'How is the President?'"[38]

But the vice presidency, once known as a "stepping-stone to oblivion,"
has become arguably the most efficient springboard into the Oval Office.

This has less to do with the qualifications that vice presidents possess than the publicity the office affords. The Constitution provides that in case of a president's "death, resignation, or inability to discharge the powers and duties of said office, the same shall devolve on the vice president."

Over the past sixty-five years, three vice presidents—Harry Truman, Lyndon Johnson, and Gerald Ford—attained the office in this manner. In Ford's case, appointed by Nixon as his vice president when Spiro Agnew resigned, he succeeded to the presidency without ever having won an elective national office.[39]

Two more—Richard Nixon and George H. W. Bush—ran subsequently and successfully for the presidency. Three more—Hubert Humphrey in 1968, Walter Mondale in 1984, and Al Gore in 2000—failed in later bids for the Oval Office, the latter two by quite narrow margins. Gore did indeed win the popular vote, though he came up short in the Electoral College as a result of a highly contested vote in Florida, a matter eventually adjudicated by the Supreme Court. Dick Cheney is the only vice president in recent memory who plausibly disclaimed any interest in converting service in that office into a future bid for the presidency.

Before 1960, Lyndon Johnson, who was the majority leader of the Senate, repeatedly said that he "wouldn't trade a vote for a gavel." But prior to the Democratic Convention that year, he asked his staff to research how many vice presidents had succeeded to the presidency. They discovered that ten had. After joining John Kennedy's ticket, Johnson responded to a question from Clare Booth Luce as to why he had accepted the nomination by saying, "Clare, I looked it up; one out of every four presidents has died in office. I'm a gamblin' man darlin', and this is the only chance I got."[40]

But the vice presidency has acquired growing weight in the scheme of practical governance. The vice president has become a regular member of the cabinet and the National Security Council, thereby obtaining a potential voice in the management of foreign as well as domestic affairs. His office is now in the West Wing. A line item in the Executive Budget ensures him a substantial staff. And, in addition, he resides in an official residence.

As the institutionalization of the office has proceeded, moreover, it has acquired greater political weight. In part, this reflects the growing tendency for so-called outsiders to run for the presidency, and their recognition of the need to balance their ticket with someone familiar with Washington rituals, knowledgeable about how the federal government works, and capable of performing substantive as well as political and ceremonial functions.

Since Jimmy Carter's presidency, vice presidents have been asked to tackle increasingly significant roles. Walter Mondale, George H. W. Bush, Al Gore, Dick Cheney, and Joe Biden were chosen in part to bolster their party ticket's national security credentials. And some observers have argued that Dick Cheney exercised influence comparable to the president's in some areas of policy during George W. Bush's first term.[41]

Yet, the procedures for selecting vice presidents remain unbelievably casual. The selection of a running mate is normally finalized hastily at the party conventions. Only one voice—that of the party's nominee for the presidency—is decisive. Rarely is the running mate chosen for his capabilities to govern. The decisive consideration is normally what he or she can contribute to the presidential nominee's victory in the general election.

Those consulted on the decision are usually few in number and are largely limited to politicians close to the presidential candidate. The final decisions are usually made under immense pressures of time. And the major preoccupation of those involved is generally with ticket balancing—weighing the political appeal of a potential nominee's geography, gender, age, ethnicity, and religion. The conventions invariably rubber-stamp the presidential candidate's choice.

Presidential nominees can select running mates to either bolster their support with the party base or broaden the appeal of the ticket to centrist swing voters and members of the other party. These choices are not mutually exclusive.

Neither Harry Truman nor Dwight Eisenhower devoted much time or effort to selecting a vice president, which they preferred to leave to their party's pros.

John Kennedy chose Lyndon Johnson, against the strong convictions of his brother and campaign chairman, Bobby Kennedy, because he needed to shore up the support of Democrats in the Old South and secure the electoral votes of Johnson's home state of Texas. He also welcomed Johnson's Protestant affiliation to balance his own Roman Catholic faith. Johnson, moreover, appeared well qualified for the job and promised to help deliver votes on the Hill.[42]

In 1968, Richard Nixon's selection of Spiro Agnew, the governor of Maryland, as his running mate revealed an electoral strategy aimed at securing a strong showing in the "rim-lands" on the periphery of the Old South.

Following a bruising fight for the nomination with Ronald Reagan in 1976, Gerald Ford was not prepared to tap the California governor as his running mate. But he did consult with him about his choice, and Reagan's nod to Bob Dole, along with the Kansas senator's broad support from veterans, the disabled, and farmers, proved decisive in Ford's selection.

Reagan considered the most unusual arrangement of all for broadening his base of support—a kind of co-presidency with his predecessor, Gerald Ford. Dubbed the "Dream Ticket," the idea created a huge buzz at the 1980 GOP Convention for a couple of days. Ford offered Reagan a wealth of Washington experience, and a reassuring presence for those independents who regarded Reagan as too radical. Ford, and close colleagues like Henry Kissinger and Alan Greenspan, evidently believed the vice presidency might permit them to hang on to significant policy-making responsibilities.

But on sober second thought, Ford recognized that the arrangement would not work, and Reagan and his political advisers decided that they had not run an arduous campaign only to cede major policy responsibilities to party rivals. His fallback was George H. W. Bush, who had put up a spirited fight for the nomination and offered geographic balance and foreign policy experience.

Bill Clinton set aside the normal ticket balancing in favor of ticket re-inforcement through the selection of Al Gore, a politician of comparable age, from another small state in the rural South. But Gore was a conservative Democrat who knew Washington well, had solid experience on national security issues, and had voted in support of President Bush to authorize the Gulf War in 1990.

Two presidents—Jimmy Carter and George W. Bush—selected vice presidential nominees whom they felt could help them govern. Carter wrapped up the nomination early in 1976 and devoted much time and attention to the process of choosing a running mate. In the end, he decided to offset his own lack of experience in Washington by picking Walter Mondale, a senator from Minnesota, whom he expected to help him in dealing with Congress and managing key foreign policy matters.

George W. Bush first asked Dick Cheney to handle the process of picking a vice president, and in the end persuaded him to accept the assignment himself. Cheney, a former White House chief of staff, GOP whip in the House of Representatives, and secretary of defense, initially demurred on grounds that he had experienced heart trouble, had two DUI convictions on his record, and came from Wyoming, a state with only three electoral votes. But Bush chose him in order to add some kind of gravitas to his own candidacy, and because Cheney's declared lack of ambitions subsequently to run for the presidency ensured his loyalty.

In 2008, many Democrats hoped that Barack Obama would select his main rival for the nomination, Hillary Clinton, as his running mate. But the lengthy nomination campaign had left some scars, and as one Obama adviser later observed, "You can't have two alpha dogs on the ticket."[43] Instead, Obama chose Joe Biden, who knew Washington, had served in the Senate for three decades, and was a respected voice on foreign policy.

TAKEAWAYS

The critical ingredient of any successful bid to secure a major party's presidential nomination is assiduous cultivation of the party faithful, who are needed to organize for a general election campaign, raise the money required to finance it, persuade potential voters of the merits of their cause, and get their voters to the polls on Election Day. Playing to the base during lengthy nomination fights impels candidates to pay at least strong lip service to the dominant foreign policy reflexes of his or her party

Platforms provide one litmus test for a party's foreign policy DNA. They are generally designed to fire up party regulars, rather than to formulate precise policy guidelines for the party's nominee.

Slavish reiteration of foreign policy proposals reflecting the preferences of the party's base may, of course, drag a candidate so far to the right or the left that they alienate the swing voters needed to win a general election. Little wonder platforms are often set aside once the party convention is over.

Incumbent presidents have a natural advantage in cultivating party regulars. After all, they can bring the wherewithal of the federal government to bear on the task. Of course, they also have a record to defend, and general elections are frequently referenda on the incumbent's record.

In peacetime, incumbent presidents rarely confront a serious intraparty challenge to their renomination for a second term. Even more infrequently does such a challenge impel major changes in foreign policy of the sort Gerald Ford felt he had to undertake during his battle with Ronald Reagan in 1976. George H. W. Bush's success abroad had a perverse political effect at home; in a safer, more tranquil world, his impressive national security credentials traded at a lower premium with the electorate.

When a major party candidate has not held national elective office before, his or her quest for the nomination arguably requires not only more extensive pandering to the party base but also greater deference to the foreign policy DNA of the party. But adroit candidates can retain a healthy measure of political maneuverability, as Dwight Eisenhower and Barack Obama demonstrated.

Although vice presidents have assumed more consequential duties, the process for their selection remains incredibly informal, even casual. But it is reassuring that five of the last six presidents chose running mates with some significant foreign policy experience. The lone exception—George H. W. Bush—possessed such experience himself. Needless to add, this does not assure vice presidents major influence over national security policy decisions. That remains dependent on their relationship with the president and his respect for their judgment.

3 CAMPAIGNS

Opportunities and Challenges

for Incumbents

FOR INCUMBENT PRESIDENTS, ELECTION DAY CONSTITUTES A deadline, a time of reckoning, an accountability moment. Like the proverbial hanging, it concentrates the mind. When a sitting president goes into campaign mode, he understands that the election will be a referendum on his policy performance during his time in office—a test of the political consequences of his foreign policy decisions.

As Harry McPherson, a wise observer of Washington's ways, once noted, at some point in his first term a president's approach to policy will move from "neutral bureaucratic" to "partisan political." Richard Nixon expressed a similar sentiment to his chief of staff, Bob Haldeman, eighteen months before the 1972 election: "We're going to have to make a shift . . . throughout our entire shop to begin a totally oriented commitment to relating everything we do to the political side without appearing to do so. The question to be asked in weighing every proposal is: Does this help us politically."[1]

The priority accorded foreign policy varies from one election to another. President Kennedy took office at the height of the Cold War—a time when the priorities seemed clear. "Domestic policy can only defeat us," he observed, "foreign policy can kill us." When the Cold War ended, President George H. W. Bush's exemplary foreign policy achievements traded at a lower premium, and he lost to Bill Clinton, whose campaign theme was, "It's the economy, stupid!"

Incumbents obviously enjoy key advantages in running for reelection. Most enjoy a free ride through the primary season and can focus their efforts on raising money for the general election campaign. Even more important, they can act; their rivals can only speak. And they have the formidable resources of the federal government at their disposal.

The national security treasure chest is indeed a sizable pork barrel. A president can beef up the defense budget, approve lucrative weapons projects, and direct foreign aid to countries that have a large diaspora in the United States. He can direct threats or propose sanctions against unpopular "pariah" countries. He can extend protection or propose subsidies to domestic industries confronting formidable competition from foreign firms. He can time foreign policy moves to maximize their potential impact on his reelection chances. The memoirs of presidents and their associates are replete with illustrative examples.

In the spring of 1948, with an election approaching, President Truman recognized Israel eleven minutes after it proclaimed its statehood, despite the firm opposition of his secretary of state, George Marshall. A variety of factors underlay his decision; political considerations—the location of substantial Jewish communities in key electoral strongholds and their demonstrated fund-raising potential—were certainly among them.[2]

In the fall of 1984, President Reagan countered Democratic criticism of his management of East–West relations with a "course correction" speech in January, and a widely publicized September meeting with Foreign Minister Andrei Gromyko at the White House.

In May 1992, officials in the George H .W. Bush administration publicly ruled out the sale of F-16s to Taiwan on the grounds that it would constitute a violation of an August 1982 agreement the United States had concluded with Beijing. Barely a month later, President Bush, now running behind Bill Clinton in the polls, announced at a plant in Fort Worth, Texas, that 150 F-16s would, after all, be sold to Taiwan. The sales promised political as well as commercial dividends in California and Texas, which were crucially important to Bush's chances for reelection. As the president informed an official from the People's Republic of China (PRC) who was visiting the White House, "This [transaction] is going ahead. It's political. Tell Deng Xiaoping that this is something I have to do."[3]

In September 1996, Bill Clinton sent cruise missiles and B-52 bombers against Iraqi air-defense installations near Baghdad. The action was provoked by Saddam Hussein's brutal attacks against his Kurdish opposition. Clinton defended the operation as the best available practical means for responding to Saddam's contempt for the UN Security Council's pledge to protect Iraqi civilians from his thuggish regime. French president Jacques Chirac criticized him for mounting gratuitous military measures to display toughness on the eve of an election.[4]

In June 2012, President Barack Obama announced that he would issue an executive order to stop the deportation of young people who had entered the United States as children of illegal immigrants. The order was immensely popular with Hispanics, and it trumped a parallel effort by Republican senator Marco Rubio to draft legislation designed to identify the GOP with immigration reform.

Of course, such measures do not always achieve their intended purpose. President George W. Bush placed a tariff on imported steel in March 2002, which was scheduled to provide three years of relief for U.S. producers against an anticipated surge in steel imports. Politics undoubtedly played some role in the decision, and large and consequential Rust Belt states like Pennsylvania, Ohio, and West Virginia were among the targeted beneficiaries.

The decision, however, precipitated controversy at home and abroad. Some Democratic leaders criticized the measures for not going far enough. Some of the president's friends complained about his deviation from his party's free-trade principles. The European Union (EU) filed a case with the World Trade Organization (WTO), which ruled against the United States and authorized stiff retaliatory sanctions. When the president refused to rescind the tariff increase, the EU approved tariffs of its own on products ranging from Florida oranges to Michigan autos—steps calculated to hurt President Bush's political prospects in states considered to be critical to his reelection. In early December 2003, the president withdrew the tariff increases. He claimed that they had served their purpose; indeed, he seemed eager to change the subject.

All incumbents tend to schedule foreign travel to dramatize their involvement in consequential diplomatic ventures, generate alluring pictures of adoring foreign crowds, or underline their efforts to utilize American power in the service of widely shared national aims. There was a time when candidates for the Oval Office felt obliged to visit "the three Is": Israel, Ireland, and Italy. In more recent campaigns, destinations like Iraq, Afghanistan, Great Britain, Germany, and Mexico have been prominent.

By the end of their tenure in office, most presidents have found their foreign policy record the object of harsh criticism. Even during the Cold War, foreign policy was occasionally a divisive and emotionally charged issue in presidential campaigns. Just as the size and role of government on domestic matters has been energetically and regularly debated, so the scope of appropriate U.S. external commitments and the proper strategies, tactics, and instruments for their pursuit have been a standard feature of presidential debates. These debates have not generally been terribly illuminating, but they reveal how incumbents expect to pursue and rationalize foreign policy involvements in the face of uncertain and unreliable public understanding and support.[5]

As reelection campaigns loom, incumbents have a record to defend, and, if possible, to burnish. Rare is the president who is prepared to admit that previous campaign pledges were naïve, misguided, or poorly executed. He is more likely to rationalize his record by exaggerating successful ventures, identifying scapegoats for failures, and quietly jettisoning initiatives, which he did not manage to launch.

Campaigning obviously takes time. It requires incumbents to crisscross the nation making their case for a second term, and dredging up the dollars needed to fund a reelection drive. Thus campaigns regularly enforce a "time-out" from a chief executive's normal foreign policy activity. They generally impel incumbents to delegate more of the management of foreign policy to cabinet members or White House officials. Campaigns affect the leverage available to a president in international negotiations. They inject a note of uncertainty into the continuity of established U.S. policies abroad.

CAMPAIGNS AS OCCASIONS FOR DELAYING, TEMPORIZING, AND OBSCURING POLICY CHOICES

It is scarcely surprising that incumbents often find it convenient to delay controversial initiatives during reelection campaign season. A few examples will suffice to indicate why.

Lyndon Johnson and the Campaign in 1964

By the fall of 1963, Lyndon Johnson was frustrated by his impotence as vice president. He feared that his political career was at an end. He was frequently treated as an object of ridicule, even contempt, by the Kennedy family, and he suspected that he might be dropped from the Democratic Party ticket the following year. When John Kennedy was assassinated in late November 1963, however, Johnson moved into the Oval Office and inherited the same thorny policy dilemmas that had troubled his predecessor.

LBJ assumed the reins of power with impressive dexterity. His urgent priority was to legitimize his ascent to the presidency and "make himself seem less like a usurper."[6] To this end, he promised to maintain the continuity of President Kennedy's policies, pressed JFK's cabinet members and White House staff to remain in their posts, and devoted the bulk of his time and attention to translating Kennedy's domestic legislative proposals swiftly into law.

Securing a record of concrete achievement happened coincidentally to be the prerequisite for Johnson to obtain the Democratic Party's presidential nomination in 1964. He was determined to run and was convinced that his campaign for the presidency should emphasize domestic accomplishments at the same time positioning him as a prudent man of peace on the world stage.

Vietnam was more than a blip on the radar screen, but it was neither Washington's central policy preoccupation nor a cause for public turmoil on America's campuses or streets. Johnson was not sure about what to do in Indochina. He wished to preserve the continuity of existing policy, but the policy he inherited from Kennedy was somewhat contradictory and susceptible to drift.

JFK had promised to pursue the Cold War with greater energy than his predecessor, Dwight Eisenhower. But by the fall of 1963, Kennedy was uncertain how to proceed in Vietnam. He had increased the number of U.S. military advisers in the South from a few hundred to more than fifteen thousand, but security conditions in the countryside were deteriorating. Kennedy appointed a prominent Republican, Henry Cabot Lodge, as the American ambassador in Saigon and gave him substantial discretion in determining the U.S. course of action. Lodge and several senior members of Kennedy's national security team in Washington became skeptical about the ability of President Ngo Dinh Diem to sustain the authority and legitimacy of his regime.

Although the president evidently harbored doubts about the wisdom of American military involvement in Vietnam, he approved a cable in late August 1963 giving U.S. support for a South Vietnamese military coup attempt against Diem. All of Kennedy's senior national security team were away from Washington at the time, and the president was in Hyannis Port. The cable conveying the decision was authorized without even convening a meeting of his senior advisers or eliciting an objective analysis of the costs and consequences of such a coup.

Kennedy subsequently had second thoughts, considered walking back the authorization of the coup attempt, and even contemplated withdrawing one thousand advisers by the end of the year. He explained his policy dilemma to Charlie Bartlett, a press columnist and friend: "We don't have a prayer of prevailing there [Vietnam]. These people hate us. They are going to throw our tails out of there at almost any point. But I can't give up a piece of territory like that to the Communists and then get the American people to re-elect me."[7] In short, at the time of the president's assassination, the Kennedy administration appeared simultaneously to be actively cultivating an option to disengage from Vietnam, while drifting, as a result of a coup d'état that it had endorsed, toward expanded involvement.

Lyndon Johnson did not resolve this confusion. On November 26, the day after Kennedy's funeral, the new president approved National Security Action Memorandum 273, which affirmed a U.S. commitment to "assist the [South Vietnamese] to win their contest against the externally directed and supported Communist conspiracy." He sent Ambassador Lodge back to Vietnam to pass this assurance to the new government in Saigon.[8] And he also signed off on the recommendation to withdraw the one thousand military advisers that Secretary of Defense Robert McNamara and General Maxwell Taylor had been persuaded by Kennedy to include in the report of their recent inspection trip to Saigon—a measure that, however, was never implemented.

Meanwhile, conditions on the ground in Vietnam continued to slip. Diem's successors in Saigon possessed limited authority and exhibited little competence. The U.S. Embassy in Saigon was wracked by divisive infighting. The Viet Cong stepped up insurgent activities in the countryside, and the U.S.–South Vietnamese Strategic Hamlet Program was mired in disarray.

The Central Intelligence Agency (CIA) reported all of this. Some military commanders in the field acknowledged it. High-level visitors from Washington were exposed to it. And some in Congress understood it.

By the spring of 1964, Johnson's national security advisers were urging him to take more robust actions to respond to North Vietnam's growing military assertiveness, and to arrest the spread of political rot in Saigon. Ambassador Lodge recommended air strikes on the North. Defense Secretary McNamara proposed the use of "selective and carefully graduated force" against North Vietnam once proper preparations and warning had been completed. The Joint Chiefs of Staff (JCS) pushed the White House to bomb the North and send American combat troops to the South. National Security Adviser McGeorge Bundy urged the president to seek a congressional resolution giving him authority to take whatever actions were deemed necessary to defend peace and security in Southeast Asia during the coming summer.[9] South Vietnam's leaders steadily pressed Johnson to "go North." And Secretary of State Dean Rusk expressed disquiet about "reports" that the president was not acting "because of the upcoming elections."[10]

Johnson shared, of course, the prevailing anti-Communist sentiments of his era, and as a Texan he was not inclined to duck a fight. But he was also deeply apprehensive about the strategic and political consequences of America's expanding involvement in Indochina. One of his closest confidantes on Capitol Hill, Senator Richard Russell of Georgia, reinforced Johnson's anxieties. So did other respected leaders of his party—Senators Mike Mansfield, Wayne Morse, Ernest Gruening, and Frank Church among them. All were squeamish about the political risks of expanded commitments in Southeast Asia, but Johnson was also determined not to "be the president who saw Southeast Asia go the way China went."

The imperative force driving President Johnson in 1964 was the impending election. "The preemptive concern," according to Bundy, was "win the election, not the war."[11] Vietnam was the only issue Republicans had to use against LBJ, and he fully expected GOP leaders—including Richard Nixon, Nelson Rockefeller, possibly Everett Dirksen, and surely Barry Goldwater— to push for stronger military actions against the North Vietnamese. He saw no political advantage, however, in using his election campaign to prepare the public for military intervention in a remote and dangerous part of the world.

The GOP's selection of Barry Goldwater as its nominee reinforced Johnson's resolve to dodge the Vietnam issue during the campaign. Goldwater inspired fierce loyalty among the conservative faithful. But the GOP remained a minority party, and moderate Republicans were not reconciled to his candidacy. Independents, among others, were alienated by Goldwater's "trigger happy" rhetoric on issues of war and peace. His off-the-cuff suggestion that the United States should "lob a nuke into the men's room at the Kremlin" alarmed many and reinforced LBJ's determination to juxtapose his reputation for "prudence" and "moderation" against Goldwater's "strident anti-Communism" and his tendency to "shoot from the lip."

For the duration of the campaign, therefore, Johnson improvised a mixed strategy toward Vietnam. He chose not to alter the policy status quo. Secretary of Defense McNamara designed a "graduated response," aimed at reconciling the administration's perceived "need to intervene against Communist insurgents with its need to minimize the risk of escalation . . . and Johnson's desire to get elected with his need to address the difficult situation in South Vietnam."[12]

Implicitly this reflected LBJ's resolve to avoid escalation of the conflict by bombing the North or deploying American combat troops, to avoid the withdrawal of U.S. military advisers behind the diplomatic cover of neutralization, to delay dramatically increased assistance to the South Vietnamese, and to duck serious discussion of the "domino theory" that many regarded as the fundamental reason for sticking with Saigon.

To maintain this approach, at a time when most members of the JCS were pressing for more robust military measures, Johnson muffled intramural struggles by narrowing his circle of principal advisers. This not only helped prevent leaks but also insulated high-level interagency deliberations from critics. When Lodge resigned as ambassador to Vietnam in order to enter GOP primaries, Johnson replaced him with General Maxwell Taylor, who could provide political "cover" with the Republicans and with the Congress.[13] The president dissuaded General Curtis LeMay from retiring as a way of obligating him to keep his hawkish views on the war confidential. He kept the chiefs on board by assuring them that he was "considering" more decisive measures—a tactic William Bundy (Johnson's key Vietnam adviser and McGeorge Bundy's brother) considered "an emotional safety valve" for those who might otherwise press the president to take actions he was anxious to avoid—at least until the election was over.

Above all, Johnson did not want Vietnam to become a central focus of the campaign, nor did he wish to be branded as the guy who either "went to war" in Indochina or "lost Vietnam." When McGeorge Bundy asked him in March 1964 what his personal thinking was about Vietnam, Johnson's response was telling: "I just can't believe that we can't take 15,000 [*sic*] advisers and 200,000 [South Vietnamese troops] and maintain the status quo for six months. I just believe we can do that, if we do it right."[14] The Democratic National Convention was six months away, and it was not difficult to deduce the motivations for his thinking.

Thus Johnson steadfastly sought to keep American military involvement in Indochina below the radar screen of the electorate. He kicked the toughest choices down the road. Those military actions he took were generally obscured from the Congress and the public by calculation, stealth, and disingenuousness.

One should not, of course, discount the serious political and moral dilemma Johnson faced. He regarded himself as merely a "trustee" of Kennedy's policy—"a political actor without real political power."[15] He recognized that a major escalation of the fighting was a momentous decision for which he (or someone else) needed the mandate of a presidential election victory. Yet he was not prepared to make the case for such a decision in the middle of his own campaign. So he steered clear of the subject as much as possible. When he did address it, his comments tended to mislead—particularly when he declared that the United States "is not about to send American boys nine or ten thousand miles away from home to do what Asian boys ought to be doing for themselves."[16]

In this context, the administration was forced to rely on less visible measures to bolster South Vietnamese morale, mollify the Pentagon, and convince Hanoi that the United States was no pushover. Covert actions were especially appealing, for they allowed the United States to apply pressure on the North and bolster morale in the South while retaining plausible deniability and limiting the risks of escalation. In the summer of 1964, the president authorized covert raids on North Vietnamese territory by South Vietnamese commandos accompanied by American advisers, plus increased surveillance patrols by U.S. naval intelligence-gathering vessels along the North Vietnamese coast.

The Tonkin Gulf incident in early August 1964 was a by-product of those activities as intelligence failures and policy misjudgments produced a naval engagement with North Vietnamese vessels. At the time, the circumstances surrounding the incident were extremely murky. Following the attack on the USS *Maddox*, Johnson withheld any reprisals, not least because of suspicions that it constituted a North Vietnamese reaction to U.S. authorized covert actions. But this left the president, in Bundy's words, "less effectively anti-Communist than he wanted to be."[17]

Johnson consequently instructed McNamara to swiftly develop a list of appropriate bombing targets in the North that could be hit if the attacks persisted. Ambiguous evidence of a further attack—later judged to be spurious—provided the occasion for both military retaliation and an urgent and successful bid for congressional support. The reprisal raids were modest, but they served Johnson's political needs.

As the incident unfolded, Kenny O'Donnell, a senior Kennedy holdover on the White House staff, and Johnson agreed that the president was being "tested" and would have to respond firmly "to defend himself not against the North Vietnamese but against Barry Goldwater and the Republican right wing." McGeorge Bundy later observed to LBJ that "separating Eisenhower from Goldwater was the real objective of the exercise."[18]

Aside from the retaliatory raids, the president exploited this "moment of high feeling" to secure his legislative aim—the Tonkin Gulf Resolution, which provided a congressional license for the later expansion of the war. Johnson's strategy paid off handsomely at home. He won the election in a landslide. Yet through half measures whose potential consequences had been neither thoroughly vetted nor publicly acknowledged, Johnson also set the country on a dangerous path. He squandered a chance to educate voters about future strategic choices in Indochina. Worse yet, the administration failed even to utilize the time to examine carefully the policy options that LBJ would later be forced to confront. For this, McGeorge Bundy must bear heavy responsibility. As national security adviser, the formulation and coordination of potential policy options clearly fell within his sphere of responsibility. Perhaps the fear of leaks forestalled analysis of sensitive alternative courses of action in Vietnam. Yet studies and simulations that supplied strong hints of future trouble in Indochina were largely ignored.[19]

Twin fears drove these decisions as they shaped Johnson's actions during the campaign. One was the president's apprehension that a candid explanation of what the United States was doing in Vietnam might set off a stampede from the Right for "victory," thereby complicating efforts to impose what LBJ considered "prudent" limits on the conflict. The other was his anxiety that public acknowledgement of the cost of an expanding intervention in Indochina would place his Great Society programs at risk. The result was that the public gave Johnson a political mandate in November

1964 with little forewarning that the American stake in Indochina was about to be dramatically increased.

President Johnson's experience in 1964 was by no means unique. The prospect of a reelection campaign often reinforces reservations about launching controversial foreign policy initiatives. Such initiatives demand presidential time that is in short supply. The potential results are inherently uncertain. It is consequently tempting to delay action on the supposition that success will be more readily achievable after securing a renewed political mandate from the electorate.

George H. W. Bush and the Campaign in 1992

President George H. W. Bush faced a similar political-strategic dilemma in 1992. Yugoslavia, without its longtime leader, Marshall Tito, was falling apart. Its dismemberment jeopardized security in southeastern Europe. Risks to the stability of the region were apparent. Pressures on the administration to take action to check the Serbs grew. The president's readiness to respond affirmatively to them did not.

As the 1992 election campaign commenced, the United States enjoyed a position of unparalleled global primacy. The president was widely admired for his deft mobilization of an international coalition to eject Saddam Hussein from Kuwait. His public-approval ratings were in the stratosphere. With the disintegration of the Soviet Union in late 1991, the United States was left without a military peer. And in the Balkans, it now had less reason to worry about Russia's close and long-standing links with the Serbs.

The president, however, faced a surprisingly tough fight for reelection. The Democrats intended to make domestic issues the principal battleground, and political experts sensed that in a post–Cold War world, President George H. W. Bush might be politically vulnerable. On the foreign policy front, meanwhile, the administration had higher priorities than the Balkans. Above all, the president hoped to define a new relationship with Moscow, advance an Arab-Israeli peace process in the Middle East, and wrap up the North American Free Trade Agreement (NAFTA) with Canada and Mexico .

President Bush and the leading members of his national security team— Brent Scowcroft, Jim Baker, Larry Eagleburger, Dick Cheney, and Colin Powell—were all wary of military involvement in the Balkans. They did not believe that vital U.S. interests were at stake in that region; they were apprehensive about the costs of intervention; they doubted that public support could be readily mobilized. Secretary of State Jim Baker summed up their view most succinctly: "We don't have a dog in that hunt."

Meanwhile, the Europeans were clamoring for a more decisive international role, and wanted to take the lead on Balkan issues through the European Community. The administration was happy to give them as much running room as they desired.

The Bush administration did not exactly wash its hands of the Balkans in the spring and summer of 1992. It pushed the Europeans to ostracize the Serbs and to undertake urgent measures to address a growing humanitarian crisis. But there were clear limits to the administration's willingness to intervene: Any use of force, it was felt, should be multilateral, authorized by the UN, and limited to the provision of humanitarian aid.

While President Bush expected to win reelection, he knew he had a fight on his hands, and he preferred to tackle the underlying problems of the Balkans, if at all, after the burdens of the campaign were behind him. Secretary of State Baker's day-to-day involvement on the issue ended in early July when he was called back to the White House to coordinate the president's faltering reelection efforts. And, of course, the president was increasingly absorbed by a campaign that proved difficult to "kick start."

In both these cases, political campaigns imposed significant constraints on American foreign policy. In 1964, LBJ sought to sustain a status quo approach in Vietnam despite pressure for action from his key advisers. He therefore sought to avert debate on a contentious issue, which he feared would complicate his reelection chances. After the election, he faced even more difficult choices without the benefit of careful analysis of the alternatives or an enlightened public forewarned of the costs and risks of action—or, for that matter, inaction.

In 1992, Bush shared his advisers' skepticism about military intervention in the Balkans, and used the forthcoming campaign as an additional excuse to leave the initiative to Europeans who seemed eager to grasp it. His opponent, Bill Clinton, criticized the administration's passivity in the Balkans and endorsed a course of action—"lift and strike" (that is, lift the embargo on arms to the Bosnians, and undertake air strikes on the Serbs)— that proved easier to embrace during the campaign than to implement once he became president.

Examples of the tendency to kick tough issues down the road are easy to multiply. In 2012, President Barack Obama was reported to have been overheard speaking on the telephone with Prime Minister Dmitry

Medvedev of Russia, explaining his limited flexibility on key bilateral issues: "On all these issues, but particularly missile defense, this can be solved but it's important for him [Vladimir Putin] to give me space. This is my last election. After my election I have more flexibility."

CAMPAIGNS AS A SPUR TO ACTION

If campaigns sometimes impel incumbents to accept a "pause" in their foreign policy activity, they can also encourage action to burnish a record of achievement on which to base a bid for a second term. Immediate events may impel an incumbent to improvise a response. But strategic plans may also be translated into a longer-term agenda on which an incumbent can seek reelection. For Richard Nixon, the conduct of foreign policy constituted the essence of his 1972 campaign. For others, electoral considerations may inspire efforts to fix established policies or belatedly honor previous campaign promises.

In 1971 and 1972, creative foreign policy provided the substance of Richard Nixon's bid for four more years in the White House. When he took office in 1969, he recognized that he would have to alter the trajectory of U.S. policy toward Vietnam if he was to have any chance of earning a second term. He presumed this would require adjustments in U.S. policy toward Hanoi and its major backers in the Moscow and Beijing.

By the spring of 1971, Nixon had clearly expressed to White House staffers his hopes of wrapping up the Vietnam War, scheduling a summit with Moscow, and organizing a visit to China by mid-1972 when the party conventions were slated to commence. He understood that this would require careful planning, a flair for the dramatic, subtle timing, and a bit of luck. He also figured that success would virtually ensure his reelection.

At the time, Nixon appeared convinced that these initiatives had to be completed by July 1972, when the party conventions would begin—a timetable that, at least with respect to the China "opening," Mao Zedong anticipated. Asked by the journalist Edgar Snow when to expect a move by Nixon, Mao responded, "The presidential election would be in 1972, would it not? Therefore . . . Mr. Nixon might send an envoy first, but was not himself likely to come to Peking before early 1972."[20]

The diplomacy of the Nixon administration was heavily driven by geopolitical calculations. But the president also believed that major adjustments in U.S. relations with the Soviet Union and China could stabilize international relations and deprive American liberals of key issues, and thus "make Nixon and the Republicans the new leaders in advocating a progressive approach to foreign affairs."[21]

Nixon's major foreign policy initiatives for 1972, moreover, were clearly shaped and carefully timed for their political effects at home. The president was in Beijing for the "opening to China" before voters in New Hampshire went to the polls. He conducted a summit meeting with Moscow and nailed down the SALT I arms control agreement before the Oregon and California primaries in late May and early June. Nixon's national security adviser, Henry Kissinger, announced that peace in Vietnam was "at hand" in late October, just days before the election. Politically, with the electoral timetable in mind, the president's diplomacy in 1972 was a tour de force.

To be sure, when Nixon entered the White House in 1969, he had expected to wrap up the Vietnam War swiftly through a negotiated settlement. But if he misjudged Hanoi's tenacity and perseverance, prodded and cajoled by Secretary of Defense Melvin Laird, he also embarked on a "Vietnamization" of the war effort, keenly aware that he needed to extricate most U.S. troops from that conflict within his first term.

American troop withdrawals—which tempered opposition at home while providing a potential incentive for greater self-reliance in Saigon— were Nixon's ace in the hole. They were subject to Washington's management at a time when little else in the combat zone was under U.S control. Nixon used periodic announcements of troop reductions to remind the public that the participation of American forces in the war was coming inexorably to an end.

In January 1972, there were still more than 130,000 American troops in Vietnam. President Nixon declared that 70,000 would be withdrawn within three months. In April, he announced another planned drawdown of 20,000. In late August, he said still another 12,000 would be brought home, leaving fewer than 30,000 there on Election Day. Those who remained were considered a source of reassurance to Saigon and a bargaining chip to trade for the return of American POWs.

The administration was especially sensitive to the timing of late 1972 troop withdrawals. The president and his key White House advisers intended to delay them as long as possible so that any adverse political or military consequences they provoked in Vietnam would occur "too late to affect the election."[22] In fact, Kissinger favored a public announcement that

U.S. troops would be out by the end of 1972 so that the final reductions could take place after the election returns were in.

The closest Richard Nixon had come in 1968 to having a "secret plan" for ending the war in Vietnam was his readiness to test Moscow's political will and ability to pressure Hanoi into settling the conflict to advance U.S.–Soviet "détente." Nixon's "opening" to China had a comparable motivation, plus the collateral effect of providing Moscow an incentive to adopt a more forthcoming posture toward Washington's bid for detente.

Nixon's initiatives failed to induce either Moscow or Beijing to substantially moderate, let alone terminate, political and material support for Hanoi.[23] But they increased the maneuverability of American diplomacy, diverted attention away from American policy dilemmas in Indochina, and underscored Nixon's ability to define the international agenda and hold the international spotlight.

Visits to both capitals were timed for maximum political advantage and staged with a theatrical flair for drama. Events were scheduled for prime-time television coverage in the United States and arranged in a fashion that underscored the president's decisive role in conducting American diplomacy. The substance of the visits was also shaped with sensitivity to the concerns of key constituencies in the United States.

This is not to suggest that Nixon took no political risks with these initiatives. Lowering tensions with China and the Soviet Union scarcely qualified as pandering to the GOP base. On the contrary, conservatives were apprehensive about Nixon's courting Communist nations, and wary of betraying old friends in Saigon and Taipei.

In negotiating the Shanghai Communiqué, as Kissinger later put it, the trick was to come up with a formula that would "encompass Taiwan but remove it as a bone of contention." This required language that would "squelch criticism from the Left in China and the Right in America."[24] He managed to finesse the U.S. position with respect to Taiwan by outlining the views of "Chinese on both sides of the Taiwan Straits" and refusing to challenge them, by putting future American troop withdrawals into the context of incremental adjustments that would unfold as "tensions in the area decline," and by leaving the U.S. Defense Treaty and its security commitment to Taiwan intact for the time being—an undertaking that Kissinger confirmed publicly in a press briefing while still on PRC soil.

The implicit linkages expressed in the Shanghai Communiqué were subtle and nuanced, and they provided a workable framework for U.S.–

Chinese coexistence, which has endured for four decades. They also worked politically in America in an election year, not least because conservative Republicans like Ronald Reagan and Barry Goldwater were enlisted to voice their public support.

With respect to the May 1972 Moscow Summit, Nixon was leery of visiting the Soviet capital at a time when North Vietnam's ongoing spring offensive was underpinned by Soviet material support. So he presented Soviet leaders with a tough choice: seek to restrain Hanoi and hold a summit with the United States, or collaborate with Hanoi at the possible cost of a break with Washington. In the end, Moscow—and for that matter, Beijing— chose to swallow Nixon's bombing of Hanoi and the mining of Haiphong harbor, without lifting a finger to help the North Vietnamese. The balance of forces was adjusted on the ground. The administration subsequently offered a new and more conciliatory negotiating stance to the North. "Vietnamization" proceeded. And Nixon won his reelection in a landslide.

Nixon thus demonstrated that an approaching reelection campaign need not impose a lengthy "time-out" from foreign policy. Political calculations did, however, precipitate one noteworthy conflict over policy priorities between Nixon and his national security's adviser. The administration first revealed in January 1972 that secret talks had long been under way with the North Vietnamese. By disclosing the talks, the president sought to juxtapose the modesty of Washington's negotiating objectives—the return of all U.S. POWs, and the survival of an autonomous government in South Vietnam—against the intransigence of Hanoi's diplomacy, which sought America's collaboration in toppling the Saigon regime as U.S. troops were withdrawn.

Publicizing American negotiating efforts, Nixon hoped, would bolster domestic support for his Vietnam policy, and convince Hanoi that it could not expect merely to stand pat throughout the election season. This preoccupation was evident in the internal deliberations about the timing of announcements. As Kissinger observed to Bob Haldeman, "If we do the peace plan early in January [1972], it'll spur the opponents to tear it to pieces. We need to do it as late as possible but before they have another rallying point."[25]

Throughout the year, the administration gradually modified its negotiating position in hopes of nailing down an agreement. Hanoi seemed interested, and by early fall conditions seemed ripe for a deal in which the United States would get a cease-fire agreement and the return of all POWs in return for the acceptance of Hanoi's troops in the South in addition to the establishment of a tripartite commission and a National Council for Reconciliation in Saigon.

At this delicate point, a breach opened between the president and his national security adviser over negotiating tactics or, to be more precise, the urgency of reaching a deal before the election. Nixon was by now convinced that his trip to China and summit with the Soviets ensured his reelection even without completing a Vietnam settlement. And, too, he worried that Kissinger's zeal to achieve an early agreement might expose him to criticism from conservatives for "signaling weakness" or "selling out Saigon."

Kissinger preferred to use the election deadline as a lever to wrap up a deal. "The Vietnam negotiations," he later wrote, "were not used to affect the election; the election was used to accelerate the negotiations. It performed the role normally carried out by an ultimatum—except that it raised no issue of prestige, and, being fixed by the Constitution, was not subject to alteration."[26]

Kissinger warned Hanoi that if it waited until after the election, it would lose its best chance for a favorable settlement. He expressed confidence that Nixon would easily win reelection, thereby earning a stronger political mandate and four more years in office. If the North remained intransigent during the run-up to the polls in November, the president, he suggested, would have less incentive to accommodate its interests, and a strong motivation to take out his anger through expanded air attacks and tougher negotiating terms.

Kissinger obviously hoped the argument would put Hanoi in a more conciliatory mood. Privately, he worried that if the issue were left unresolved, Congress would seek after the election to attenuate American involvement in Indochina by imposing harsh limits on assistance to Saigon. He believed, moreover, that an agreement was within reach, and concluding it before November would clear the decks for the administration to pursue other priorities in Nixon's second term.

While Kissinger was close to an agreement in late October, South Vietnamese president Nguyen Van Thieu did not share his sense of urgency. When he saw the terms in Kissinger's draft, he refused a swift endorsement and played for time by insisting on numerous amendments.

Ironically, Thieu's dilatory tactics gave Kissinger time to whittle down Hanoi's intractable positions on a variety of subsidiary issues.[27] But Hanoi, seeking to contrast its own negotiating flexibility with Thieu's rigidity, leaked the contents of the negotiations to the press on October 25. Nixon, unwilling to risk an upheaval among his supporters on the Right, signaled to Hanoi that an agreement would have to be delayed. The election took place before agreement could be reached.

Each of the parties made a different bet on the outcome of the election. Nixon sought to diminish the risk of offending his conservative base, presuming that he would win without a settlement of the war. Kissinger tried to use the prospect of Nixon's likely victory to prod Hanoi to wrap up a deal. He thought that he could inoculate the administration against charges of a sell-out of Thieu by insisting on terms that would leave the Vietnamese president in office when American troops were withdrawn, and by promoting a Council of National Concord and Reconciliation that could not act without Thieu's concurrence.

He figured that President Thieu was not in a strong position to object; Nixon now held a large lead in the polls, and the South Vietnamese government would retain no leverage with the United States if George McGovern were to win. President Thieu doubtless recalled that he had managed to stare down Lyndon Johnson before the 1968 election. He presumably hoped that in the clutch, Nixon would not ignore the pleas of an ally. Hanoi evidently anticipated that as the election neared, Nixon's political uncertainties might be translated into additional negotiating leverage and less demanding terms for a settlement.

In the end, Nixon had the winning hand. He was less concerned about the GOP's right-wing conservatives—"where, after all, were they to go?"—than about centrist swing voters. In this respect, he was lucky in having George McGovern as his opponent. The South Dakota senator exuded little appeal to independents, and he alienated conservative Democrats. Nixon wound up, as Theodore White later put it, "triangulating" the Democrats out of their favored issues by "Vietnamizing" the war, promoting détente with the Communists, negotiating arms control agreements with adversaries, reducing the defense budget, and even stealing the liberals' thunder on several domestic issues. The assassination attempt that disabled George Wallace also served to avert an expected split vote among conservatives. Meanwhile, the fractious Democrats self-destructed, and Nixon won the election in a walk.[28]

Richard Nixon proved that a bid for reelection need not constitute a distraction from foreign policy. On the contrary, by stimulating and dramatizing diplomatic initiatives to advance American interests abroad, he harvested tangible political advantages on Election Day.

CAMPAIGNS AS OPPORTUNITIES AND INCENTIVES FOR COURSE CORRECTIONS

Nixon chose to run on his foreign policy record. For other incumbents, an approaching moment of accountability may drive efforts to tidy up their foreign policy record, belatedly fulfill past campaign promises, or signal "course corrections" in the light of changing circumstances abroad or shifting priorities at home.

Bill Clinton and the Balkans in 1995

Bill Clinton ran in 1992 as a post–Cold War "domestic policy" candidate. But he also criticized what he characterized as President Bush's diffidence in the face of a crisis in Bosnia, and he promised to "do whatever it takes to stop the slaughter of civilians" there. He argued that history demonstrated "that you can't allow the mass extermination of people and just sit by and watch it happen."[29] He promised "assertive multilateralism" and hinted broadly that, if elected, he would consider "humanitarian intervention" in the Balkans by lifting an arms embargo on the Bosnians, while utilizing American air power to strike Serb positions—an option designed to level the military playing field known as "lift and strike."

By mid-1995, however, with a reelection campaign approaching, the United States remained sidelined in the Balkans. Secretary of State Warren Christopher's meek effort to mobilize European support for "lift and strike" in the spring of 1993 had fizzled completely, leaving American policy adrift while the president devoted himself to what he considered more urgent matters.[30] A wide variety of excuses were offered to rationalize U.S. inaction—the doubts of advisers, the priority of domestic concerns, the squeamishness of the Europeans, the hypocrisy of the UN, the misgivings of Boris Yeltsin, and the forebodings contained in Robert Kaplan's book *Balkan Ghosts*.[31]

To Republican critics, Clinton's policy in the Balkans provided a metaphor for the administration's irresolute foreign policy. Dick Morris, the political consultant on whom Clinton increasingly relied, recognized the growing chaos in Bosnia as a major political liability and told the White House staff in the summer of 1995 that if the conflict was not settled, "Clinton's reelection might be in peril."[32]

The president acknowledged to his White House aide, George Stepha-nopoulos, his growing apprehension that a Bosnian denouement could be "dropped in during the middle of the campaign."[33] And as he observed a few months later, "If we let the moment slip away, we're history."[34] This con-clusion was fortified by public reactions to the brutal atrocities committed by the Serbs at Srebrenica as well as a major GOP victory in the 1994 mid-term congressional elections.

Clinton consequently ordered his advisers to come up with a more en-ergetic and effective Bosnian policy. Several developments facilitated timely policy adjustments. For one, the French and Croatians—the latter bolstered by covert arms supplies—demonstrated that the Serbs were vulnerable to attacks on the ground. For another, polls suggested that while Americans remained reluctant to introduce ground troops into the Balkans, they were more comfortable with the use of air power to restrain or punish the Serbs. The Pentagon also began to come around on that issue. And with Senator Bob Dole, the likely GOP candidate, urging a lifting of the arms embargo on Bosnia, a veto-proof margin for that measure appeared within reach on the Hill.

Fortunately for Clinton, Tony Lake, his national security adviser, mobi-lized interagency support for a more plausible and promising endgame strategy in the Balkans.[35] Richard Holbrooke, the new assistant secretary of state for European affairs, pressed aggressively for a more energetic and purposeful diplomacy. Most important, the president displayed a belated readiness to invest some of his own political capital into a major push for a settlement.

The Bosnian Serbs were warned that they would be bombed if they under-took new assaults in Bosnia. The Bosnian Muslims were reminded that if they refused to negotiate, they were on their own; that is, the United States would lift the embargo, but that was all. The Europeans were informed that we had embarked on a new course and were invited to join, but they were given no veto over American policy. This calculus provided the parties with the necessary incentives to bargain; the negotiations in Dayton were han-dled skillfully by Richard Holbrooke and his team.

The story of those negotiations has been told elsewhere.[36] Suffice it to say, its success turned a political liability into an electoral asset for Clinton in the 1996 campaign. Dole's GOP candidacy ironically provided essential political cover for Clinton throughout the Dayton negotiations and the campaign itself. As Holbrooke put it, Dole "ignored every opportunity to exploit the issue because . . . he did not want to hurt a policy with which he 'basically agreed.'"[37]

The Dayton agreement did not eliminate all politically delicate choices for the administration in Bosnia. On the contrary, its provisions required American participation in the International Peacekeeping Force (IFOR). The U.S. military was not keen on assuming such duties, and the president was reluctant to shoulder an open-ended obligation to keep American forces in the Balkans. Thus he publicly set a twelve-month time limit on the deployment of contingents attached to IFOR, even though all knowledgeable experts recognized that this was hopelessly unrealistic. The U.S. troops remained in Bosnia for years, but the limited pledge served the president's more immediate campaign needs.

Once Clinton determined that the Balkans fiasco had to be neutralized, he discovered that foreign policy provided an arena in which he could act decisively and with greater freedom from congressional constraints. The success accomplished at Dayton helped him ameliorate a reputation for foreign policy bumbling. The low casualties sustained in the Balkans encouraged the administration's contemplation of other humanitarian interventions. The active role that Clinton played in fostering reconciliation among rivals in the Balkans encouraged him to play a more active mediating role vis-à-vis other conflicts (for example, between the British and Irish, the Indians and Pakistanis, the Cypriots and Turks) during his second term. Such endeavors appealed to his hopes of earning political kudos at home for tempering strife abroad.

George W. Bush and Iraq in 2004

In 2003 and 2004, President George W. Bush and his political adviser, Karl Rove, expected to capitalize politically on the administration's swift and dazzling military victory in Afghanistan and its success in ousting Saddam Hussein.

Even when the stabilization of Iraq proved a more vexing aim, Bush bet on the public's reluctance to toss out an incumbent president in the midst of a shooting war. Highlighting national security issues was expected, as usual, to put the Democratic nominee on the defensive.

Yet a campaign based merely on the slogan "Stay the Course" appeared inadequate, given the growing difficulties on the ground. The U.S. military engagement in Iraq looked less like "mission accomplished" than a potential quagmire.[38] Some policy adjustments appeared essential due to the growing apprehensions about the intensifying insurgency in the Sunni heartland, and the many questions about the effectiveness and the durability of the U.S. occupation.

Its first overseer, Lieutenant General Jay Garner, was swiftly and unceremoniously replaced within weeks of the invasion. His successor, a former career diplomat, L. Paul "Jerry" Bremer, chose to announce dramatic but ill-considered decisions to dissolve the Iraqi army and impose a deep purge of civilian members of the Iraqi Baath Party within days of his arrival in Baghdad.

To make matters worse, no weapons of mass destruction were found. Saddam Hussein's links to al-Qaeda remained uncorroborated. American allies, with the notable exception of the British, put relatively few "boots on the ground." The intensity of sectarian strife made Iraq appear an unlikely candidate for swift transformation into a vibrant democracy. And Democratic Party criticisms of Bush's foreign policy seemed to be gaining traction. This was the context in which the president began improvising adjustments to the policy in Iraq. They took a variety of forms:

• Withdrawals of American troops, pushed by the Pentagon and field commanders, were postponed as it became clear that existing force levels were insufficient to stabilize the country.

• America's proconsul in Baghdad, Jerry Bremer, who published a September 2003 op-ed in the *Washington Post* that was not cleared by his superiors, left the White House anxious and irritable. It laid out an extremely complex plan for transforming Iraq into a constitutional democracy at a pace that was far too leisurely to fit comfortably into the president's reelection campaign plans. Bremer was consequently subjected to more rigorous supervision by a hard-nosed NSC staff member, Bob Blackwill, on behalf of Condoleezza Rice, Bush's national security adviser.

• By mid-November, the administration announced a new and compressed timetable for returning sovereignty to the Iraqis. As Rice told Bremer in late 2003, "I don't think the political situation in Washington will support another year of the current status." Transferring sovereignty by late June 2004 would formally end the occupation of Iraq before the Republican and Democratic conventions commenced.[39]

- Plans for fashioning an indigenous Iraqi political structure were also revamped. The American-appointed Iraqi Governing Council (IGC) was abolished, and a UN official, Ibrahim Brahimi, a former Algerian foreign minister, was enlisted to select and "bless" a new interim government to which sovereignty could be transferred.

- The training of Iraqi security forces was accorded higher priority and given more generous budgetary support. This did little to curb violence or shift the security responsibilities to the Iraqis in the short term, but it did mute public interest in the issue, at least for a while.

- In April 2004, a looming military showdown with the Shi'a militia in Faluja was postponed at the behest of the IGC and Brahimi, despite the misgivings of U.S. commanders, until shortly after the November election.

- Greater attention was given to Iraq's economic reconstruction, and Saudi Arabian cooperation was solicited to flood the market with oil in order to keep gas prices stable through the campaign and to help finance additional helicopter deliveries to the Pakistanis.

- The administration also pushed other Arab countries to display progress on political reform to underline the seriousness of its grandiose plans for the "democratization of the Greater Middle East."

- The administration pushed back the date for completing the Robb-Silberman Commission Report—which examined intelligence reporting on weapons of mass destruction—until March 31, 2005, well after the election was over.

These steps hardly added up to a wholesale policy reversal in Iraq. In the aggregate, however, they constituted a course correction that was more than cosmetic. The adjustments were doubtless inspired by events in Iraq. They arguably had a more immediate and decisive impact at home than in Iraq, where sectarian violence continued to intensify for many months after the presidential election.

George W. Bush also proved to be an agile campaigner. As the war went sour, he altered the central narrative of his quest for reelection. Instead of hailing his success in the war, he portrayed the election as a choice between an incumbent with the guts to make unpopular decisions in pursuit of the national interest, and a rival whose record on the war was marked by ambivalence and uncertainty. Bush relentlessly portrayed John Kerry as a "flip-flopper," who voted in favor of authorizing the war but against the appropriations needed to fight it to a successful conclusion. The ploy appeared to work. The GOP mustered a superior effort to mobilize its base and get its voters to the polls on Election Day. And the electorate rewarded the incumbent with a modest majority.

Ronald Reagan and the Soviet Union in 1984

Election years almost invariably prompt policy adjustments when the nation is at war. But course corrections are also facilitated by elections during peacetime. One of the most dramatic occurred in early 1984 as Ronald Reagan prepared to campaign for reelection.

Reagan's declaratory policy toward the Soviet Union underwent an intriguing adjustment during his reelection campaign. In his first term, Reagan had characterized the Soviet Union as an "evil empire," and he did not shrink from confronting it. He dramatically expanded the U.S. defense budget, launched the Strategic Defense Initiative (SDI), and augmented assistance to "freedom fighters" resisting Soviet-supported regimes in places like Afghanistan and Nicaragua. He displayed little interest in arms control agreements and held no meetings during his first term with the leaders of the Soviet Union. Not that he was disinterested in such meetings: to those who criticized his failure to meet Kremlin leaders, his rejoinder was simple, "They kept dying on me." During his first term three Soviet leaders— Leonid Brezhnev, Yuri Andropov, and Konstantin Chernenko—had passed away.

Yet, on January 16, 1984, with an election year just under way, Reagan heralded a fundamental shift in his thinking about policy toward the Soviets. In a major speech, he underscored the dangers of war and the necessity for steps to preserve the peace. The tone was conciliatory, the stated objective to dispel misperceptions, and the emphasis on confidence-building measures. Secretary of State George Shultz described these remarks as "comprehensive and operational."[40]

Having expressed doubts about Soviet intentions throughout his first term, President Reagan now publicly acknowledged the possibility that Moscow needed reassurance about U.S. aims. He set out areas of common concern and identified possible fields for collaboration. He demonstrated interest in exchanges with Soviet leaders at the highest level. And he asserted a very ambitious objective whose achievement required Soviet cooperation. "My dream," the president affirmed, "is to see the day when nuclear weapons will be banished from the face of the earth."[41]

Critics dismissed the speech as mere campaign rhetoric—"damage control" aimed at voters who were upset by the administration's hawkish Cold War policies. Secretary of State Shultz responded to such criticism by noting bluntly that President Reagan "didn't need the Russian embrace to get reelected."[42] And in retrospect, it is clear that the speech was much more than a tactical ploy: it foreshadowed a major adjustment of policy. Its themes reappeared in the UN General Assembly speech Reagan gave the following fall. It was complemented by Reagan's expressed interest in a summit meeting with Premier Chernenko, an invitation to Foreign Minister Andrei Gromyko to visit Washington in September 1984, and, following Chernenko's death, a swift offer to Mikhail Gorbachev of a meeting without preconditions as soon as he assumed office.

Political calculations were not absent as a motive for policy adjustment. Stuart Spencer, Reagan's most trusted political adviser, warned that one of the president's few vulnerabilities in 1984 was the perception by voters that he might risk confrontation or even conflict with Moscow. Walter Mondale's charge that Reagan—as president—had never met with a Soviet leader seemed to strike a nerve with voters. Nancy Reagan was known to have pressed the president to speak more softly toward the Soviet Union. Secretary of State George Shultz and key White House advisers, including Jim Baker and Mike Deaver, as well as historian Suzanne Massie, a personal favorite of the president, urged a more forthright display of interest in constructive engagement with Moscow.

Yet electoral concerns were by no means the whole story, or even the main story. For that matter, there was no unanimity of political views on the issue among Reagan's chief advisers. Casper Weinberger, Bill Casey, and Ed Meese remained highly influential insiders at the time, and none of them was pressing for a more conciliatory policy stance toward the Soviet Union. In fact, prior to the New Hampshire primary, the political priority was on firing up the GOP's conservative base, rather than mollifying independents, let alone Democrats. In any event, the economy was strong, 1984 looked like a Republican year, and the White House exhibited little fear of the Democrat's likely nominee, Walter Mondale.

Major motivations were substantive and strategic. Accordingly, in his diaries Reagan noted that the speech was carefully prepared "to offer a level-headed approach to peace to reassure the eggheads & our European friends that I don't plan to blow up the world."[43] The "correlation of forces" (as the Soviets described the balance of power) had changed to America's advantage. In 1980, Reagan had worried about a "window of vulnerability." That window had now closed.

In late 1983, such concerns had been replaced by fears of misperceptions in Moscow; CIA assessments warned Reagan that there was evidence that some in the Kremlin feared an American surprise attack. In his 1990 autobiography, Reagan acknowledged that he had begun to realize that "many Soviet officials feared us not only as adversaries, but as potential aggressors who might hurl nuclear weapons at them in a first strike."[44] The public remarks of Soviet leader Yuri Andropov appeared increasingly paranoid. And President Reagan was convinced that having restored the U.S. military posture and the vitality of key alliances, the time had come to reassure the Soviet leadership about American intentions and to begin negotiations from a position of strength.

This confluence of events reinforced Reagan's natural disposition to engage his Soviet counterparts directly. He had sought earnestly to initiate a open correspondence with Soviet leaders in a channel independent of the stale official exchanges between the Washington and Moscow bureaucracies. He was consistently urged by Secretary Shultz to seek anew to engage Moscow's leaders.

It was also typical of Ronald Reagan to regard a political campaign as an occasion to outline his ideas on the key issues. He had no reason to disguise or conceal his policy priorities, and he was confident of his own persuasive powers. The campaign thus offered a welcome opportunity to mobilize public support for a more intensive engagement with America's principal foreign adversary once the election was over.

CAMPAIGNS AS A POTENTIAL GAME CHANGER IN NEGOTIATIONS

Negotiations are a core element in America's engagement with the world, and their conduct is shaped naturally by the political circumstances in which they unfold. Elections constitute a wild card. They may occasionally provide a helpful deadline—an urgent incentive to complete a difficult negotiation—but they can also expose the terms of bargaining to unwelcome partisan scrutiny and criticism. They are certainly a distraction for top officials in an administration and may even deprive them of the time required to wrap up a complicated deal. Alternatively, an election may put an incumbent president under pressure to make concessions he might regard as tactically unwise or substantively unwarranted, however politically convenient.

As noted earlier, U.S. negotiations with Panama over the return of the Canal were "slow-balled" throughout the 1976 campaign in order to reduce the risk of their "politicization" during a volatile political season. Despite the Ford administration's best efforts to handle the issue in a low-key way, the inevitable leaks provoked both major party candidates, as Henry Kissinger later acknowledged, to "strain the limits of truth" in affirming their red-blooded patriotism without entirely forfeiting prospects for forward movement once the elections were over.[45]

We have also seen how Kissinger attempted to utilize the 1972 election as a deadline for wrapping up an agreement to end the Vietnam conflict. In the end, the tactic failed because of Saigon's dilatory tactics and President Nixon's conviction that pressing South Vietnamese President Thieu was not worth running the political risks with his conservative base.

We have seen how the Iranians ran out the clock on the Carter administration's effort to secure the return of American hostages in Tehran, perhaps to demonstrate the ability of its radical regime to seal the fate of an American administration.

George H. W. Bush had better luck in using the 1992 election as a prod to get the trilateral NAFTA negotiations accelerated. He initially hoped that the negotiations, which commenced in June 1991, could be ratified by the Senate before the Democratic Convention the following July. Such a tight schedule proved to be unrealistic in a complicated trade negotiation. It took time to sort out the agenda, organize working groups, identify the critical issues, consult with concerned interest groups, and define potential trade-offs. But the campaign still provided the administration with a convenient "action forcing event" against which to pursue an important foreign policy achievement.

President Bush perceived no major political risk in pressing for an agreement during the campaign. He believed in free trade and regarded the creation of an embryonic hemispheric market a worthy, even historic, objective. The quest for a NAFTA agreement could be honestly portrayed as extending a helping hand to a friendly neighbor. As such, trade liberalization could alleviate pressures in Mexico for massive emigration to the United States.

The U.S. business community—a generally reliable supporter of the GOP—saw in NAFTA the promise of a broader North American market.

The likely opponents of such a deal—labor unions and environmental activists—were bulwarks of the Democratic Party and unlikely to vote for Bush anyway. Promoting NAFTA also provided a means of putting Bill Clinton, who had made public remarks supporting such an agreement, on the spot. If he now chose to reverse his position and oppose the accord to accommodate political support groups, he could be accused of "waffling"— a charge on which he was considered vulnerable.

Nor was America's negotiating leverage undercut by the election. The Mexicans wanted an agreement; it could facilitate the liberalization of their home market and enhance their political status in the hemisphere. If elected, the Democrats were likely to drive a harder bargain, if they pursued the agreement at all. The Canadian prime minister Brian Mulroney was a close friend of President Bush, and he saw clearly the advantages of putting the agreement to bed as quickly as possible.

By midsummer 1992, the proximate aim was to finish up the agreement by the time the GOP Convention commenced in August. The ministers and head negotiators convened in Washington on July 29 for a make-or-break bargaining effort. They emerged on August 11 with a signed accord. In truth, the agreement was not entirely finished. The Bush administration, in response to congressional pressures, acceded to requests to seek side agreements improving the terms on labor and environmental issues. Meanwhile, by late summer, Ross Perot's third-party candidacy had acquired some momentum, and the president's standing in the polls had receded. This complicated the task of drafting mutually agreeable side letters on the remaining issues. American lobbyists with an axe to grind on NAFTA were reluctant to cut final deals with a U.S. president whose time seemed to be running out. The environmentalists in particular began holding back in hopes that they could strike a better deal with a Democratic president.

In the end, President Bush got only half a loaf. Although a NAFTA text was completed, side letters on labor and environmental issues remained unresolved on Election Day, so the agreement ultimately wound up on President Clinton's desk, and he had to decide on what terms he would ask Congress to implement the NAFTA agreement. Nonetheless, George H. W. Bush demonstrated that a sitting president could push a complicated, controversial negotiating effort forward in the midst of a tough, uphill re-election campaign. And the resulting agreement was ratified later despite his defeat.

Presidents pursuing tough international deals while running for re-election may also seek to insulate a negotiation from electoral politics by soliciting the support of their political rival. But it is a tough sell.

In 1976, Gerald Ford sought Jimmy Carter's assent for bargains that his administration was attempting to work out in southern Africa. Henry Kissinger went to Dean Rusk, the former secretary of state for Presidents Kennedy and Johnson, with a request for Jimmy Carter's help. Rusk's response was wary. He suggested that cooperation might be possible, "if things develop favorably in Africa."[46] But he also urged Kissinger to get African leaders on board and to consult carefully with congressional Democrats. It was a politically loaded request. A diplomatic success in southern Africa would certainly attract favorable press reviews and possibly enhance Ford's electoral prospects. The Democratic candidate discerned little advantage in promising support for a controversial administration venture during the heat of a campaign, particularly when the credit for success might be harvested by his opponent.

Thus Rusk's advice, however reasonable in principle, was difficult to implement in practice. The Africans had little incentive to make extensive commitments to an administration that might not be around for long. Predictably, they temporized. Carter, meanwhile, asserted a tough campaign line on human rights issues, and this diminished South African prime minister John Vorster's readiness to be helpful on Rhodesia and Namibia. Eventually, the planned Geneva Conference, where Kissinger hoped to unveil new and promising arrangements with respect to Rhodesia and Namibia, simply "ran into the sand," and the Carter administration picked up later where Ford and Kissinger left off.[47]

George W. Bush faced a different negotiating dilemma with respect to North Korean nuclear weapons while preparing for his bid for reelection in 2004. He resolved it by changing the negotiating venue without adjusting the administration's substantive approach.

His administration inherited a 1994 Agreed Framework accord, which froze North Korea's plutonium program in return for deliveries of heavy fuel oil and assistance in financing the construction of two light-water nuclear reactors. Intelligence reports indicated, however, that Pyongyang was circumventing the terms of the agreement by developing an alternative source of fissionable materials by enriching uranium.

The administration confronted the Democratic People's Republic of Korea's (DPRK) representatives on this issue in late 2002. When the North

Koreans did not credibly deny Washington's allegations, the United States suspended its deliveries of heavy fuel oil. This prompted Pyongyang to withdraw from the Treaty on the Non-Proliferation of Nuclear Weapons (NPT), expel International Atomic Energy Agency (IAEA) inspectors, resume the reprocessing of spent fuel rods, and continue its clandestine work on uranium-enrichment technology.

The Bush administration sought further to isolate North Korea and to impose tougher economic sanctions on it. It presumed hopefully that its invasion of Iraq would pressure the DPRK to suspend its nuclear activities lest they provoke a similar military response from the United States. Instead, North Korea accelerated its nuclear activities, and this left the president confronting a tough 2004 election campaign in which he would be asked to explain how his policy toward Pyongyang left its expanding nuclear program subject to no regulation or restrictions.

The Democrats sharply criticized the administration's abandonment of the Agreed Framework. Since Bush planned a campaign that relied heavily on mobilizing his party's conservative base, the administration could scarcely replicate the kind of trade-offs embodied in that agreement—that is, a renewed "freeze" of DPRK nuclear activities in return for U.S. economic concessions—because leading GOP officials had trashed it for a decade.

The administration found a middle ground by promoting a new negotiating framework—the Six Party Talks. These proposed to bring North Korea's neighbors—South Korea, China, Japan, and Russia—into the negotiating process. Ostensibly, this would increase prospects for isolating North Korea in the talks, thereby heightening pressure on it to terminate its nuclear activities. It was also hoped that it would give Pyongyang's neighbors a stake in enforcing any agreements that might subsequently be reached.

At the same time, however, the administration paid heed to its own conservative constituency by keeping its negotiator, James Kelly, Bush's assistant secretary of state, on a very short leash. He was permitted no substantive flexibility and, in fact, was instructed to avoid all contact with North Korean representatives unless delegates from other countries were present. As Kelly observed with a mixture of irony and irritation, "A monkey could have performed the mission."

The Six Party Talks met in June 2004 but registered no progress. Still, the new venue served its political purpose by tempering Democratic criticism during the campaign. Ironically, although the Six Party Talks were designed to isolate North Korea on the nuclear issue, U.S. negotiators often found themselves the odd man out, pressured to take a more conciliatory line not only by the Chinese but by the South Koreans as well.

Needless to add, the North Koreans were able to adapt to the new venue. Their strategy was consistently designed to identify differences in the interests and priorities of their adversaries, and to exploit them in order to buy time and utilize it to operate their nuclear reactor, reprocess plutonium, test their missiles, and augment their work on uranium-enrichment technology. And so they did. Following the 2004 elections, the Six Party Talks did appear for a time to yield more serious negotiations, but in the end, the talks neither produced verifiable agreements nor prevented Pyongyang from testing nuclear devices and long-range missiles. They have been suspended since 2008.

MANAGING INTERNATIONAL CRISES DURING CAMPAIGNS

Incumbent presidents doubtless prefer to pursue reelection campaigns in tranquil international circumstances. International crises are unpredictable: they cannot be ignored, they divert a president's time and attention away from the campaign, and the political fallout can add a further element of uncertainty to the election.

If well managed, of course, crises can also provide a political bonanza for the incumbent. They play, after all, to a sitting president's potential advantage. Crises concentrate media attention on the White House. They underline the president's capacity to act, and they usually prompt people to "rally around the flag," which generally means rallying around the president. They give the incumbent an excuse for cutting back on campaigning with no loss of news coverage. Ultimately, of course, the size of the political dividend depends on how the crisis turns out. A few examples illustrate the possibilities.

Harry Truman and the Berlin Blockade in 1948

In 1948, Harry Truman was a deeply unpopular president, facing an uphill battle for reelection. Clare Boothe Luce declared him "a gone goose."[48] The polls supported her contention. The Republican candidate, Thomas Dewey, the governor of New York, shared her belief.

In the impending campaign it appeared that foreign policy would trump domestic issues. The core questions involved the East–West struggle and the president's management of relations with Moscow.

In the late spring and early summer of 1948, Truman faced a crisis over Berlin, which was provoked by Joseph Stalin. The Soviet dictator was responding to a decision made on June 19 by the Western allies—the United States, Britain, and France—to transform their respective occupation zones into a single economic unit and to implement a currency reform within this enlarged region in order to strengthen the German economy.

While it was recognized that this step toward Germany's partition would precipitate Soviet ire, Stalin's decision to blockade all rail, highway, and water traffic into and out of Berlin evoked surprise as well as consternation and anguish in Washington. The blockade was announced on the very day Thomas Dewey was chosen as the GOP candidate to challenge Truman.

Uncertain of Stalin's motives, the Truman administration was initially baffled as to how it should react. Lucius Clay, the military governor of the American occupation zone, wanted to defy Stalin by pushing an armored column through to Berlin. President Truman and his national security team were not so certain that Stalin would take the bluff. They were mindful that U.S. conventional forces in Europe were weak, the American atomic arsenal was modest, and the possibility of general war could not be ignored.

They preferred to look at other policy options. Those initially considered—closure of the Panama Canal to Soviet ships, or a blockade of the Soviet port of Vladivostok—were rejected; their efficacy and effectiveness seemed dubious.

Truman was determined to "stay in Berlin, period." This sentiment was not shared by key military figures like Army general Omar Bradley and Air Force general Hoyt Vandenberg. Nor was it endorsed by leading Soviet specialists like George Kennan and "Chip" Bohlen. British and French leaders also expressed doubts. But Truman, General Marshall, and others found an ingenious means of responding through a hastily contrived airlift, which supplied Berliners with food and, eventually, fuel. The airlift neutralized the Soviet blockade, earned the United States the enduring respect of West Germans, and forced the policy initiative back on Stalin's shoulders. He had to consider whether to take a further step up the escalation ladder with all the risks of war that this entailed. In the end, Stalin blinked. By the spring of

1949, when Stalin finally chose to lift the blockade, the Western allies had signed the North Atlantic Treaty (NATO).

To what extent, one may ask in retrospect, were Truman's decisions concerning Berlin shaped by electoral considerations? He had attempted to insulate his foreign policy from partisan attacks by appointing General George Marshall—who was widely regarded as resolutely nonpartisan—as secretary of state. One of Truman's principal biographers, David McCullough, concluded that he never agonized over how his decisions on Berlin would play politically, how they might affect his standing in the polls, or how partisan political advantage might be derived. "For all the political heat and turmoil of the moment," he quoted George Elsey, a naval intelligence officer assigned to the White House, as recalling that the staff there "had no direct role whatever in any decisions or in the execution of any of the carrying out of the airlift."[49]

Attending to his presidential duties, it turned out, proved to be good politics, because, as Jim Rowe, a prominent attorney who had served Franklin Roosevelt, observed at the time, "In times of crisis the American citizen tends to back up his president." McCullough added, "So by such reasoning, the Berlin crisis, if kept in bounds, was made to order for Truman."[50]

It is not clear that Truman accepted that view at the time. He regarded the crisis as an unwelcome burden and lamented the distraction it presented. As he noted in a letter to Winston Churchill on July 10, 1948, "I am going through a terrible political 'trial by fire.' Too bad it must happen at this time." Then he added, "Your country and mine are founded on the fact that the people have the right to express themselves on their leaders, no matter what the crisis."[51]

Truman enjoyed one signal advantage. Some politicians in those early days of the Cold War honored the maxim "Politics stops at the water's edge," and Senate Republicans like Arthur Vandenberg steadfastly supported the airlift. So did Thomas Dewey, Truman's rival in the election. He shared the president's internationalist instincts, backed the administration's decisions to furnish aid to Greece and to undertake the Marshall Plan, believed in a strong defense, and readily endorsed the Berlin airlift.

In order to encourage bipartisan support, Undersecretary of State Robert Lovett had quietly shared confidential State Department cables with John Foster Dulles, Dewey's presumptive secretary of state, through the summer and fall. He did so to encourage continuity of policy rather than to ingratiate himself with the predicted winner in the presidential sweepstakes.[52]

In truth, Dewey's differences over foreign policy were more acute with Robert Taft than with Harry Truman. And since Dewey thought he had the election in the bag, he considered it prudent to say as little as possible on such issues. This helped give the president a political "pass" on crisis management, which in any event he handled skillfully. His actions helped Berlin to survive, forced the Soviets eventually to back down, and bolstered his own reputation for courage and resolution. And he surprised virtually everyone—including Dewey—by winning his bid for reelection in November.

Dwight Eisenhower and the Suez Crisis in 1956

President Dwight Eisenhower confronted a comparably challenging foreign policy crisis during his campaign for reelection in 1956. Indeed, he faced a double crisis, since the Soviet Union intervened to crush the Hungarian Revolution at just the moment when Britain, France, and Israel invaded Egypt in an attempt to reverse Nasser's takeover of the Suez Canal.

As noted in chapter 2, the 1952 GOP platform proclaimed an interest in "rolling back" Soviet influence in Eastern Europe. Ike was pressed anew at the 1956 Republican Convention to endorse another strong platform plank on the subject. Nikita Khrushchev's recent denunciation of Stalin's excesses created a new situation in Central Europe, and GOP conservatives were buoyed by the efforts of regimes in Hungary and Poland to test the limits of Soviet tolerance for their autonomy.

In the Middle East, Eisenhower had pursued a cautious course. He sought consistently to avoid being drawn into the Arab–Israeli dispute. He had refused to sell arms to either side and had attempted to sustain friendly ties with the Egyptian leader, Gamal Abdel Nasser, who had persuaded Washington to help finance construction of the Aswan Dam to hasten his nation's economic development. To burnish his nonaligned credentials, however, Nasser also decided in the spring of 1956 to recognize Mainland China and to purchase arms from Czechoslovakia.

These decisions angered Washington, particularly Secretary of State Dulles, who had the lead on Middle East issues during the summer of 1956 when President Eisenhower was sidelined by an attack of ileitis. The administration abruptly canceled funding for the Aswan Dam in late July. Dulles evidently believed at the time that this would put Nasser and his Soviet patrons "in a hell of a spot."[53] But Nasser responded by nationalizing the Suez Canal, and inviting the Soviets to finance the dam.

This provoked the British and French, who clandestinely encouraged Israel to attack the canal. They presumed this would provide them a convenient excuse to intervene, ostensibly to "protect" the canal, although their underlying motive was to depose Nasser and reestablish Franco-British control over it.

The 1956 GOP Convention convened in late August in San Francisco as these tumultuous events were beginning to unfold. Ike faced no challenge for the GOP nomination; his bid for a second term was approved by acclamation. In addition, he had already decided to shoulder only limited campaign obligations, while leaving the heavy political lifting to his vice president, Richard Nixon, and other surrogates.

He could afford to do so. He had compiled an impressive record of accomplishment during his first term and remained extraordinarily popular. He had also experienced serious health problems during the previous year and faced pressing challenges overseas. Still, his acceptance speech contained no reference to Suez or an impending crisis in the Middle East.

While a surface calm prevailed in the Middle East during the early fall, Britain, France, and Israel were secretly planning a military assault on Egypt. The Israelis initiated the attack on October 29, just a week before the U.S. election.

This infuriated Eisenhower. He instructed Dulles to warn Tel Aviv that "we're going to apply sanctions, we're going to the United Nations, we're going to do everything that there is so we can stop this thing."[54] His exchanges with the British and French were equally tough and icy. He noted in a hastily called press conference that in concert with Israel, London and Paris had violated the 1950 Tripartite Agreement, which committed Britain and France, along with the United States, to maintain the status quo in the Middle East on matters related to borders and arms sales.[55] The administration knew that the French had already been selling military aircraft to the Israelis in numbers substantially exceeding those to which Washington had agreed. The fact that the sales were handled through clandestine channels compounded Washington's chagrin and Ike's resentment.

Clearly, the administration had underestimated the durability of its European allies' colonial reflexes. And while Ike publicly declared that concerns about the Jewish vote would not diminish the White House's resolve to preserve peace in the Middle East, he assumed incorrectly that the Israelis would not directly confront its American benefactors in the face of such admonitions.[56]

Eisenhower's furious reaction was compounded by Washington's parallel preoccupation with escalating turbulence in Central Europe, where the Poles and Hungarians demonstrated rising resistance to Soviet domination. Moscow's sudden move to oust Imre Nagy's regime in Hungary by force in early November put Eisenhower clearly on the spot.

Many voters considered "roll back" in Eastern Europe as the litmus test of a Republican president's willingness and ability to deliver on the GOP's platform pledge to "liberate" Soviet satellite states. But the president confronted a very practical problem: how to respond to political developments in an area the Soviet Union regarded as within its own "sphere of influence," and in which it enjoyed overwhelming conventional military superiority.

Eisenhower deplored the Soviet intervention but feared that an East–West confrontation might lead down a slippery slope to war. He consequently turned down requests from the CIA to drop supplies and arms to Polish and Hungarian resistance forces. In doing so, he exposed himself to harsh criticism from conservatives for timidity, and from liberals for hypocrisy.

Ike's focus was heavily riveted on the Middle East, where the British, French, and Israelis were waging a military assault on Egypt. He sniffed the "scent of colonialism" in their attack, and he reacted angrily against their conspiracy. He was determined to teach them all that they could neither trifle with him nor expect the United States to accommodate a fait accompli.

In truth, on the substantive issues involved, Ike's policy instincts were substantially more moderate than those of Secretary of State Dulles. The president considered Nasser's seizure of the Suez Canal as a lawful exercise of the right of eminent domain. He regarded a military response to this action as reckless and foolish. He parried Dulles's proposal that an international consortium be created to run the canal on the grounds that no evidence existed that Egyptians were incapable of operating the canal. He dismissed the counsel of those insisting that long-standing U.S. allies deserved our faithful support by noting, "Nothing justifies double-crossing us." And he took seriously the Tripartite Agreement's pledge to "support any victim of aggression in the Middle East," even if this put us in confrontation with old friends.

The British, French, and Israelis all misjudged the president's intentions and resolve. London was presumably convinced that Ike would back an ally on a matter it considered vital. Paris apparently assumed that its NATO connection would insulate it from Washington's ire. The Israelis perhaps anticipated that our election would box the president in, despite his explicit disclaimers.

Ike devoted himself thoroughly to these twin crises, declaring that he did not care about how their outcome might affect his electoral prospects—always good politics—and he took decisive action. He affirmed the Tripartite Agreement, which in this case committed the United States to support Egypt as the victim of aggression. He instructed his ambassador to the UN, Henry Cabot Lodge, to table a resolution in the Security Council calling on all parties to avoid the use of force. When the British and French vetoed it, he advanced an identical "Uniting for Peace" Resolution in the General Assembly, the first time such a tactic had been attempted since the Korean War. It passed by a 64–5 margin.

When alerted that Israel's attack on Egypt imperiled Europe's oil supply, Eisenhower responded that those who had begun the operation should be left to "work out their own oil problem—to boil in their own oil."[57] He refused to provide aid. In addition, he had the Treasury Department block British access to dollar accounts in the United States, thereby increasing pressure on the pound in world markets. When Britain sought a U.S. loan to help defend the value of its currency, the administration promised to make such aid available only when the British accepted a cease-fire and withdrew their troops from Suez.

Eisenhower's insistence on the primacy of legal obligations in siding with the Arabs versus Israel placed the United States with the Third World in opposition to America's European allies—a posture that took nearly everyone by surprise, particularly at a time when the Soviet Union was using military force to quell a rebellion on NATO's frontier. The president imposed sanctions on Israel on the eve of a U.S. election in the face of harsh domestic criticism not only from Lyndon Johnson, the Democratic Senate majority leader, but also from William Knowland, the GOP minority leader.

And when Soviet premier Nikolai Bulganin threatened to fish in troubled waters by sending Soviet troops to the Middle East, Eisenhower treated the threat as an empty bluff and stared Moscow down. He insisted, moreover, that any UN peacekeeping forces dispatched to the Middle East exclude units from *all* the major powers.

Repudiating allies, confronting Israel, and ignoring Hungary's call for help were not easy actions for an incumbent president to take within days of an election. Eisenhower's press secretary, James Hagerty, observed years later that the allies evidently could not imagine that "an American president would dare to interfere and, in effect, try to stop a war between the Arabs and Israelis, when the Israelis were going to win, in the closing days of a national election."[58] Andrew Goodpaster, Ike's military aide at the time, subsequently remarked that they had ignored a more salient fact: a president in our system was obliged to demonstrate that his actions in a crisis were not colored by domestic political calculations.[59]

Throughout the crisis, Eisenhower focused on national interests that he considered vital—keeping the Russians from establishing a foothold in the Middle East, preventing Moscow and others from exploiting Arab nationalism at America's expense, sustaining the flow of oil from the Gulf, and averting avoidable risks of war in Central Europe.

Keeping his eye on the ball proved to be good politics. In the election, Ike doubled his 1952 margin over Adlai Stevenson, winning by more than 10 million votes and yielding only seven states in the Electoral College.

There can be no doubt that Eisenhower benefited from the predictable "rally around the flag" effect at a moment of international crisis. Yet in retrospect the striking feature of the episode is the limited impact political considerations appeared to exert on the administration's crisis management.

Or perhaps Ike merely recognized instinctively, as had Truman, that effective crisis management was the best politics. His resistance to militant calls for roll-back from the conservative wing of his own party appeared a display of prudence to moderate swing voters. He also prevailed in the domestic debate over Middle East policy because reliance on the UN and international law as reference points for American actions resonated with the general public. In the mid-1950s these swing voters clearly controlled the outcome of presidential elections. Ike's policy instincts suited the political needs of a candidate who sought their votes.

Jimmy Carter and the Iranian Hostage Crisis in 1980

Harry Truman and Dwight Eisenhower got a political boost from their handling of an international crisis during a reelection campaign. Jimmy Carter did not. When American diplomats in Tehran were taken hostage in November 1979, it was immediately apparent to the president's advisers that "the press will be looking at this in the context of the campaign."[60] They were right. At the time, however, few imagined that a full year later the hostages would continue to languish in captivity. This, for all practical purposes, sealed President Carter's hopes for reelection.

For a time, the hostage crisis predictably boosted support for the president. He survived Ted Kennedy's challenge in the primaries and won his party's nomination. But by the time the Democrats held their convention in August 1980, the uncertain fate of the hostages was fast becoming a metaphor for national weakness and diplomatic futility.

In the course of the general election campaign, the political dynamics of the hostage issue changed. Ronald Reagan, Carter's opponent, did not criticize him for conciliatory gestures toward the shah (as had Ted Kennedy), but for weakness in defending America's honor and prestige.

In retrospect, it is clear that Carter paid a huge political price for his inability to secure a timely and safe release of the hostages. Several features of his policy contributed to that result. For one, Carter initially devoted his time and attention single-mindedly to the crisis. He even cancelled plans to campaign outside the national capital. Inadvertently, this may have increased Tehran's leverage in negotiations with the United States.

For another, the president made it publicly clear that his overriding aim was the safe return of all the hostages. Coercive measures were contemplated only as a last resort. This relieved the hostage-takers of the need to worry about their own safety and further diminished American bargaining power.

Beyond the premium the administration placed on patience and restraint, it displayed a surprising amateurishness in its early diplomatic efforts. Ramsey Clark, a fringe figure at best, was dispatched as an intermediary; the Ayatollah Ruhollah Khomeini refused even to allow him into Iran. French interlocutors were engaged as middlemen, but they delivered nothing beyond Iranian excuses for inaction and requests for additional American concessions. No one could verify whether their contacts in Tehran had genuine access to Iran's leaders or their designated representatives. As President Carter once noted in exasperation to his chief of staff, Hamilton Jordan, "It looks like we have everybody in the world roped into our scenario—our government, the UN, French lawyers, Argentinians, Panamanians, the Revolutionary Council—and it's starting to look like the only person not involved is the Ayatollah Khomeini."[61]

When force was attempted in late April 1980, it took the form of a flawed rescue mission. The concept was problematic, and the execution botched: helicopters malfunctioned, the rescue team never reached Tehran, its mission was aborted in the desert, and eight American soldiers died in vain. Thereafter, the administration appeared bereft of any coercive option.

In the end, the administration provided the Iranians no compelling incentives to come to terms. No firm deadlines were established, no menacing ultimatum issued, no credible threats designed, none of the inducements offered worked.

Arguably, Reagan positioned himself in a helpful way during the general election campaign. Apart from occasional barbs suggesting that the administration's handling of the crisis was inept, he did not dwell much on the subject. This presumably reflected a political judgment that if the issue were resolved before the election—and right up until election eve his advisers expressed anxieties about an "October surprise"—Carter would harvest the political benefit. Thus why increase its potential value by highlighting the issue? The press managed in any event to keep the spotlight on the hostage crisis.

When in September 1980 the Ayatollah Khomeini appeared to endorse more conciliatory conditions for the release of the hostages, Reagan issued a carefully prepared statement suggesting that the United States should accept most of them (e.g., unfreeze Iranian assets, provide a declaration of nonintervention). He added that the disposition of the shah's assets should be handled in accordance with the "due process of law" and insisted that the hostages "must be released immediately upon the conclusion of an agreement without delays, the introduction of additional demands, or waiting for fulfillment of the agreement."[62]

Reagan's position reinforced the cards in Carter's hand. The GOP candidate's reputation for toughness, his assertions that he would not negotiate with terrorists, hints that a Republican administration would contemplate coercive options—all could be used by the president and his representatives to urge Iran to settle promptly, since the price for an accommodation would presumably go up if Reagan took office. Indeed, Carter's representatives suggested that if Carter's overtures were spurned and he lost the election, Tehran would face during the presidential transition an angry, possibly vindictive incumbent determined to inflict vengeance on those whom he considered responsible for denying him reelection.

In its frantic efforts to resolve the crisis, the administration did indeed take some punitive actions against Iran. It cut off the flow of Iranian oil to the United States, froze Iranian assets, broke diplomatic relations, and sponsored UN resolutions that condemned Tehran. It sought, albeit without much success, to mobilize allied support for sanctions. The president occasionally indulged in muscular rhetoric, though mainly to assuage the anger of Americans he feared would push for tougher actions "whose wisdom or efficacy he doubted."[63] At the time, many critics dismissed these steps as "too little, too late," and they did not produce the desired effect in Tehran.

President Carter also periodically sweetened proposed offers for settlement. In September 1980, for example, he made it clear that if the hostages were returned, the United States would deliver military equipment for which the Iranians had already signed contracts—Carter's version of "arms for hostages." He affirmed U.S. willingness to normalize relations with Tehran once the hostages came home, and he promised America would desist from any future "meddling" in Iran's internal affairs.

Nothing worked. In fact, the Iranians mocked the administration by escalating their own demands. They insisted that the shah be returned for trial, that his assets be confiscated, and that he apologize for the crimes he committed against the Iranian people. They persisted in their obduracy through Election Day and beyond.

Over time, the hostages became a wasting asset for the mullahs. They had served their essential purpose in galvanizing domestic support behind Khomeini and his radical Islamist regime. Gradually, Tehran's hostage-holding began to alienate other Muslim governments in the Middle East. And after Saddam Hussein attacked Iran, Tehran paid a stiff price for its inability to replace or secure spare parts for its made-in-America military equipment.

Ultimately, the Iranians overestimated their leverage and overplayed their hand. They correctly perceived that Carter needed a resolution of the issue to get reelected. They presumably figured that as the election drew closer, they could drive the price of a deal higher. But by this reckoning, they should have been prepared to settle in late October or early November.

Gary Sick, a member of the Carter NSC staff, subsequently alleged that Reagan campaign operatives took out "insurance" against an October surprise by arranging their own "arms for hostages" deal with Iran through the Israelis.[64] As Americans later learned, Bill Casey, Reagan's campaign manager, was not particularly squeamish about trading arms for hostages with Iranian middlemen. The Israelis had the motive and the means to encourage such covert operations. Indeed, Yitzhak Shamir's government sold the Iranians American-made military equipment in the fall of 1980 in defiance of promises it had made to the Carter administration.

Whatever the plausibility of Sick's claims, however, subsequent congressional hearings found no convincing evidence to support them. Nor did Warren Christopher, Carter's principal negotiator with Iran, accord the allegations any credibility in his own memoirs.[65]

Perhaps the Iranian political system was in such disarray in 1980 that it was incapable of organizing a coherent and decisive response against the American electoral deadline. Perhaps the Ayatollah Khomeini and his associates were determined to demonstrate, as Howard Teicher and Bruce Reidel later argued, that they could bring down a U.S. administration in retribution for America's overthrow of the regime of Mohammad Mossadegh in Iran in 1953.[66]

These are hypotheses. There is no conclusive proof. But the eventual timing of the hostage release, minutes after President Reagan was finally inaugurated, suggests that for whatever reason, the Iranian authorities were resolved to humble President Carter, and that they believed that it was safe, if not necessarily wise, for them to do so.

Zbigniew Brzezinski had warned Carter in the weeks following the hostage-taking that if the president allowed the crisis to settle into a "state of normalcy," it "could paralyze . . . [his] Presidency." It did, and Carter paid the political price.

In truth, of course, as in 1956, President Carter confronted a twin crisis, for in December 1979 the Soviet Union invaded Afghanistan. This compounded the administration's political dilemma. The invasion made its earlier analysis of the Soviet threat appear misguided and naïve. Its policy had failed to deter. Its sanctions appeared more symbolic than real. One of the few with bite—an embargo on grain shipments—seemed to hurt American farmers more than Soviet consumers.

The Carter administration did undertake significant covert action to bolster the anti-Soviet resistance in Afghanistan, and this was continued and expanded by President Reagan. The fact that it was covert rather than open and visible, of course, meant that Carter reaped no political benefit from it during the election. Ironically, moreover, the Iranians were to become a tacit partner in providing support to the mujahedeen fighters who resisted Soviet forces in Afghanistan.

President Carter was a prime victim of the hostage crisis. He settled for protracted, patient negotiations for their release despite damage to the nation's prestige, the decline of his own popularity, and the weakness it signaled to others who thought ill of the United States. If at times his restraint seemed almost craven to some, in the end his patience was rewarded when all of the hostages returned home, though not in time to save Carter's bid for reelection.

Truman and Eisenhower turned successful crisis management into electoral advantage. Carter did not. The reasons are not particularly mysterious. Crises play to a president's advantage if he plays a strong hand and if things turn out well. In dealing with Iran, Carter's efforts were inconclusive. In coping with the Soviet invasion of Afghanistan, his response appeared ineffectual. The voters drew their own conclusions by denying Jimmy Carter a second term.

TAKEAWAYS

When incumbents bid for reelection, the domestic implications of their foreign policy records become a matter of greater political concern, and White House political advisers acquire potentially greater influence on these policies.

Anticipating that a bid for reelection will become a referendum on his record, an incumbent president has strong incentives to burnish his legacy by addressing previous campaign promises that have been neglected, and introducing course corrections that appear timely, exaggerating claims for what has been accomplished, and formulating excuses for external projects that did not work out.

During reelection campaign season, incumbent presidents are prone to exploit foreign policy situations to demonstrate their toughness on national security, their cunning in negotiations, their vision of the United States as an exemplar of rectitude, and their determination to encourage other countries to become "more like us."

Reelection campaigns usually slow the pace of foreign policy activity and disrupt temporarily the rhythm of policy making. Negotiations are often slow-walked, controversial projects delayed, and tough choices deferred.

Even worthy aims enjoying broad public support may be pursued with less urgency when the president is preoccupied with securing a renewal of his political mandate. In most cases the balance between pursuing domestic objectives and foreign goals will shift temporarily toward the former. President Nixon's campaign in 1972 was the rare exception that underlines the rule.

International crises during a campaign generally play to an incumbent president's natural advantage. This is why contenders so often worry about October surprises. But to extract political benefits from crises, a president must play his hand prudently and avoid the appearance of exploiting it for domestic purposes.

A reelection campaign need not hamstring a president's ability to manage an international crisis effectively. But it highlights events beyond the White House's control, which can exert a potentially decisive impact on voter preferences. In the end, of course, that is what elections are often about—testing the ability of an incumbent to shape unforeseen events to America's advantage.

4 CAMPAIGNS

Opportunities and Obstacles
for Challengers

IT IS HARDER TO ASSESS THE IMPACT OF A CHALLENGER'S campaign on foreign policy, since he has no record to defend. His foreign policy consists essentially of words—a party platform, an occasional speech, a series of press releases, carefully crafted answers to questions at staged political events, the contents of attack ads, occasionally offhand, unscripted remarks on the campaign trail, in addition to comments and speeches offered during brief visits to a few foreign capitals.

The foreign policy pronouncements of contenders are frequently crafted to highlight overseas problems and the fecklessness of the incumbent in responding to them. They reflect a view that foreign policy consists mainly of thinking up bold and imaginative schemes for improving those conditions without much consideration of the means needed to accomplish them.

The foreign policy ideas advanced by contenders during general election campaigns are naturally designed to bolster their credentials as a plausible commander in chief and their chances of winning the presidency. Like their rivals—whether an incumbent or another challenger—they articulate promises designed to appeal to a wide range of demographic cohorts. They vary greatly in their specificity. More attention is devoted to their appeal at home than their efficacy abroad. Less emphasis is focused on painful choices, difficult trade-offs, or the financial and opportunity costs of the policies they advocate.

Examples of such campaign promises are legion.

- In pursuit of his 1968 "southern strategy," Richard Nixon considered South Carolina to be critical, and he actively courted Senator Strom Thurmond with promises of relief from foreign textile imports.
- In his 1980 campaign, Ronald Reagan hoped to attract Farm Belt voters by promising an end to the grain embargo that President Carter had imposed on the Soviet Union following its invasion of Afghanistan in 1979.
- In 1992, Bill Clinton harshly criticized President George H. W. Bush's decision to turn back Haitian refugees and promised, if elected, greater leniency in granting them asylum.
- Democratic challengers routinely offer trade relief to Rust Belt manufacturing industries; GOP contenders instinctively promise to open vibrant foreign markets to U.S. exporters.
- Many candidates direct sharp criticism at the Chinese—the Democrats for their indifference to environmental issues, their persecution of political dissidents, and their exports of labor intensive goods; the Republicans for their reliance on abortion as an instrument of population control, their harassment of religious minorities, and their robust increases in military spending. Candidates of both parties have recently targeted their geopolitical assertiveness.
- In every election in recent decades, candidates of both major parties have pledged generously to support Israel's security and prosperity.
- Needless to add, virtually all contenders express patriotic sentiments with varying degrees of nationalistic fervor.

PAYING FOR CAMPAIGN PROMISES UP FRONT

Only after elections are won, does the piper need to be paid. By then, sober second thoughts may have dawned on the president-elect. Yet pressure to acquit campaign promises promptly is often intense, and the price for doing so can sometimes be unexpectedly high.

To honor his pledge to Senator Thurmond, Nixon sought to exact a "promise" from Prime Minister Eisaku Satō of Japan to provide textile import relief in 1969 negotiations over the return of Okinawa. To his subsequent consternation, he learned that the Japanese regarded Sato's commitment to be at most a "best efforts" pledge. The payback was unsatisfying, and lingering mistrust between Tokyo and Washington was an unintended by-product of this misunderstanding.

Following Reagan's election in 1980, his secretary of state, Al Haig, and others urged him not to lift the grain embargo—the one sanction that appeared to have some real impact on Moscow. They hoped to defer sanctions relief to the Soviets as long as they continued to occupy neighboring Afghanistan, or alternatively until the United States secured other foreign policy concessions in return. For Reagan, however, a promise was a promise, and he chose to follow through despite the misgivings of some advisers.

Clinton's pledge of generous treatment of Haitian "boat people" exposed him to the "law of unintended consequences." Shortly after his election, the number of Haitians heading for the United States on small boats increased dramatically, precipitating frenzied opposition from other southern governors fearful that their states were about to be inundated by destitute immigrants. Clinton rescinded his promise even before his inauguration.

Even more adverse consequences have accompanied the hasty acquittal of other campaign promises. Presidents Kennedy and Carter both learned the hard way.

When John F. Kennedy launched his campaign for the presidency in 1960, he was scarcely a novitiate in foreign policy. A member of a distinguished, cosmopolitan family, JFK possessed an exemplary war record, had traveled extensively, published a widely acclaimed book on foreign policy, and served on the Senate Foreign Relations Committee. But he had been an observer of diplomacy, not a practitioner with operational experience.

Representing a new generation eager to take the reins in Washington, Kennedy organized his campaign around the theme of "change," and placed foreign policy at the center of his appeal for political support. He sought to exploit public disquiet over Soviet success in putting the first man in space, developing a more powerful generation of long-range ballistic missiles, accomplishing rapid economic growth, and extending its influence in the Third World. As a candidate, JFK complained that American prestige was in decline and that its diplomacy lacked vision and dexterity. He did not disparage the containment doctrine; rather, he promised to implement it more energetically.

Above all, he warned of an ominous "missile gap" with the Soviet Union, and pledged to close it. It was a plausible allegation in the wake of Moscow's launch of *Sputnik*. But the charge was mistaken. Eisenhower and Nixon knew at the time that the planned introduction of the Polaris submarine ballistic missile system would give the United States a survivable deterrent force that could operate close to Soviet territory—a capability for which Moscow had no effective counter. Yet this highly classified information was not disclosed to challenge Kennedy's assertion, which took on a life of its own in the course of the campaign.

Just weeks before the election, moreover, Kennedy's campaign also issued a position paper, which essentially called for a U.S.-backed ouster of Havana's Marxist dictatorship. Kennedy dismissed Nixon's alternative—an economic embargo—as "too little, too late." He promised a four-point program, which emphasized efforts "to strengthen the non-Batista democratic, anti-Castro forces in exile and in Cuba itself, who offer eventual hope of overthrowing Castro." Thus far, he added, "these fighters for freedom have had virtually no support from our Government."[1]

At the time, Kennedy had not been briefed about a sensitive, covert program to train Cuban exiles for possible action against Cuba.[2] Nixon was familiar with its details but chose not to let this out of the bag for security reasons. Instead, the vice president ironically chose to argue that illegal intervention in internal Cuban affairs would violate American treaty obligations and international law, and alienate America's friends in the hemisphere.[3] Nixon suggested a quarantine "as utilized in Guatemala"—a bit of legerdemain that left his own options open, since the Eisenhower administration had in fact overthrown the Jacobo Arbenz regime in Guatemala in 1954 through a covert CIA operation.[4]

The election was tight. The first presidential debate, in which Kennedy's performance exceeded expectations, was arguably decisive. The margin of victory was slim; JFK won.

With the benefit of hindsight, it appears that Kennedy's campaign left him vulnerable to at least several potential "traps" when he took office in January 1961. While the alleged missile gap failed to materialize, he was loath to acknowledge that his campaign had misrepresented the strategic balance. To close the nonexistent gap, Kennedy doubled the production rate of land-based intercontinental ballistic missiles from thirty to sixty per month, and boosted the Polaris submarine-launched ballistic missile (SLBM) fleet from twenty-nine to forty-one. He also quickly lifted the cap that President Eisenhower had imposed on defense spending and replaced deterrence based on "massive retaliation" with a strategic doctrine of "flexible response," from which the U.S. Army, with its more than 200,000 additional recruits, was the principal beneficiary.[5]

Kennedy's forthright promises to extend assistance to anti-Castro Cubans produced even more serious consequences. They strengthened the CIA's resolve to press for his approval of contingency plans, which the Eisenhower administration had initiated for a covert invasion of Cuba.

It was not, of course, inevitable that the Kennedy administration succumbed to early policy mistakes (e.g., the missile gap and the Bay of Pigs fiasco). But like several other successful challengers for the presidency, he slipped up during his early months in office on banana peels dropped during his own campaign.

President Carter experienced a variation on this theme with his 1976 campaign promise to withdraw U.S. ground troops from South Korea. Campaign promises to undertake substantial changes in U.S. policy toward China occasioned troublesome slipups in relations between Washington and Beijing in the early months of the administrations of Ronald Reagan, Bill Clinton, and George W. Bush.

One should not dismiss campaign promises on foreign policy as mere cynical ploys to get elected. Some are earnestly implemented following the election despite sober second thoughts or the prudent counsel of political advisers or executive branch officials. Some are quietly modified or delayed. Some are mercifully abandoned. The point is that campaign promises look a lot different when sitting in the Oval Office than they do out on the campaign trail.

CAMPAIGNS AS A HARBINGER OF A PRESIDENT'S FOREIGN POLICY

Whatever the logic or motivation behind a challenger's campaign promises, generally they are not an especially reliable guide to the policies he will pursue once in office. There are a variety of reasons for this. The most important of these is perhaps obvious: during campaigns, challengers are so preoccupied with figuring out how to win the election that they have little time to focus in much detail on how to fix the nation's problems overseas. While contenders offer visionary plans and soaring rhetoric, once in office they quickly discover that much of America's diplomacy involves determined efforts to improvise in the face of unforeseen developments. They learn, as Abraham Lincoln once acknowledged, that they rarely control events, but are often controlled by them.[6]

Contenders' campaigns generally focus on goals, often without serious acknowledgment of the priorities among those objectives or the resources needed for their implementation. Party platforms and presidential debates elide such choices; press releases ignore them; candidates finesse them. Yet the enduring challenge of foreign policy is the need to allocate resources, which are scarce, among aims, which are legion.

Even if a challenger is inclined to outline a broad foreign policy agenda, he has few incentives to offer concrete plans for advancing it. Detailed proposals are as likely to spur opposition as elicit support, and events will probably reshape the contours of the problems well before a new administration is in a position to act. Hence, his campaign rhetoric generally reflects a harsh assessment of the world as it is, and it offers an inspiring "vision" of the world as he hopes it will become.

American exceptionalism pervades most contenders' campaigns. We operate our society and our government on the basis of principles, which Americans regard as universal. It is consequently natural for candidates to presume that a key mission of U.S. foreign policy is to transplant our values, institutions, and political practices to the rest of the world. Foreigners listening in on our campaigns may regard this reformer's reflex as a habitual tendency to interfere in others' domestic affairs. But it is an inclination that is as characteristic of Congress as of most presidents. It is shared by partisans of both major parties.

Some presidents are content to rely on the appeal of our democratic rule of law to inspire emulation by others. Most recent incumbents have been inclined to a more interventionist approach to encourage other countries to look "more like us." President George W. Bush argued in his second inaugural address that "[t]he survival of liberty in our land increasingly depends on the success of liberty in other lands." His secretary of state, Condoleezza Rice, put his sentiments in a slightly different way: "The fundamental character of regimes now matters more than the international distribution of power."[7]

The premises of this policy outlook—that democracies are inherently peaceful, that market economics lead inexorably to political pluralism, that economic interdependence discourages strife—are assumed to be so widely accepted that they scarcely need to be articulated, let alone explained. Most contenders for the presidency—like the incumbents they hope to replace— assume that the United States is the "indispensable nation," and that voters welcome reassurances that we intend, above all, to remain Number One.

Thus contenders for the Oval Office tend relentlessly to project optimism about America's ability to set the world's ills aright, to spread peace, to open foreign markets, and to advance democracy around the world. Little wonder that campaign promises are laced with wishful thinking, or that hopeful rhetoric often obfuscates tough policy choices.

One of the ironies of the 2008 presidential campaign was that the Democratic contender, Barack Obama, denounced George W. Bush's record while gradually embracing a similar "freedom agenda." For that matter, Bush's second inaugural riff on "banishing tyranny from the world" constituted an extreme variation on Bill Clinton's post–Cold War quest to replace "the containment of communism" with "the enlargement of democracy" as the core aim of U.S. foreign policy.

Beyond this, many of the detailed promises that surface in presidential campaigns amount to marketing ploys. Contenders float policy ideas that have been massaged carefully by election specialists—many of them unembarrassed by any serious familiarity with the substance of foreign policy. Public statements and press releases are painstakingly tested with focus groups. Their political impact is examined through constant polling. Political advisers regularly spin the candidate's pronouncements for the media.

Only after an election is over is the victor obliged to acknowledge the "retroactive weight" his campaign promises acquired,[8] and to surround himself with people who can help him govern, rather than get him elected. Only then are campaign pledges more carefully scrutinized for their strategic logic, operational feasibility, financial cost, and impact on other priorities.

Other features of our general election campaigns limit the likelihood that contenders will articulate the conceptual premises that will guide their foreign policy plans. The 24/7 cable news cycle is one. It encourages "gotcha" politics rather than a careful examination of the conceptual underpinnings of policy proposals. It fosters rhetorical excess and political polarization.

It propels candidates toward more uncompromising positions. And it invites personal attacks on rivals rather than the thoughtful exposition of ideas.

Major party candidates now have a bevy of well-informed foreign policy advisers poised to help the campaign (and collaterally maneuver for jobs in the next administration). But they seem to occupy themselves primarily with positioning their candidate in response to events, drafting talking points for their myriad public appearances, and crafting assaults on their opponent's perceived shortcomings. Mobilizing broad public support for a specific foreign policy agenda rarely appears to be a high campaign priority.

Party platforms express a party's philosophy and contain scores of policy proposals. They offer contenders an opportunity to define a foreign policy agenda. Yet in practice these documents are designed mainly to fire up the party activists rather than provide a serious blueprint for a candidate's external strategy. Few voters would claim an even cursory familiarity with their party's platform.

Few candidates, moreover, consider themselves tightly bound by its provisions. Dwight Eisenhower recognized the value of his 1952 platform in disarming critics within the Taft wing of the GOP. Yet his chief speechwriter, Emmet Hughes, openly acknowledged that he had never bothered to read the document. John Kennedy organized his campaign around general themes—change, hope, victory, peace—rather than the explicit pledges of the Democratic platform, which he believed raised "too many unwarranted hopes and unnecessary fears" and was encumbered by "too many antagonistic specifics that could not be fulfilled."[9]

Campaign debates offer voters an opportunity to test a candidate's understanding of foreign policy. At least one debate in each campaign is regularly devoted to the subject. But in preparing for such debates, the primary objective of most contenders is to avoid a costly mistake rather than make the case for specific policies.

An exception occurred in a 2008 CNN/YouTube–sponsored Democratic Party debate in Charleston, South Carolina. Barack Obama was asked if he would "be willing to meet separately without preconditions with the leaders of Iran, Syria, Venezuela, Cuba, and North Korea in order to bridge the gap that divides our countries." Obama's response was crisp and specific: "I would, and the reason is this, that the notion that somehow not talking to countries is a punishment to them—which has been a guiding diplomatic principle of the Bush [administration] and is ridiculous."

The premise of Obama's remarks—that the essence of diplomacy requires precise communication designed to establish the basis of agreement or disagreement as the case may be, and that it is especially important in dealing with countries with which we experience deeply divergent interests—appears cogent. But its expression in this form provoked weeks of criticism, and some backpedaling by the candidate.[10]

More generally, the candidates therefore voice pronouncements that are longer on principles and shorter on details. Moreover, presidential debates are often a greater test of style and self-confidence than of relevant experience or seasoned judgment.

The format of the debates can be inhibiting. Time is limited. The questions are often superficial. Follow-up queries are relatively rare. And the candidates' answers are frequently banal. Misleading premises or hyperbolic claims are rarely challenged with the tenacity they deserve. The focus is more on outlining appealing aims than explaining how they can be accomplished and at what cost

But the main reason why contenders' campaign promises are a poor guide to a future administration's plans is that few contenders possess extensive knowledge of the world beyond our borders. Dwight Eisenhower, Richard Nixon, and George H. W. Bush were noteworthy exceptions. More often than not, presidents take office without the benefit of substantial experience abroad, and most acquire their foreign policy training on the job.

Those with such experience tend to be somewhat cagey about disclosing how, if elected, they intend to proceed on specific foreign policy issues. The Eisenhower and Nixon campaigns of 1952 and 1968 are especially instructive in this regard. Both ran for office when the United States was involved in a divisive Asian war. In each case, national security policy was a decisive issue in the campaign, but neither contender described his foreign policy plans in detail.

Ike's criticism of Truman's strategy in Korea became increasingly pointed during the campaign. Yet he provided few indications of how he intended to alter it. He justified his reticence on two main grounds. It would be inappropriate, he maintained, to formulate specific proposals before visiting the war zone. And he refused to divulge his plans at a time when it could possibly complicate President Truman's efforts to conclude ongoing truce negotiations with the Chinese and North Koreans.

Ike's late October 1952 pledge to "visit Korea" electrified the voters. He declared that immediately after the election he would forgo the diversions of politics and concentrate on the job of ending the Korean War. "That job," he announced, "requires a personal trip to Korea. I shall make that trip. Only in that way could I learn how best to serve the American people in the cause of peace. I shall go to Korea."[11]

The announcement appealed both to those who yearned for an all-out victory and to those eager for a swift disengagement of American troops. He left all options on the table, promising to make his policy decisions only after surveying the situation on the ground. Harry Truman derided Ike's promise as a "gimmick," but his pledge to make Korea his number-one priority resonated with the public, and without foreclosing any policy options he won the election in a walk.

Nixon inherited from Lyndon Johnson an ill-conceived war in Vietnam, the continuing ostracism of mainland China, an escalating arms race with the Soviet Union, and a stalemate fraught with danger in the Middle East. During the 1968 campaign Nixon criticized the Johnson administration's record on all these fronts. He intended to adjust the U.S. approach to each policy challenge. Yet few details of his plans for course corrections—in either the content of foreign policy or the process of policy making—found their way into his campaign speeches.

Nixon was especially crafty in disguising his plans for handling the war in Indochina. Instead of outlining an alternative policy, he promised "new leadership" and an "era of negotiations." He highlighted the Johnson administration's shortcomings while keeping his own plans to himself. He allowed the media's inference that he might have a "secret plan," but resisted all pressures to reveal its contents. He made no promise "to visit Vietnam." Instead, he insisted that going public with his plans would alert Hanoi to them, while complicating President Johnson's diplomacy. Nonetheless, he did play aggressive defense against the possibility of an October surprise in the 1968 Paris peace talks.

Nixon was certainly aware of activities undertaken by a prominent Republican, Anna Chennault, to discourage President Nguyen Van Thieu from playing along with Johnson's Vietnam strategy by participating in the Paris peace talks. Nixon may well actively have encouraged Chennault's efforts. If so, however, he was leaning against an open door. President Thieu had little interest in joining negotiations, which included representatives of the Viet Cong. Known to favor Nixon over Humphrey, Thieu required no persuasion from Chennault on that score. In the event, the initial promise of Johnson's bombing halt fizzled, public opinion turned, the Paris talks remained stalemated, and Nixon won the election by a hair.

George H. W. Bush's campaign in 1988 presented a somewhat different story line. In that year, the United States was generally at peace. Bush commenced his run for the Oval Office as a sitting vice president. And to his good fortune, the Reagan administration was wrapping up its second term on a high note of East–West comity.

Like Eisenhower and Nixon, Bush possessed impressive foreign policy credentials. Some regarded his quest for the presidency as a bid for Reagan's "third term." He ran on the record of an administration in which he had played a dutiful role. Yet Bush and his closest associates, James Baker and Brent Scowcroft, harbored serious misgivings about some of Reagan's foreign policy priorities. Once in office, they introduced noteworthy adjustments in them. During the 1988 campaign, however, Bush had little incentive to publicize such differences, and, with one exception, he did not.

In the summer of 1988, the Reagan administration sought to negotiate what amounted to a plea bargain with Manuel Noriega, the Panamanian dictator. In return for his agreement to leave Panama, the United States offered to set aside a Justice Department indictment against Noriega for drug trafficking. The State Department dispatched a senior diplomat, Mike Kozak, to test the possibility of striking such a deal.

I attended several NSC meetings in which this was a central issue, and indeed defended the State Department's case for the Kozak talks. I discovered personally the intensity with which Vice President Bush opposed these negotiations. Apart from his substantive misgivings about the plan, he was convinced it would play poorly with the domestic law-enforcement community. The police chief of Los Angeles, Daryl Gates, was a particularly outspoken critic of the venture. While candidate Bush generally sought the presidency as a loyal steward of the Reagan legacy, he openly challenged the president on this issue within the administration and publicly declared his opposition to it on the campaign trail.

CAMPAIGNS: CHALLENGES FOR CONTENDERS

For contenders, campaigns pose four main challenges and opportunities. They test the candidate's credentials as a commander in chief. They provide an opportunity to torch the incumbent's (or challenger's) foreign policy record. They offer an occasional chance to amend promises designed to secure the nomination of their party in order to court centrist votes needed in the general election. And they supply an invitation to advance a foreign policy agenda. How much of this agenda will survive if the contender is elected is, of course, another matter.

Campaigns as Tests of Foreign Policy Credentials

To be elected, it is widely assumed, a candidate must be considered by voters as a credible commander in chief and a plausible manager of U.S. diplomacy. From the late 1960s until the end of the Cold War, any serious contender for the presidency required a defensible military record. Dwight Eisenhower, John Kennedy, Richard Nixon, Gerald Ford, Jimmy Carter, Ronald Reagan, and George H. W. Bush all passed muster.

Democrats generally faced a tougher test than Republicans due to their party's reputation for being soft on national security. Military service, while a necessary credential, was not sufficient. George McGovern was among the most decorated pilots in World War II, yet he was also buried in 1972 in one of the biggest presidential election landslides ever.

The termination of the draft in 1973 tended to lower this bar, and with the disintegration of the Soviet Union, military service diminished further as an electoral asset. Indeed, in 1992 Bill Clinton won the Democratic Party nomination and the general election despite allegations of draft dodging. And he prevailed that year over a genuine war hero—George H. W. Bush—in the first post–Cold War election. Among more recent candidates for the presidency or vice presidency, Barack Obama, Mitt Romney, Jack Kemp, Dick Cheney, Joe Biden, Sarah Palin, and Paul Ryan had no record of military service. George W. Bush, whose stint in the Air Force National Guard was completed in the United States, defeated Al Gore and John Kerry, despite their tours of duty in Vietnam.

Those with lengthy tenure in the Congress discover that legislative experience is a mixed bag for candidates seeking a national office. It can provide not just familiarity with national security issues but also experience in dealing with them. Service on the Foreign Relations, Armed Services, or Intelligence Committees can be particularly valuable in this regard. Yet prolonged service in the Senate or House also brings with it an extensive voting record, and given the pattern of horse-trading that marks legislative activity, such records usually expose evidence of logical inconsistencies, political incorrectness, and past support for causes no longer in the mainstream.

Recent contenders lacking strong national security credentials have found resourceful ways of coping. Bill Clinton's campaign in 1992 highlighted the slogan "It's the economy, stupid," and he devoted only 141 words out of his 4,000-word acceptance speech at the Democratic Party Convention to foreign policy. George W. Bush's early and somewhat bewildered efforts to answer questions about foreign leaders prompted campaign advisers to surround him with experienced hands from the GOP's deep foreign policy bench. Both won election in a post–Cold War world of relative international tranquility by campaigning mainly as aspiring domestic policy presidents.

As both major parties have turned more recently to governors as their presidential nominee, these contenders have attempted to bolster their foreign policy credentials by selecting running mates with foreign policy experience. With such considerations in mind, Walter Mondale, George H. W. Bush, Al Gore, Dick Cheney, and Joe Biden were picked by Jimmy Carter, Ronald Reagan, Bill Clinton, George W. Bush, and Barack Obama, respectively.

Challengers regularly seek to burnish their foreign policy credentials through foreign travels, meetings with respected international figures, and endorsements from prominent leaders in politically consequential countries. Barack Obama certainly bolstered his foreign policy credentials in 2008 by embarking on an extensive midsummer trip to the Middle East, South Asia, and Europe. This allowed him to mix it up with American GIs in key war zones, hold his own with foreign heads of state, burnish his standing with well-known Israelis, and demonstrate his ability to draw huge and rapturous crowds in Europe.

Needless to add, timing can be crucial. When international tensions are high and the security of the nation at risk, this credentialing exercise takes on greater importance. When peaceful conditions reign, it diminishes in salience. In midsummer 2012, Mitt Romney traveled to London, Tel Aviv, and Warsaw to highlight his successful management of the 2002 Winter Olympic games, indulge in some tough talk on Iran, demonstrate close ties with prominent Israeli leaders, and be photographed with the Polish icon Lech Walesa. Romney's rhetorical miscues played poorly in the press, but the trip scarcely altered his standing in public-opinion polls.[12] He subsequently selected as his running mate, Paul Ryan—a congressman from Wisconsin whose main expertise was on domestic issues.

Campaigns as Opportunities to Expose and Criticize an Incumbent's Record

Presidential campaigns tend to be backward-looking. They provide challengers a chance to disparage the record of the incumbent. John Kennedy criticized the Eisenhower administration for its complacency and torpor, while promising renewal and change. Richard Nixon capitalized on widespread public animosity toward Lyndon Johnson's debacle in Vietnam by offering an "era of negotiations." Jimmy Carter exploited public uneasiness with the Nixon/Ford/Kissinger brand of realpolitik, while pledging a post-Watergate cleanup and the promotion of human rights around the world.

Ronald Reagan exploited Carter's weak response to Iranian hostage-taking and the Soviet Union's invasion of Afghanistan by promising to build up America's defenses and restore America's prestige. Bill Clinton assailed George H. W. Bush for alleged passivity in the face of ethnic cleansing in the Balkans and the suppression of pro-democracy protests in China by the "butchers of Beijing." George W. Bush attacked Clinton's humanitarian interventionism in Somalia, Haiti, and the Balkans, and pledged to pursue a "more humble, less arrogant" foreign policy. Barack Obama criticized George W. Bush's conduct of the "global war on terror," and pledged to extricate U.S. troops from Iraq while stepping up counterinsurgency activities against al-Qaeda in Afghanistan and Pakistan. Mitt Romney chastised President Obama for displaying weakness in the face of foreign enemies, but he concentrated his main fire on his failure to boost domestic economic growth.

Challengers generally devote more attention to castigating the policies of their rivals than to explaining their own plans. Still, these criticisms serve to identify overseas issues contenders believe deserve greater attention and occasionally supply hints as to how they plan to tackle them.

Campaigns as Chances to Modify Promises Made During the Struggle for the Nomination

Attracting swing votes imposes different requirements than mobilizing the base. Hence, general election campaigns often provide challengers an opportunity to modify promises they made while seeking their party's nomination. The 1980 Reagan campaign illustrated the pressures and problems associated with managing this pivot after the party convention.

During his quest for the nomination, Ronald Reagan made no secret of his desire to implement a "Two Chinas" policy. He even heralded an upgrade in U.S. official representation in Taipei. But once the general election campaign commenced, he faced strong pressures to amend his position from within the GOP.

A fellow Republican, Richard Nixon, had, after all, initiated the "opening to China." In 1972, he had signed the Shanghai Communiqué, which defined what was subsequently labeled America's "One China" policy. Moderates in the GOP were eager to keep the door open for constructive ties with Beijing—in order both to pursue commercial opportunities and to constrain the Soviet Union geopolitically. George H. W. Bush, Reagan's running mate, shared such views and had indeed represented them to the Chinese while directing the U.S. Liaison Office in Beijing for the Nixon administration.

Reagan's campaign advisers considered it prudent to navigate their candidate back to a centrist position on this issue, and he felt the vice presidential nominee was just the man to manage this challenge. With this in mind, George H. W. Bush and a small band of advisers, including Richard Allen and James Lilley, set off for China shortly after the GOP Convention. They intended to reposition the candidate on the China issue while securing the understanding of key Beijing leaders that some adjustments in U.S. policy were to be expected.

While in the Chinese capital, Bush and Allen, who was to become Reagan's first national security adviser, urged the Chinese to accommodate the expectation that the United States intended to treat Taiwan with greater dignity and accord it a somewhat higher political profile. They also admonished their hosts to stop attacking Reagan's campaign.

Chinese leaders responded stiffly, reminding Bush of what they portrayed as solemn yet unfulfilled commitments made to China by past U.S. administrations. Even as George Bush was meeting with Deng Xiaoping, aides brought the Chinese leader news bulletins reporting that Ray Cline, described as "a leading Reagan adviser on China policy," had affirmed the candidate's intent to reestablish diplomatic relations with Taiwan. This undercut the Bush delegation's case, while reinforcing Chinese suspicions of President-elect Reagan.

On the trip home, the delegation drafted a nuanced approach to the China issue intended for Reagan's use as a policy statement. Reagan agreed dutifully to read it to the press. But when invited by reporters to interpret its meaning, he affirmed his resolve to define more flexibly than had President Carter the rules of "unofficiality" for dealing with Taiwan. This put him back in the soup with Beijing.

Throughout the campaign, ambivalence shrouded Reagan's intentions vis-à-vis China. Whatever he might express in prepared remarks, his personal policy reflexes were clear. He felt that the Carter administration had been "lily livered" in its reluctance to stand up to the Chinese. He believed that the bureaucracy interpreted the rules of engagement with Taiwan in a nit-picking, custodial fashion. He did not like to be told to turn his back on old friends in Taiwan, and he intended in fact to make some policy adjustments.

At the same time, Reagan planned to confront Soviet assertiveness more directly than had his predecessor, and he recognized the value of China's help in establishing a favorable balance of power, monitoring Moscow's missile testing, and funneling assistance to anti-Soviet forces in Indochina and Afghanistan. Once in office, the new president had to confront the resulting policy dilemma: how to enlist China's help in coping with the Soviet Union while ignoring or defying its interests on matters related to Taiwan.

Wishful thinking can be indulged in campaigns; governance imposes a harsher dose of reality. It should not have come as a surprise. Deng had been blunt in warning Bush and Allen that "Reagan's tough stand on the USSR will not cause China to swallow his position on Sino-US relations and Taiwan."[13] A People's Liberation Army (PLA) officer had put the matter even more straightforwardly: "Don't give us that stuff about Russia and polar bears. Taiwan is a real issue, and don't forget it for one minute."[14]

During the campaign, Reagan was more successful in muting opposition to his views about China on the home front than in eliciting understanding for them in Beijing. He essentially invited a test of wills, and he got it. But the chickens came home to roost, of course, only after he entered the White House. Reagan's administration eventually found its equilibrium on China policy, but it took the better part of two years and the negotiation of a third major communiqué with the People's Republic of China (PRC) on arms sales to Taiwan that was arguably more restrictive than American policy under Jimmy Carter.

Of course, most campaign promises are casual IOUs, which can be implemented only if the challenger wins the election. Needless to add, many are jettisoned when their practical consequences are confronted. For example, challengers regularly bid for Jewish support by promising to move the U.S. embassy in Israel from Tel Aviv to Jerusalem—a suggestion that those elected to the Oval Office have been consistently persuaded to abandon given the potentially adverse impact it would have on the U.S. negotiating position on Israeli–Palestinian issues.

Campaigns as Occasions to Set Agendas

Campaigns can, of course, expose the genuine priorities of an administration-in-waiting. Any contender who plans to undertake major reforms is well advised to mobilize the case for specific changes during his campaign, above all to convey seriousness to the "permanent government"—that is, the bureaucracy—whose help he will need to implement his plans.

George W. Bush sought to make national defense an issue in the 2000 campaign in order to lay the foundation for a future change in policy. His plans were somewhat inchoate, but there were strong motivations for change. Bill Clinton's evident reluctance to push national missile defense was one. Critics of the Pentagon also persuaded Bush that the military services were hidebound, wed to the past, and forever planning "to win the last war." Bush also sympathized with the uniformed military's complaints about being diverted too often into peacekeeping and "nation-building" missions.

In September 1999, he gave a speech at The Citadel in South Carolina, which laid the predicate for future reform efforts. As he later told Steve Hadley, his deputy national security adviser, if he ran and failed to mention the subject, when he subsequently went to the Joint Chiefs to secure their assistance, they would simply say, "Who are you? You've just been elected. You'll be gone in four years. We'll be here. Thank you very much."[15]

However, "If I go to the American people and say, 'I'm going to reform the Defense Department. Here's why. Here's what I'm going to do.' And when I get elected and go to the Joint Chiefs and I say, 'The American people have just elected me to reform the Defense Department. Where do we start?'"[16] That makes a big difference.

President Bush did appoint a secretary of defense, Donald Rumsfeld, who shared his desire for reform. But their ideas about a lean force structure still encountered the resistance of a strong inertial force—the military bureaucracy. And within months, Rumsfeld was rumored to be frustrated and even ready to leave.

After September 11, things changed. In Afghanistan, the United States relied on the kind of agile forces that Rumsfeld favored. But as internal turmoil emerged there and in the wake of America's invasion of Iraq, insistence on keeping U.S. forces lean proved incompatible with the objective of fostering "stabilization," let alone successfully protecting the local population or countering a nascent Sunni insurgency. By the time Bush's tenure was over, he was enmeshed in two costly nation-building campaigns that required sizable surges of U.S. troop levels. In both Iraq and Afghanistan, the conflicts were protracted, the costs high, and the results of nation-building exercises inconclusive.

RECURRENT DEMOCRATIC AND REPUBLICAN PARTY CAMPAIGN THEMES

Some features of challengers' campaigns recur with striking regularity, and they can have consequential effects on the foreign policies of those elected. Two familiar patterns are particularly worthy of note. One is the tendency of Democratic nominees to counter their party's reputation for being soft on national security by seeking to outflank Republican opponents from the right on defense and foreign policy. The other is the inclination of Republican nominees, viewing the management of foreign policy as their party's strong suit, to disparage incumbent Democratic presidents' records so disdainfully as to foreshadow wholesale reversals of course. The "Anything but Carter" and "Anything but Clinton" campaigns of 1980 and 2000 provide examples.

Democratic Campaigns: "Outflanking the GOP from the Right"

John F. Kennedy designed the template for such campaigns in 1960. He accused Eisenhower of presiding over a "missile gap," and promised to bolster the U.S. nuclear deterrent and broaden conventional force options, tackle the Communist threat in Cuba, and augment America's alliances and counterinsurgency capabilities.

Harry Truman, Jimmy Carter, Bill Clinton, and Barack Obama improvised variations on this theme. Each managed to win the presidency. George McGovern, Fritz Mondale, Michael Dukakis, Al Gore, and John Kerry either foreswore this game or played it poorly. All lost their bids for the White House.

Truman's address to Congress in 1948 requesting funding for the Marshall Plan, restoring the draft, and proposing universal military training foreshadowed a tactic utilized by many successors. And he also expressed interest in forging a Western military alliance. James Chace characterized his speech as "disguised to outflank the Republicans on the right and on the left to neutralize Henry Wallace." In 1976, Jimmy Carter, a former naval officer, enjoyed a convincing national security credential, and his rival, Gerald Ford, appeared politically vulnerable, having been pummeled by Ronald Reagan in the primaries. On national security issues, Carter ran a hybrid campaign, appealing on some issues to the right and on some to the left of the incumbent.

He set forth a tough critique of Ford's East–West policy, suggesting that the Russians were exploiting "détente" and that the president had offered insufficient resistance to Moscow's advances. He also covered his flanks on the right by affirming the importance of America's Cold War alliances and indulging in a bit of demagoguery on the Panama Canal issue—positions that appealed to southern Democrats.

The strong defense of containment made good political sense. The Cold War was still on. The Soviet Union had achieved strategic parity and was overplaying its hand in local contests for influence in the Third World. The Democratic Party retained a strong Henry "Scoop" Jackson wing whose members were hawks on national security matters but liberal on domestic issues. Remnants of the postwar tradition of bipartisanship persisted; most members of Carter's national security team—Cyrus Vance, Zbigniew Brzezinski, and Harold Brown—were in fact members in good standing of the same foreign policy establishment as the officials they replaced.

At the same time, Carter mollified his party's liberals by rejecting GOP-style realpolitik, promising to pursue ambitious arms control initiatives, pledging to focus U.S. economic assistance on ameliorating "basic human needs," and underlining his intent to promote human rights and democracy around the world.

Carter thus fashioned a national security playbook featuring some elements of policy continuity and some prominent breaks with the past. Whereas Ford and Kissinger had focused on East–West issues, Carter expressed emphatic concern about North–South matters, while downplaying their Soviet dimension. Ford and Kissinger's diplomacy sought systematically to utilize linkage to secure leverage in negotiations with Moscow, but Carter pledged to use such leverage to press for reforms in Soviet domestic practices. Ford was prepared to settle for a relatively modest strategic arms control deal with the Soviets; Carter promised to strive for deeper cuts.[17] Ford and Kissinger had accomplished interim, partial agreements in the Middle East; Carter set his sights on more expansive breakthroughs. Although Carter expected to preserve America's alliance with South Korea, he also outlined plans for withdrawing American ground troops from the peninsula.

Thus Carter tacked to the right on some national security issues, while consolidating the support of his party's liberal constituency on others. The combination provided him an effective means of solidifying the party's northern base, at the same time attracting significant support in the more conservative, nationalist, pro-military South.

In 1992, Bill Clinton ran essentially on domestic issues. He recognized that foreign policy was George H. W. Bush's strong suit, and in the general election campaign he merely sought to fight the foreign policy debate "to a rough draw, or at least something short of a rout."[18] He did not exactly position himself to outflank Bush from the right. Rather, he promised more actively to promote American "values" abroad, while portraying the incumbent as too accommodating to the Chinese, too diffident toward the plight of Haitian refugees, too supine in trade negotiations with the Japanese, and too passive in the Balkans.

Clinton pledged to do "whatever it took" to stop the slaughter of innocent civilians in Yugoslavia, arguing that history shows "that you can't allow the mass extermination of people and just sit by and watch it happen."[19] He maintained that with the end of the Cold War, Beijing's strategic value had declined and thus America could afford to use its power, backed by threats of economic sanctions, to push the "butchers of Beijing" to implement democratic reforms. And he promised to "get tough" with those countries that were running large merchandise trade surpluses with the United States. As expected, the election's outcome was shaped decisively by domestic issues, but Clinton could not so easily ignore or abandon his foreign policy promises, and once in the Oval Office, some came back to haunt him.

We saw in chapter 3 how Barack Obama's critique of President George W. Bush's invasion of Iraq assisted his bid for the Democratic nomination. It was framed as a realist indictment of a Bush policy rather than as an ideological assault on the incumbent. As E. J. Dionne noted later, it sounded "more like Brent Scowcroft than MoveOn.org."[20] This facilitated Obama's adroit pivot during the 2008 general election campaign to a hard-nosed insistence that America step up its military effort in Afghanistan, where he was determined, he affirmed, to break "the cycle of American neglect, Pakistani duplicity, and Afghan dysfunction."[21]

Obama upped the ante in Afghanistan, thereby investing greater American prestige in the outcome of the conflict. For practical purposes, he embraced a counterinsurgency strategy for which the Bush surge in Iraq (which he had opposed) provided the template. Without perhaps realizing it, the strategy he initially adopted was labor intensive, demanded patience, depended for its efficacy on high-quality intelligence, and would require a local partner possessing effective authority and legitimacy. And a successful outcome would remain highly problematic unless the Afghan frontier with Pakistan could be closed. Little wonder he harbored second thoughts before the end of 2009.

Of course, these judgments and their consequences would be tested only if Barack Obama won the election. In the meanwhile, this "realist" stance, plus his publicly declared readiness to attack al-Qaeda leaders and operatives in Pakistan and deny Taliban forces a safe-haven there—if necessary, without Islamabad's assent—served to bolster Obama's credentials as a hard-nosed, tough-minded potential commander in chief.

Advertising "toughness" and a determination to protect American interests abroad clearly helped these Democratic candidates get elected. It also exposed them to painful policy dilemmas once in office. Such campaigns obliged successful challengers to accord a higher degree of priority to foreign policy than they might find comfortable. It also put them on record for supporting robust foreign policy commitments that provoked disquiet among their more liberal constituents, who preferred to spend more money on domestic priorities, who were uneasy about open-ended overseas commitments, or who regarded the use of force to promote foreign policy objectives distasteful.

In each case, contenders' campaign rhetoric established predicates for actions that, once in office, the new incumbent found inconvenient to carry out or at odds with their domestic political priorities. Each candidate promised significant change in the field of foreign policy. And they all discovered that change was a lot more complicated and costly to engineer than they had foreseen. Some initiatives blew up in their faces; some ran out of gas when found too difficult to implement; some were swiftly and judiciously buried.

Republican Campaigns: "Anything but . . ."

Political polarization between the Democrats and Republicans deepened in the 1960s and 1970s. As a consequence, changes of party control of the White House implied larger discontinuities in U.S. foreign policy. As the GOP acquired a seeming hammerlock on the White House from the late 1960s to the early 1990s, it came to regard a strong national security policy as a core competence, which the Republican Party alone possessed. Its campaign criticisms of the Democratic Party's legacy in foreign affairs grew shriller.

Public criticism is a natural means of holding any administration accountable for its performance while in office. Without pressure from the other party, administrations are loath to concede policy errors. Foreign policy problems are unlikely to be fixed if they remain unacknowledged. Insofar as presidential campaigns generate thoughtful criticisms of existing policies, they can prepare the political ground for necessary and timely adjustments.

On occasion, however, challengers are inclined to ratchet up the criticism, claiming that their rivals can do virtually nothing right—voicing contempt for the incumbent, scorn for his record, and doubts about his competence. These tendencies have increased alongside the growing intensity of partisanship. One result has been "Anything but . . ." campaigns run by Ronald Reagan in 1980 and George W. Bush in 2000. Each reflected neoconservative views.

In 1980, things were not going well in America's relations with the world. The Iranians held American diplomats hostage. The Soviets occupied Afghanistan, and both Moscow and Havana were assertively meddling in Third World disputes. Central America was a cauldron of unrest. Europe and Japan were challenging America's competitiveness. Energy prices were skyrocketing, propelled by turmoil in the Middle East, and the American economy was gripped by "stagflation."

Reagan boldly articulated the dissatisfaction these trends evoked within the American body politic and rode it to a landslide victory in the election. He claimed that the Carter administration had allowed American military strength to atrophy, dismissed its arms control proposals as shams, and accused the incumbent of soft-peddling Soviet perfidy and responding lamely to its assertiveness.

Judged against the conventional wisdom of the time, some of Reagan's policy instincts were quite unconventional. He evinced little enthusiasm for arms control and was quite prepared to foster an intensified arms race with Moscow, confident that the United States could not only outspend the Soviet Union but also expose the structural weaknesses in its system. He regarded "Mutual Assured Destruction" as an abominable strategic doctrine, and strategic defenses appealed to him. He yearned deeply—if silently at this juncture—for the elimination of nuclear weapons.

He believed that previous administrations had been too deferential to the Chinese and Russians, and too critical of long-time allies like Taiwan. He was eager to subsidize "freedom fighters" prepared to resist the Soviet Union. He considered Russia an "evil empire" and was prepared to say so publicly. For all these reasons, the foreign policy establishment regarded him as suspect, even potentially dangerous.

Implicit in his comprehensive critique of Carter's policies lay a resolve to reverse many of his priorities, and once he laid claim to the Oval Office, he proceeded to do so. But, at Richard Nixon's suggestion, he also chose Al Haig to be his secretary of state, and in doing so ensured some measure of continuity in the realm of foreign policy. Haig, after all, was an experienced Washington hand who had participated for several decades in the management of U.S. national security policy.

This notwithstanding, Reagan embarked on a major acceleration of defense spending and more proactive resistance to Soviet assertiveness in the Third World. He downplayed arms control and proposed using economic assistance to push market-oriented reforms in developing countries. His rhetoric on foreign policy matters was more combative than that of recent predecessors, and it provoked predictably critical reactions from some allies as well as adversaries. In some areas, there was greater policy continuity than met the eye. The Carter administration had in the late 1970s begun to increase the defense budget, chart a more robust security role in the Middle East and Persian Gulf, and undertaken some substantial measures to combat the Soviet challenge in Afghanistan, though the covert character of the latter actions left the public unaware of their scope and effectiveness.

In 2000 George W. Bush organized his "Anything but Clinton" campaign primarily around proposals for domestic reform—promises of tax cuts, K-12 educational reform, and faith-based social policy initiatives. Unlike Reagan, he did not personally foreshadow fundamental discontinuities in national strategy. He did promise "a less arrogant and more humble" foreign policy.

To neutralize doubts about his ability to manage America's external relations, he promised to surround himself with an experienced cadre of foreign policy professionals. He picked a former secretary of defense, Dick Cheney, as his running mate, and was seen regularly during the campaign with Colin Powell, whom he hinted would be tapped to manage major national security responsibilities. Reliance on such familiar figures was expected to provide reassurance to the press and public, and the tactic seemed to work.

It was also apparent from his selection of foreign policy advisers for the campaign—the so-called Vulcans—that other significant adjustments of national security policy were likely.[22] Condoleezza Rice, Paul Wolfowitz, Richard Perle, Richard Armitage, Dov Zakheim, Bob Zoellick, and Bob Blackwill occupied various places along the political spectrum from realism to neoconservatism. But all regarded Clinton's foreign policy with a skepticism bordering on disdain.

They were especially critical of what they considered the Clinton administration's inability to apply power purposefully. They mocked its "assertive multilateralism" and were dismissive of its tendency to define environmental degradation or public-health pandemics as matters of national security. They lamented the fact that Saddam Hussein remained in power in Iraq and were instinctively supportive of Ariel Sharon's hawkish government in Israel. They promised to devote more attention to long-standing allies like Japan and were eager to consign Clinton's "strategic partnership" with China to the dustbin of history.

They had no intention of ratifying agreements recently signed by the Clinton administration like the Comprehensive Test Ban Treaty, a proposed International Criminal Court, or robust measures to curb carbon dioxide emissions. These were regarded either as unwarranted restrictions on America's economic competitiveness or undesirably impediments to its diplomatic maneuverability. Those who knew the Bush foreign policy inner circle thus foresaw portents of dramatic change in the content and style of its foreign policy management.

During the campaign, moreover, George W. Bush, was publicly critical of some of the main lines of his predecessor's overseas priorities, but he scarcely foreshadowed major reversals of course. He pledged to accelerate national missile defense, promised to cultivate stronger relations with the

Great Powers, and outlined plans for transforming the structure of U.S. military forces. He also expressed skepticism about the virtues of "humanitarian intervention," and misgivings about nation building and peacekeeping as appropriate missions for U.S. troops. Yet even these course corrections were expressed in a relatively low-key fashion, and he certainly accorded priority to domestic concerns.

The Bush campaign team was scarcely opposed to the Clinton administration's penchant for interventionism. In the "unipolar," post–Cold War world, both major parties appeared partial to using U.S. power to reshape the global system. But Democrats and Republicans were disposed to intervene on behalf of quite different causes. Liberal internationalists were preoccupied with mitigating such root causes of instability as hunger, humanitarian disasters, and ethnic cleansing, and they were prepared to utilize force, if necessary, to address these issues. Conservative interventionists were more focused on sustaining America's geopolitical hegemony and recognized the use of force as a legitimate means for accomplishing that aim.

The major factor underlying these ABC campaigns was the self-confidence of GOP leaders that they were superior custodians of American interests abroad. They considered themselves as more seasoned and experienced in the management of U.S. equities overseas. They felt they had a better understanding of how the world worked and how to advance American interests in it.

TAKEAWAYS

For presidential contenders, a general election campaign is in part a credentialing exercise testing their plausibility as a commander in chief and foreign policy leader. Since the end of the Cold War, the bar for this test has been lowered. But its importance in determining a contender's election chances still varies with the gravity of external threats to the nation's security.

The overheated rhetoric of campaigns tends to exaggerate the scope of U.S. interests overseas, and to downplay the limits of American influence beyond our shores. Contenders regularly trash the record of the incumbent, portray the world as dangerous, and characterize American foreign policy as in need of dramatic course adjustments. Their proposed fixes reflect soaring aspirations pursued with strategies that remain vague and costs which are generally unspecified.

Relatively few challengers bring deep foreign policy experience to their quest for the Oval Office. Those who do often hesitate for political reasons to articulate their strategic plans with clarity, acknowledge the limits of American power, or indicate how they plan to allocate scarce resources among a variety of external objectives.

General election campaigns rarely illuminate the country's most pressing foreign policy challenges. Platforms are formulated primarily to fire up the party faithful. Foreign policy debates are more a test of style and self-confidence than of substantive knowledge and prudential judgment. Proposed policy initiatives are shaped more for their appeal at home than their efficacy abroad. Many foreign policy promises thrown out in the heat of the campaign warrant sober second thoughts, substantial modifications, or even a quiet burial, once the election is over. And some campaign promises, if swiftly and slavishly implemented, turn out to be banana peels on which the victor may easily slip.

Still, prolonged campaigns are a test of character, and they expose for the voters the nature of a contender's policy reflexes, the breadth of his political instincts, and the quality of his judgment.

5 PRESIDENTIAL TRANSITIONS

TRANSITIONS TEND TO BE UNRULY AND HIGHLY UNCERTAIN affairs, particularly when political control of the White House changes hands. As Jimmy Carter once observed, "A change of administrations in Washington, especially where one party throws out the other, rises like a thunderstorm over a picnic. Panic is the dominant feature. Thousands of political appointees, who may have been in power for up to eight years, scramble for the exits, and for jobs in the private sector. Thousands of new political appointees sweep into town with one eye on the new era and the other looking under every rock for unpleasant surprises."[1]

Transitions can be awkward for both the incumbent and his successor, since their interests are by no means naturally aligned. The former is understandably focused on "shoring up the past" and burnishing his legacy; the latter on putting an administration together in order to "embark . . . on the future."[2]

Still, the incumbent may need the help of the president-elect to finish his tenure on a high note. His successor will naturally worry that requests for such assistance might constrain his own future policy flexibility.

Presidents-elect are impelled by law and custom to avoid premature engagement in diplomacy. In any event, their hands are full. During the transition, an incoming president must form a cabinet and begin to fill hundreds of subcabinet slots. He must distribute patronage to the party faithful and decide which positions to reserve for career officials in the interest of bureaucratic competence or policy continuity. He must establish priorities among campaign promises and settle on a policy-making structure that is personally comfortable and operationally efficient. And he must align the party machinery with his policy aspirations, open up effective lines of communications with the Congress and press, bind up the intraparty wounds left by the campaign, and, if an "outsider," introduce himself to Washington society.

Needless to add, there are a host of personal matters to attend to, like recuperating from an exhausting campaign, straightening out personal finances, and moving the family to Washington. The president-elect will hope, moreover, that during the transition, he can build a certain political momentum for a fast start once he is inaugurated. It is in the context of this whirlwind of frenetic activity that he will face occasional requests for policy collaboration from the incumbent, or experience paranoia that his predecessor is either laying policy traps to trip him up or narrowing policy options to box him in. It is scarcely surprising that missed signals and policy mishaps are occasional by-products of transitions.

Of course, the conduct of foreign policy cannot be suspended during a transition, which is roughly the ten-week period between an election and the inauguration of a president. There is unfinished business to wrap up. Events overseas continue to demand a response from Washington. Some foreign governments are eager to conclude arrangements while the outgoing president remains in office; others are impatient to establish official contacts and initiate business with his successor.

Some of the problems caused by transitions result from choices made by presidents-elect (to those we shall return in chap. 6). The balance of this chapter is devoted mainly to actions undertaken by incumbents *after* their successors are elected—that is, the challenges and choices facing lame ducks. They occasionally achieve fruitful diplomatic collaboration with their successors, but this is difficult and the results of such attempts are generally modest and sometimes unfortunate.

It takes a strong ego to seek the presidency and unusual political sensitivity to acknowledge that one's time in office is about up. The dilemma of what to try to accomplish during a transition is real. For a lame duck, custodial work is normally the order of the day, though it is not particularly bracing. Outgoing presidents sometimes promise a sprint to the finish line, but they are rarely successful in adding much luster to their records in their final months in office.

Henry Kissinger poignantly described the painful realities of an administration's waning days:

> The surface appurtenances of power still exist; the bureaucracy continues to produce the paperwork for executive decisions. But authority is slipping away. Decisions of which officials disapprove will be delayed in implementation; foreign governments go through the motions of diplomacy but reserve their real attention for the next team. And yet so familiar has the exercise of power become that its loss is sensed only dimly and intermittently. Days go by in which one carries out one's duties as if one's actions still matter.[3]

In light of their waning power, it is generally prudent for lame duck incumbents to approach their remaining duties with modesty. It's too late to launch controversial initiatives. Long-term planning is feckless when one's time in office is so limited. Delicate negotiations are difficult to sustain, let alone commence, once the voters have conferred a political mandate on another. Even routine matters become more difficult to manage, since during transitions the attention of senior national security officials tends to drift toward either maintaining their current positions or on nailing down a new and promising assignment—inside the government, or beyond it.

POLICY-MAKING OPTIONS FOR LAME DUCK PRESIDENTS

The president remains in office for more than two months following the election of his successor, and his actions (and his counsel) can be quite consequential for his successor. What's a lame duck to do?

Responding to Crises

Problems arise during transitions that cannot just be put on hold. I recall one, which came up during and following the 1980 election. That fall, South Korea's military regime tried opposition leader Kim Dae Jung for treason and consorting with North Korea. He was convicted and sentenced to death.

At the time, I was serving as the principal deputy to the assistant secretary of state for East Asia and the Pacific, Dick Holbrooke. We immediately signaled to Republic of Korea (ROK) generals that carrying out this sentence would have a catastrophic impact on our alliance. This seemed to deter the execution of Kim, at least until after the U.S. election. It was also evident, however, that the ROK military regarded President Carter with distaste and hoped for his defeat.

After Reagan's electoral victory, we learned from sensitive intelligence reports that senior generals in South Korea now felt free to carry out Kim's sentence before President-elect Reagan was inaugurated. The implications of this were extremely worrisome. We knew that the Carter administration's leverage on the government in Seoul was limited. We also understood that there was bad blood between people in the upper ranks of the outgoing and incoming administrations. Consequently, prospects for overt cooperation during the transition did not appear promising.

Nonetheless, Holbrooke and I arranged to meet informally in late November with leaders of the Reagan national security team, Richard Allen and Fred Ikle, in the transition team's office. We conveyed a simple, stark message: the United States had succeeded in dissuading senior South Korean generals from killing Kim Dae Jung for several months, but now his life depended on an urgent signal conveyed in the name of the president-elect. Without that, we feared Kim might be executed before the new administration took office. We shared sensitive intelligence reports to underline the seriousness of the problem and the urgency of our request.

Dick Allen knew the Koreans well, and we felt that he and Fred Ikle instinctively understood the foreign policy implications of Kim's execution. They thanked us for the heads-up but also affirmed, as transition teams invariably do, that the country could have only one president at a time; that until January 20, 1981, members of the transition would exercise no official authority; and that responsibility for foreign policy would remain exclusively in the incumbent's hands. They made no promise to get involved but acknowledged that they had their own contacts with the Koreans, and would welcome further information about administration actions and Korean responses to them.

I was in touch with Dick Allen in the weeks that followed. He did not disclose details about conversations he or other members of the transition team might be having with the Koreans, but I sensed that a discrete, parallel effort might be under way to avert Kim's death.

I later learned that Allen had conferred with President-elect Reagan, who authorized him to "handle the matter in his own way." Allen then contacted President Chun Doo-hwon and informed him that Reagan was opposed to the execution of Kim, which, if it occurred, could produce quite drastic consequences "like a bolt of lightning out of the heavens."

The South Koreans took the warning seriously. They also sensed a bargaining opportunity and sought an invitation for Chun to attend Reagan's inauguration. Allen parried that request but offered a different "carrot"—a working visit for Chun to Washington early in President Reagan's tenure, provided that Kim's death sentence was commuted. It was, and Kim Dae Jung left Seoul shortly thereafter to take up a fellowship at Harvard. When Chun visited Washington in early February 1981, the press criticized President Reagan heavily for "coddling dictators." But the deal—never made public at the time—saved Kim's life.

This episode serves as a reminder not only that foreign governments are extremely attentive to our election cycle but that occasionally tacit cooperation on foreign policy issues can be arranged between outgoing and incoming administrations during a period of transition. It helped in this case that the objective was limited and clear, and that key members of the outgoing and incoming administrations not only recognized that significant national interests were up for grabs but that timely action was required to protect them. It was also crucial that the contacts between members of the Carter administration and the Reagan transition team were managed discretely, with the focus on achieving a practical result rather than worrying about who would get the political credit or blame.

During the same Carter–Reagan transition, Bill Casey, Reagan's campaign manager, turned down a request from Lloyd Cutler, a key Carter adviser, for a public pledge that the incoming administration would not offer the Iranians any terms for the release of hostages more favorable than the Carter administration had put on the table. This did not prevent a tacit, unchoreographed "good cop–bad cop" routine that facilitated the ultimate return of the hostages.

Such tacit or implicit cooperation was possible because the president and his successor shared an objective: resolving the crisis as quickly as possible consistent with the nation's honor. Jimmy Carter wanted the satisfaction of getting the hostages back during his tenure; Reagan was eager to avoid inheriting a problem that could skew his foreign policy priorities.

Carter's resentment at the Ayatollah Ruhollah Khomeini's intransigence throughout the campaign increased his readiness to beef up U.S. diplomacy with more robust threats. Reagan's campaign hints of drastic actions against hostage-holders implicitly strengthened Carter's bargaining leverage during the balance of his term. The combination, further reinforced by objective factors impelling Tehran to settle—above all, the Iran-Iraq War—ultimately produced a salutary result. The details of the deal were fashioned by Deputy Secretary of State Warren Christopher with the assistance of Tunisian intermediaries. The Iranians agreed to the deal, though they stubbornly withheld release of the hostages until Ronald Reagan had taken the oath of office.

Reagan did not even agonize over the decision Carter's deal left on his plate: whether to honor the terms of the agreement. He did so immediately, without apparent hesitation or extended reflection. To be sure, U.S. relations with Iran remained estranged, but that was due to conflicting historical memories and divergent national interests, not to differences over the negotiations carried out by Carter and Christopher during the transition.

More robust and formal collaboration was achieved by George H. W. Bush and Bill Clinton during the transition following the 1992 election when a humanitarian mission to deliver food to starving Somalis was launched. At the time, Somalia was a country marked by a combustible mixture of massive starvation, civil discord, gross violations of human rights, and a breakdown of institutions. Conditions had become sufficiently desperate by midsummer that the Bush administration had closed its embassy in Mogadishu, evacuated American citizens, and suspended economic aid.

During the presidential election campaign, the food crisis in Somalia deepened. In response, the UN passed a series of resolutions providing for the supply of food and the dispatch of UN forces (led by the Turks) to safeguard its delivery. In August 1992, reflecting concerns provoked by heavy media coverage of starving Somalis and criticism of the administration's alleged passivity in the face of a major humanitarian crisis, Congress urged the president to seek further UN actions, particularly to protect those delivering relief supplies.

The Bush administration agreed to support additional UN Security Council Resolutions, and to supply food in unarmed aircraft—an operation that was suspended in September when an American aircraft was fired on. The deliveries resumed in October, but they did not proceed smoothly.

Local warlords stole food supplies from warehouses and hijacked relief agency trucks; UN representatives appeared beleaguered and ineffectual against the backdrop of daily television reports of starving children and lawless factions.

By fall, it had become increasingly clear that a Somalian faction, led by General Mohamed Farah Aidid, was a major force to be reckoned with in the capital, Mogadishu, and that UN Secretary General Boutros Boutros-Ghali was keen on building up UN forces in Somalia to implement an ambitious humanitarian mission, for whose accomplishment, however, he articulated no clear strategy. There things stood when American voters denied President George H. W. Bush a second term.

Ironically, Bush's defeat liberated him to take more decisive action. Attacks on the Pakistani UN unit laid the predicate. The commander of the U.S. Central Command (CENTCOM), Joseph Hoar, developed contingency plans for a mercy mission—Operation Restore Hope—that the JCS chairman laid out for President Bush just weeks after the election. It was based on the premise that U.S. Army "boots on the ground" would provide greater assurance that food would be delivered safely and efficiently.

The plan appealed to the president, who assumed that it could be accomplished within his remaining time in office. "I don't want to stick Clinton with an ongoing military operation," he noted. Some members of his national security team were more skeptical; Secretary of Defense Dick Cheney feared that it was easier to get U.S. forces in than to get them out. "We can't have it both ways," he said. "We can't get in there fully until mid-December. And the job won't be done by January 19."[4] Until late November, moreover, the Joint Chiefs of Staff were reluctant to deploy ground troops. These cautionary notes notwithstanding, the president moved ahead.

At an NSC meeting on November 25, Bush agreed that food would be delivered by a U.S.-led coalition. Under the plan, the United States would deploy up to 30,000 forces to secure Somali ports, airports, and roads to facilitate food deliveries. The troops were to be under American operational control in accordance with precise, strict rules of engagement. Their duties were to be handed off to the UN within at most several months.

The mission that President Bush authorized was specific in character and limited in duration. He encountered, however, persistent differences with Boutros Boutros-Ghali, who relentlessly pressed the United States to interpret its responsibilities expansively to include classic nation-building tasks:

disarming Somali factions, defusing land mines, training a civilian police, and creating a civil administration.[5]

On December 3, 1992, the Security Council unanimously authorized armed intervention, and a week later American troops began landing in Somalia. Their mission was to create—in concert with other UN forces—"a secure environment" for the distribution of food. No time frame was specified, but President Bush still hoped to see the mission concluded by January 20, when his term ended. No senior member of his administration contemplated an open-ended commitment, or intended to formulate or implement a "political solution" for Somalia.[6]

In retrospect, it is clear that the decision to intervene was heavily influenced by media pressure, but still, the administration was swayed by other considerations as well. During the election campaign, there had been much talk about promoting American "values" as well as American "interests" in a post–Cold War world. With the election over, the Bush national security team, still pressed to quell the widening chaos in Yugoslavia, chose to deflect that pressure by acting instead in Somalia, where it believed a military intervention would be easier to circumscribe "in mandate, duration, and scope."[7] One of President Bush's motives was also "to spare President-elect Clinton from having to immediately confront a messy problem needing military action."[8]

Prior to taking action, President Bush consulted with President-elect Bill Clinton, who readily agreed to the plan. It seemed an easy call at the time. "Humanitarian intervention" fit neatly into the convictions of the Democratic Party, which was marketing its brand of "liberal internationalism." Mounting an intervention under the aegis of the UN was consonant with Clinton's declared support for "assertive multilateralism." The Democratic transition team seemed comfortable working with the Bush administration, which had a well-deserved reputation for operational effectiveness.

At the outset, moreover, the intervention in Somalia went quite smoothly. American troops secured the ports without casualties. Food was efficiently distributed to desperately needy people. Other nations joined the coalition. By the time Clinton was inaugurated, leaders of the warring Somali factions had agreed to attend a peace conference, and U.S. troops were scheduled to withdraw within a few months. Boutros Boutros-Ghali had appointed an American, the retired navy admiral Jonathan Howe, as his special representative to oversee military operations in Somalia. The international forces under Howe's control were continuing to expand.

Nonetheless, the venture was hardly routine or without risk. The United States had never before launched an armed intervention essentially for humanitarian purposes.[9] Twenty-six thousand U.S. troops were involved—scarcely an insignificant military undertaking. Several senior officials, including Brent Scowcroft and Colin Powell, made no secret of their uneasiness about the venture. Above all, famine in Somalia continued to be exacerbated by feuds among competing factions, and no one had figured out how the United States, once engaged on the ground, would be able to withdraw "without turning the country back to the same warlords whose rivalries had produced the famine in the first place."[10]

President Bush was clear regarding his intentions. He consistently emphasized the limits on the intervention's scope and duration. He repeatedly expressed his resolve to avoid drift into a wider nation-building enterprise. And he engaged the Clinton transition team on the matter in a timely way.

Still, the intervention was launched without a specific request from Somali authorities and unfolded without the explicit approval of Congress. When the president announced the mission, no mention was made of vital national interests, no precise guidelines were specified for determining when the mission would be concluded, and no exit strategy was formulated for a "worst-case" contingency. The source of the food distribution problems in Somalia were essentially political, but it was unclear how "a secure environment for food distribution" could be created without addressing the underlying sources of institutional dysfunction and governmental instability in the country. The operation did unfold during a period of transition in which the incumbent president was preparing to relinquish the reins of government, while his successor was absorbed by the urgent necessities associated with organizing a new administration.

The subsequent mutation of what was conceived as a limited-liability commitment into a considerably more ambitious venture in nation building was no doubt affected by the distractions that are an inevitable by-product of transitions. Still, the trouble only surfaced later, and one cannot say that the "mission creep" that occurred in the spring of 1993 was inevitable or unavoidable.

Thus it is evident that successful collaborations on foreign policy issues between outgoing and incoming administrations are attainable. Nonetheless, they entail risks, and the results are by no means inevitably salutary.

"Advising, Encouraging, and Warning"

Since Harry Truman invited Dwight Eisenhower to the White House to discuss orderly transition arrangements in December 1952, formal meetings between the incumbent and his successor have become a ritual of American political life. To the public, they convey a reassuring sense of national unity. Among officials, they help facilitate an orderly transfer of power. If well managed, they may accelerate the learning curve of the incoming president.

With varying degrees of intellectual acuity and political sense, lame duck incumbents have "advised, encouraged, and warned" their successors on matters of policy and occasionally personnel in a manner somewhat similar to the roles Walter Bagehot attributed to the British monarch.[11] Formal meetings between outgoing and incoming presidents can be used to flag problems demanding early action, brief successors on sensitive intelligence operations, and share impressions of world leaders.

The formal encounters between a lame duck and his successor have invariably been respectful, though not always particularly cordial. Truman's meeting with Eisenhower in 1952 was stiff; Dean Acheson described Ike's look as "grim and frozen" throughout the session. When picking up President and Mrs. Truman to accompany them to his inaugural, President-elect and Mrs. Eisenhower refused even to enter the White House for tea. Yet Ike largely preserved the internationalist policy Truman had established. On the one specific request he received for diplomatic help, Eisenhower readily provided a public endorsement of Truman's demand for "voluntary repatriation" of POWs in the ongoing Korean Truce negotiations.

In 1960, Eisenhower was stung by John Kennedy's campaign claim of a "missile gap." Kennedy, in turn, came away from his two transition meetings with President Eisenhower unimpressed by his mastery of the policy issues but dazzled by Ike's personal charisma. He concluded that it would be politically imprudent to risk his disapproval. There was a hint of gloom in their substantive exchanges. Ike's forebodings about Southeast Asia and his fear that failure in Indochina would lead to "falling dominoes" in neighboring countries cast a definite shadow over the Kennedy administration's policy making in its early stages.

Eisenhower also broke diplomatic relations with Cuba during the transition, and encouraged the president-elect to support "to the utmost" those who were struggling against Castro.[12] With respect to mainland China, Ike warned Kennedy against seating the PRC in the United Nations or extending its government diplomatic recognition.[13] On these and other matters, JFK did not regard Ike's approval as essential, but on major foreign policy issues he feared that Eisenhower's disapproval would be "devastating."

Lyndon Johnson was bereft of any formal transition. When President Kennedy was assassinated, LBJ inherited his predecessor's advisers and policy priorities.[14] Instead of sweeping the slate clean and handpicking his own team, Johnson requested that Kennedy's entire staff stay on, and devoted his first year in office essentially to implementing JFK's domestic legislative priorities and preserving continuity in his foreign policy.

The Johnson–Nixon transition was surprisingly smooth, given their long history of partisan rivalry. Their shared Cold War policy reflexes contributed to this result. So did their mutual respect for the rituals of governance. Yet Nixon spurned several specific requests to help burnish Johnson's foreign policy legacy, apprehensive that these steps would limit his own diplomatic maneuverability.

Jimmy Carter recalled President Ford's slashing 1976 campaign attacks with bitterness but appreciated his gracious management of the transition. It was facilitated, as was the Johnson–Nixon transition, by close personal connections across party lines among members of the foreign policy establishment who inherited key senior official positions. Still, however civil the transfer of power, Carter had his own foreign policy priorities and little disposition to embrace what he considered the Nixon/Kissinger/Ford brand of realpolitik.

In his transition meeting with Ronald Reagan, Jimmy Carter outlined a long list of issues at a level of specificity that the president-elect appeared to find mind-numbing. Carter came away feeling that Reagan, who took no notes, was aloof and inattentive. In truth, Reagan revered the institution of the presidency and requested a copy of Carter's talking points. The president-elect was impressed by Carter's diligence, but Reagan's policy perspectives and priorities, which were generally at odds with Carter's on both domestic and foreign policy, were not altered by the briefing.

The Reagan–Bush transition was more informal in many respects, since Bush as vice president had been an integral member of the Reagan team. One of Bush's biographers described the transition as a virtual "co-presidency."[15] That overstates the matter considerably; in fact, I was serving as undersecretary of state for political affairs at the time, and in that department at least, the transition was not regarded exactly as "a friendly takeover." Indeed, it became gradually clear that the new GOP team intended substantially to redefine some of President Reagan's key foreign policy goals.

By most accounts, Bill Clinton's transition was among the most undisciplined on record. Strife between his campaign staff and his transition team was acute. He did not get around to selecting a White House chief of staff until late December 1992. Yet when George H. W. Bush first met with his successor, the meeting went twice as long as scheduled. Clinton described it as "cordial and helpful," and the exchange on foreign policy "particularly insightful."[16] Unfortunately, this did little to head off major policy discontinuities heralded by the new president's campaign rhetoric on such issues as China, Somalia, Haiti, and Bosnia.

Bill Clinton's get-together with George W. Bush was respectful, but there was little meeting of the minds or meshing of foreign policy priorities. Clinton presumed the new administration would initially concentrate on national missile defense and Iraq, which Bush confirmed. Clinton urged his successor to focus instead on al-Qaeda, Middle East diplomacy, North Korea, nuclear competition in South Asia, and—only then—Iraq.[17] Bush did not respond, and the encounter did nothing to alter his resolve to implement what amounted to an "anything but Clinton" approach to foreign policy.

George W. Bush's one-on-one meeting with Barack Obama took place within two days of the election and was marked by an atmosphere of civility and cooperation. An orderly transition was facilitated by Bush's establishment of a bipartisan White House Transition Coordinating Council. The council was designed to encourage reliance on "best practices" introduced in previous transitions to ensure comprehensive briefings by the director of national intelligence and facilitate a speedy security clearance process for key transition personnel.[18]

Subsequent press leaks suggested that Bush asked for Obama's help on a free-trade agreement with Colombia in return for Bush administration measures to help the auto industry. These rumors were denied by both sides. Obama, having run on a promise of change that tapped heavily into his party's disdain for President Bush's record, the president-elect was scarcely inclined to buy into the Bush policy agenda. Yet second-term adjustments in Bush's policies toward Iraq, Iran, North Korea, Afghanistan, Pakistan, and the Israeli–Palestinian struggle set the stage for a surprising degree of policy continuity during the early phase of the Obama administration.[19]

In these personal encounters between incumbents and their successors, efforts to influence foreign policy priorities generally enjoyed indifferent results. This is not particularly surprising. Campaigns focus candidates on the issues that differentiate the parties, and presidents-elect are understandably wary of dropping or modifying major campaign promises of policy change before they are even sworn in.

In their final months in office, lame duck presidents confront choices beyond what advice to give to their successors. Above all, they must decide whether to coast to the finish line or to tackle unresolved problems with a renewed sense of urgency in hopes of bolstering their legacy.

Taking the Heat for a Tough Decision

On rare occasions, an outgoing president may offer to hasten the implementation of a tough decision during the transition, and to take the political heat for it, rather than defer action until after his successor's inauguration. Such charitable acts are relatively rare. They may not be welcomed by the president-elect as a result of doubts about his predecessor's sincerity or competence.

In 1980, President Carter planned to carry out arms transfers to Saudi Arabia.[20] The proposed sales included F-15 aircraft, fuel tanks that increased their range, Sidewinder air-to-air heat-seeking missiles, a bomb rack designed to improve accuracy, and some type of Airborne Warning and Control System (AWAC) aircraft—presumptively the less sophisticated E-3A version. Needless to add, this decision provoked the ire of the Israelis and a predictably adverse echo from the Congress.

At the time of the 1980 election, the Carter administration had not yet provided the necessary notification of these sales to the Congress. But the secretaries of defense and state—Harold Brown and Edmund Muskie, respectively—were not only committed to the decision but also eager to move ahead promptly with its execution. They consequently notified the Reagan transition team of their readiness to proceed with required notifications to Capitol Hill in order to get the matter completed before their tenure in office ran out.

The transition team considered the offer, but in the end demurred. Al Haig, President-elect Reagan's nominee for secretary of state, doubted that the Clinton administration would prevail on the issue with the Congress (even though it was controlled by Democrats), and he was skeptical about whether, once dead, the offer to the Saudis could be revived. He put his case to Reagan, who agreed.[21] They had subsequent reasons to regret their decision.

In pursuing this arms sale on its own, the Reagan team fell victim to a telling feature of transitions: lapses of institutional memory. Secretary of State-designate Haig paid scant attention to the specific assurances the Carter team had made to the Israelis in 1978: that the United States "did not intend to sell weapons systems" to Riyadh "that would increase the ground attack capability of Saudi F-15s."[22]

By Christmas, Haig had informed the Israelis that the Reagan administration planned to go ahead with the sale. Having committed itself to stick with Carter's decision, Reagan's team inherited responsibility for its consequences. And when the new administration went public with its plans to sell the planes to Saudi Arabia in early February 1981, the Israelis fiercely criticized the decision and put in their bid for compensation.

The moral of the story is clear: Where transitions are concerned, good intentions are rarely sufficient. It takes two to pass a policy smoothly from one administration to another.

Deferring Tough Calls

The prospective end of an incumbent president's tenure may indeed encourage him to leave tough problems to his successor "like a land-mine in a field of weeds." In his account of farewell visits with Harry Truman and Dean Acheson in late 1952, George Kennan recalled wryly, "They had in their eyes, the faraway look of men who know that they are about to be relieved of heavy responsibilities and who derive a malicious pleasure in reserving their most bitter problems for those who are about to displace them."[23]

Eisenhower refused to authorize armed U.S. intervention when the French were run out of Indochina in 1954. Yet when he met with John Kennedy during the transition in mid-December 1960, he insisted that forceful intervention might now be necessary. "If the situation is so critical," Kennedy responded, "why didn't you decide to do something?"

"I would have," Ike replied, "but I did not feel I could commit troops with a new administration coming to power."[24] So he punted, but not without a stern warning to Kennedy about the potential costs of inaction. He did the same, as we shall see, with respect to plans for covert action against Castro.

It is easier, evidently, to recommend tough actions if someone else will be held accountable for their execution.

At the time, Kennedy's more immediate preoccupation was with a neighbor of Vietnam. He sought to get "some commitment from the outgoing administration as to how they would deal with Laos . . . particularly . . . some idea as to how prepared they were for military intervention."[25] In response, Eisenhower described Laos extravagantly as "the cork in the bottle of the Far East. If Laos is lost to the free world, in the long run we will lose all of Southeast Asia. . . . You are going to have to put troops in Laos. With other nations if possible—but alone if necessary."[26]

This advice was especially unwelcome. Even before the meeting, the president-elect had commented to Ted Sorensen, "Whatever's going to happen in Laos, an American invasion, a Communist victory or whatever, I wish it would happen before we take over and get blamed for it."[27]

Only sixty days later, JFK declared to a nationwide television audience, "Laos is far away from America, but the world is small. Its own safety runs with the safety of us all . . ."—tougher language than Ike had ever publicly used.[28] But Kennedy by no means slavishly followed Eisenhower's advice. He pursued a negotiated coalition arrangement in Laos, a course that Ike had opposed firmly.

Providing Policy Options to a Successor

On occasion, administrations prepare policy options they foreswear themselves but pass along to a successor. The Eisenhower's administration's development of contingency plans for covert anti-Castro operations in Cuba fell into this category. The Bay of Pigs saga has been told many times. Our interest here is in why Eisenhower's national security team accelerated the pace of contingency planning against Cuba *after* his successor had been elected

Dwight Eisenhower set aside his administration's watch-and-wait approach toward Castro well before the 1960 election. Planning for covert operations to replace Castro had commenced by the spring of 1960. The language of the CIA's "Plan of Action Against the Castro Regime" affirmed that its objective was to establish a government "more devoted to the interests of the Cuban people and more acceptable to the U.S. in such a manner as to avoid any appearance of U.S. intervention."[29] The original concept was relatively modest; it involved training about twenty Cuban guerrilla leaders, who would, in turn, train other insurgents to link up with indigenous guerrillas operating in the Escambray Mountains in Cuba.

By Election Day 1960, the plan had changed dramatically. It now proposed a conventional military assault on Cuba by an exile force with the expectation that this would spur a wider indigenous rebellion on the island. The plan presumed that U.S. personnel would not be involved in combat operations but could perform a variety of support missions.

During the campaign, Vice President Nixon was aware of the plan and expressed no objections to it. John Kennedy was not officially briefed on the matter but learned of it informally through Governor John Patterson of Alabama, who had approved a CIA request to send 350 Alabama National Guardsmen to train Cuban exiles for an invasion of Cuba.[30]

Kennedy's victory and an impending change of party control of the White House did nothing to slow down agency planning. On November 16, CIA director Allen Dulles presented an updated version of the plan to the 5412 Committee, an interagency group created by the NSC to oversee covert intelligence operations. The plan now contemplated an amphibious landing, the swift declaration by the exile force of a provisional government, and a request for immediate American help.

This plan was briefed to President-elect Kennedy on November 18 and augmented by a more detailed presentation on November 29. When the latter briefing ended, Kennedy merely told Allen Dulles to "carry the work forward."[31]

Meanwhile, Eisenhower allowed the planning to proceed but withheld formal approval. Though he was generally sympathetic, he continued to raise critical questions: whether the scale and boldness of the plan was compatible with the principle of "plausible deniability," whether the actions envisaged could be effectively implemented by an exile force of modest size, and whether the broad political front the CIA was supposed to be organizing could generate significant appeal within Cuba.[32] And in the final weeks of his administration, plans for Project Zapata, as it was called, underwent further adjustments.[33]

In December, it changed again in order to provide for attacks to take out Castro's air force before putting the exile force ashore. The location of the proposed landing was also altered to simplify logistic support. But the new locale, which was farther from the Escambray Mountains, made it harder for the force to fall back on guerrilla warfare if a popular revolt failed to materialize. Meanwhile, support requirements were beefed up to include air attacks from a base in Nicaragua, naval amphibious ships to put Cuban units ashore, and air cover for the assault force—all of which implied a substantially greater U.S. role. By early January 1961, the plan foresaw airlifting a provisional government-in-exile into Cuba almost immediately after a beachhead was established.

Throughout the transition period, the proposed operation strayed farther and farther from its initial premises. With each revision of the plan, U.S. "fingerprints" on its military dimensions became more difficult to conceal. As the CIA placed more and more rightist Cuban exiles in key positions in the paramilitary force or political front, the chances of sparking a widespread internal insurrection within Cuba diminished.

Why, though, was this planning effort hastened even as a change of political control in the White House loomed? A variety of considerations contributed to this outcome.

The White House, having successfully orchestrated the ouster of governments in Iran in 1953 and Guatemala in 1954, regarded covert action as a necessary and appropriate instrument for deterring or countering Soviet inroads in the developing world. Now Cuba appeared an appropriate target for "regime change." A general consensus existed among most senior leaders of both major political parties that a Communist regime in Cuba, aligned with Moscow, could not be tolerated. The question was how to dislodge the Castro regime without undermining other important U.S. objectives.

The postelection impetus for intensifying work on the plan came from the operational side of the CIA. Its principal architects—Allen Dulles, Richard Bissell, and Tracy Barnes—not only believed in the efficacy of their proposed operation, but also feared that the longer its implementation was delayed, the greater the risks that Castro would consolidate his political power and augment his country's military capabilities.

Those within the intelligence community who were likeliest to have expressed misgivings or encouraged doubts about the plan were effectively frozen out. Potential skeptics like Richard Helms, chief of operations in the Directorate of Operations; Deputy CIA Director Robert Amory, who managed the analytic side of the agency; and James Angleton, the head of the counterintelligence division, were all kept out of the loop. The reservations, moreover, of Pentagon skeptics—including Secretary of Defense Thomas Gates, Undersecretary James Douglas, and the counterinsurgency expert, Edward Lansdale—were essentially ignored. This left CIA operators in

charge of the intelligence judgments that were critical to the plan's rationale and justification·

Meanwhile, President-elect Kennedy's heated anti-Castro rhetoric during the 1960 campaign reinforced the supposition of agency planners that
the Kennedy administration would be receptive to at least some variation
of their emerging plan . . . once that administration assumed office.

And finally, President Eisenhower was confident that he could control
the content of the plan and the timing of its execution during his watch.
When Ike was briefed by Richard Bissell on the proposed operation in the
summer of 1960, his White House military aide, Andrew Goodpaster, recalled admonishing him, "Mr. President, if you don't watch it, that plan will
take on legs of its own." Eisenhower snapped back, "Not while I am president," to which Goodpaster pointedly observed, "Yes, Mr. President. That's
the problem. You won't be president much longer."[34]

In the end, Ike never signed off on the operation. In his memoirs, he affirmed that he withheld formal approval because of the lack of unified exile leadership, which could generate significant appeal within Cuba.[35] This
notwithstanding, he passed on to his successor a detailed proposal dated
December 6, 1960, for a conventional invasion near Trinidad, Cuba, which
included a specified D-Day—in March 1961—and an explicit timetable for
specific invasion-related events.[36] But Ike was unwilling to launch a risky
operation like this during the twilight days of his presidency. He did not
want to turn over the reins of government "in the midst of a developing
emergency."[37]

So he confined the CIA to contingency planning. But in his last meeting
with Kennedy on January 19, 1961, without pressing his successor to implement a specific CIA plan, he did express his firm belief that the United
States "had to support to the utmost" those who struggled against Castro,
and this meant "to do whatever is necessary" to assure their success.[38]

Arthur Schlesinger Jr. later maintained that Eisenhower bequeathed to
Kennedy "a force of Cuban exiles under American training in Guatemala,
a committee of Cuban politicians under American control in Florida, and
a plan to employ the exiles in an invasion of their homeland and to install
the committee on Cuban soil as the provisional government of a free
Cuba."[39]

That was a reasonably accurate description of the covert action plan that
Ike passed along to his successor. But it makes all the more perplexing the
question as to why neither Kennedy nor his close advisers did anything to

slow down the planning exercise, pending their own detailed review of its premises, its contours, its potential benefits, and its inherent risks.

Enlisting Help to Burnish One's Record

Lame ducks face uphill battles securing the assistance of their successors in bolstering their foreign policy records. This does not necessarily discourage them from trying.

In late 1968, President Lyndon Johnson was eager to move forward with the Paris peace talks in Vietnam. President-elect Richard Nixon was reluctant to lean on South Vietnamese leaders to show up for the negotiations. Many believe that he actively discouraged them from doing so.

Saigon hardly required such outside counsel and advice. The day after the 1968 election, Vice President Nguyen Cao Ky told U.S. Ambassador Ellsworth Bunker that it would take several months for the South Vietnamese government to review even the procedural issues in the talks—a time frame that would delay any substantive engagement during President Johnson's remaining time in office.

With but one exception, Nixon resisted requests to apply pressure on South Vietnam to get the Paris talks going. It involved a largely symbolic issue that nonetheless possessed some substantive importance—the shape of the negotiating table. The South Vietnamese government opposed any arrangement that implied equivalent status for the National Liberation Front, the insurgents who sought to supplant their regime. In mid-January 1969, with hopes of breaking a lengthy stalemate, the Soviet Union proposed on behalf of the North Vietnamese a compromise: a circular table without name cards or markings. This would permit the North to speak of "four sides" (North Vietnam, the National Liberation Front [NLF], the United States, and South Vietnam) while the South Vietnamese could speak of "two sides" (the allies and the Communists).

The motives of Hanoi and Moscow were pretty clear. They hoped presumably to break the procedural deadlock while LBJ remained in office, fearing that if the stalemate dragged on until after the inauguration, a new administration could either claim credit for its resolution (thereby bolstering public support for its policy) or use a continued impasse to justify an end to the existing bombing halt.

In the end, William Rogers, Nixon's secretary of state–designee, persuaded the president-elect to agree to Moscow's proposal. Henry Kissinger thought this was a mistake, for it gave the outgoing administration a minor success that was meaningless yet doomed the incoming administration to an immediate deadlock on tougher substantive matters, which soon sparked a renewal of the domestic debate about Vietnam.[40]

On other more consequential Johnson requests, Nixon was less accommodating. When LBJ signed the Non-Proliferation Treaty (NPT) in July 1968, he invited fifty-two nations to send representatives to Washington to mark the occasion. He planned to utilize the ceremony to announce that the United States and the Soviet Union planned to kick off talks on strategic arms limitations with a summit meeting in Leningrad on September 30. The joint announcement, scheduled for August 21, never took place. It fell victim to the Soviet invasion of Czechoslovakia.

Despite Nixon's victory in November, neither LBJ nor the Soviets had relinquished hopes for a Johnson–Alexei Kosygin summit and the Strategic Arms Limitation Talks (SALT) to follow. With that in mind, Johnson sought Nixon's help in convening a special session of Congress to secure Senate ratification of the NPT as a prelude to a summit. Nixon and Kissinger both found the proposal objectionable.[41]

Nixon begged off on grounds that the NPT was controversial with several key GOP senators. He and Kissinger considered the convening of a summit meeting during the transition "grandstanding" designed to polish Johnson's tarnished legacy.[42] They doubted that much could be accomplished. If such a meeting merely produced a spirit—as in the "spirit of Geneva"—it would be ephemeral and redound in their view to the Soviet Union's advantage. In any event, they planned to apply linkage among foreign policy issues in negotiations with Moscow, and this would require the sort of careful preparation that was incompatible with a last-minute summit.

Nixon and Kissinger suspected, moreover, that the Soviets were eager to lock the United States into the principle of strategic arms control before a new president took office. They also felt that a meeting in December or January would come too soon after the Soviet invasion of Czechoslovakia, and make the United States appear too eager to forgive and forget—a perception that would play poorly in Western Europe. Above all, they considered the notion of a lame duck administration tackling sensitive national security measures for whose implementation Nixon would inherit responsibility bizarre.

The Nixon–Kissinger team consequently let Johnson know that they opposed a summit during the transition, and that if one were scheduled Nixon would state publicly that he would not be bound by its results. The idea swiftly died.

George H. W. Bush was similarly skittish when he learned that Mikhail Gorbachev planned to visit the United States to give a speech at the UN in December 1988, just weeks after Bush's election. Through the Soviet Embassy, Gorbachev sought a meeting with President Reagan and Vice President Bush, now the president-elect. President Reagan and Secretary of State George Shultz reacted favorably to the idea of such a valedictory meeting. Bush and Brent Scowcroft worried that Gorbachev might have a trick up his sleeve. Colin Powell, as national security adviser, responded more cautiously with a "weary sigh."[43]

Assurances were sought from Moscow that nothing of substance would be raised on the grounds that it was too late to tackle such issues with Reagan but too early to take them up with Bush. The meeting on Governor's Island in New York Harbor came off without a hitch, and Bush's apprehensions notwithstanding, Gorbachev played no diplomatic games and offered no new proposals.

Attempting to Bolster a Foreign Policy Legacy Even Without Help

As an incumbent's time in office runs out, his concern about history's verdict on his tenure inevitably grows. This adds an element of urgency to second-term foreign policy endeavors, even after the election of a successor. Since a president retains his authority until a successor is sworn in, nothing in the law prevents him from undertaking assertive actions through his very last day in office.

We have seen that Lyndon Johnson sought to leave office on a high note, but that Richard Nixon generally refused the role of "enabler." Other presidents, with the end of their tenure in sight, often barrel ahead hoping to complete priority security or diplomatic objectives or to lock in progress that has been achieved.

George H. W. Bush was one president who, as it were, sprinted to the finish line, determined to utilize his remaining time in office to wrap up as much unfinished business as possible. Following Bill Clinton's election in November 1992, Bush sent U.S. troops to Somalia to protect food deliveries, bombed Iraq to contain Saddam Hussein's influence in Kurdish and Shi'ite areas, issued a clear warning to President Slobodan Milosevic that the United States would respond militarily if the Serbs initiated armed conflict in Kosovo, worked steadfastly to advance the Uruguay Round trade negotiations, and signed the Start II Treaty, the NAFTA agreement, and a chemical weapons accord.

Bill Clinton was even more ambitious, though less successful. Following the 2000 election, he pushed two major initiatives: efforts to mediate a comprehensive Israeli–Palestinian agreement, and to negotiate with North Korea a moratorium on DPRK missile tests, deployments, and sales.

If the last-ditch effort to foster peace in the Middle East proved quixotic, Clinton's motivations in launching it were understandable. He had invested substantial political capital over many years in promoting Arab–Israeli peace. In the view of his national security team, the Camp David summit meeting in July 2000 had come tantalizingly close to producing a breakthrough. The growing frustration of both Israeli and Palestinian leaders with the incrementalism of the Oslo Agreement approach was clearly observable. And the president had devoted considerable effort to promoting the resolution of foreign disputes.

Nor did he call for renewed negotiations without outside prodding. Ehud Barak, Israel's prime minister, pleaded with Clinton to give negotiations with Palestine Liberation Organization (PLO) leaders one more shot. The Palestinians, though less forward-leaning on the subject, also supplied encouragement. And Clinton's top Middle East advisers—Dennis Ross, among others—appeared more than game to roll the dice one last time.

Within days following the 2000 election, President Clinton met with both Yasir Arafat and Ehud Barak at the White House.[44] Both expressed interest in making one more attempt to reach an agreement; both allowed the inference that a deal was within reach; both claimed they possessed the political courage to conclude it. And both agreed to send delegations for comprehensive talks to be held at Bolling Air Force base in Washington, D.C., in mid-December.

When those talks quickly stalled, Clinton informally tabled American "parameters" for a settlement of all the core issues—borders, security, refugees, and Jerusalem. These parameters did not constitute American preferences; they reflected U.S. negotiators' judgments as to what was required of each of the parties to achieve a settlement.[45] They were no surprise to the parties; they had been on the table since September and had been explained with precision by Dennis Ross. The Israelis and Palestinians were expected to accept these parameters by December 27. A failure to respond would be considered a "no," as would anything approximating a "maybe."

Unprecedented steps were demanded of Barak and Arafat. The Israelis would have to accept a divided East Jerusalem, the withdrawal of their military presence from the Jordan Valley, and an independent Palestinian state with roughly 97 percent of the West Bank and 100 percent of the Gaza Strip. The Palestinians, in turn, would have to relinquish the cherished "right" of their refugees to return to Israel (except under conditions established by Tel Aviv), while accommodating the continued presence of 80 percent of the Israeli settlers who had claimed land in the West Bank, plus the residual right of Israel to intervene militarily on their territory in the face of demonstrable provocations.

Against this backdrop, prospects for a deal were never even close to a slam dunk. Still, all key members of the Clinton national security team— Sandy Berger, Madeleine Albright, George Tenet, Bill Cohen, and Dennis Ross—considered the risks acceptable. Whether all these advisers found the logic or necessity of a last-minute drill of this sort compelling is not clear; some perhaps chose to embrace it in hopes that a further predicate could be laid for future Middle East diplomacy.

While Barak's negotiating style could be irritating, he acknowledged the need for compromise, conditioned his people to the prospect of concessions required for a deal, and secured the approval of his Security Cabinet to negotiate—albeit with some reservations—on the basis of Clinton's "parameters."

Arafat, however, equivocated by seeking "clarifications," insisting on delays, and using Arab friends to support his dilatory tactics. Whether he ever seriously considered signing onto a deal remains uncertain. His diffidence about even participating in the July 2000 Camp David summit had been clearly evident, as was his distrust of Barak. He sought neither to prepare the Palestinian people for the necessity of concessions nor to conceal his fear that accepting an agreement would amount to signing his death warrant.

Perhaps he calculated that given Barak's decision to withdraw Israeli Defense Forces from Lebanon in the face of Hezbollah pressure, he could afford to play a waiting game. Such a negotiating stance certainly exposed him to fewer political risks and was consistent with his usual disposition to defer tough decisions.

Was this endgame started too late with too little time? Not in the view of Dennis Ross. In his comprehensive account of the negotiations, *The Missing Peace*, he recalls that American bridging ideas were on the table for months. Barak and Arafat encouraged a renewed effort to seal a deal. A deadline—the inauguration of a new president—was clear, if tight. Variations on a comprehensive and final settlement were offered (e.g., a joint letter to Clinton summarizing the points on which the Israeli and Palestinian negotiators had reached agreement, and which might serve as a point of departure for Clinton's and Barak's successors). The White House arranged frequent meetings with Arafat to assuage his inflated sense of amour propre. The administration attempted to generate some modest and belated pressure from moderate Arab leaders to push the Palestinian leader toward a decisive response.

In the end, Arafat walked away from a settlement whose terms would never be matched by Barak's likely successor, Ariel Sharon. He simply ran out the clock, thereby vindicating yet again his reputation as a leader "who never missed an opportunity to miss an opportunity." But still, knowledgeable observers did not absolve the Israelis for their own share of the culpability for the breakdown.

Was the effort to pursue a deal right up to the end of Clinton's tenure feckless or counterproductive? Some of the ideas contemplated in January 2001 did expose an unseemly air of desperation, most particularly the president's readiness to make a trip to the Middle East to meet with Barak and Arafat during his last week in office but only on condition they previously meet to reconcile their remaining differences. Arafat's answer—that other commitments prevented him from attending such a meeting—went, as some observed, "well beyond mere insolence."

Clinton's warnings to Arafat were vindicated. Ehud Barak was rejected by Israeli voters, and his successor, Ariel Sharon, refused to deal with the PLO leader. Violence flared anew. The peace process atrophied. The Israelis sought unilateral solutions for their problems in the occupied territories. And George W. Bush's administration turned its attention to Iraq, fortified U.S. links with Tel Aviv, and cited Clinton's failed effort as justification for a more passive approach to the Israeli–Palestinian peace process.

Clinton's last-ditch effort was a long shot at best. As long as the outcome of the U.S. election remained inconclusive, which was well into December, a possibility remained that he could pass along whatever progress was attained to his vice president, Al Gore, whose views on the key issues closely mirrored his own.

Once George W. Bush's victory was confirmed, the president and his advisers believed that they could extract bargaining leverage from their lame duck status. Both Barak and Arafat regarded Clinton highly as a so-called honest broker. In arguing to both of them—"Seize the moment, I won't be around much longer"—the president evidently presumed that he could inject a decisive note of urgency into the negotiations. He and his staff heavily embroidered this theme. If the chance for a deal slipped away, they argued, the next administration would take office with its legitimacy sullied by the contested outcome in Florida, and its political capital low. It was unlikely to invest it in a peace process that had just failed. Hence, they argued, grab the only deal likely to be on the table for some time.

The president and his negotiating team were also persuaded that the alternative to a continuing last-ditch mediating effort was a further descent into violence. The intifada had resumed in September 2000 and appeared in danger of spiraling out of control.

The venture failed in the end. A key negotiator, Dennis Ross, acknowledged shortcomings in the administration's hyperactive attempt to keep the peace process alive. He noted that active mediating efforts, which both Palestinians and Israelis welcomed, "should have been dependent on public conditioning for compromise, on each side fulfilling commitments and behaving in a way that fit the objectives of the negotiating process."[46] These failings, however critical, were not a by-product of the transition. They were, as Ross conceded, consistent features of U.S. Middle East diplomacy.

Bill Clinton was not the only president to pursue a Middle East breakthrough during his final year in office. Ronald Reagan, George H. W. Bush, and George W. Bush pursued somewhat similar efforts. Each commenced intensive diplomacy on Israeli–Arab issues late in their tenure. In each case, their diplomatic efforts resembled what George Shultz described as a "two-minute drill." All saw the foes of Middle East peace agreements literally run out the clock, leaving their successors to pick up the thread later.

The Middle East peace process was not the only issue on which President Clinton pursued last-ditch diplomacy. During his final months in office, he and his national security team also actively sought a moratorium on North Korea's development, testing, deployment, and sale of mid- and long-range ballistic missiles.

With U.S.–North Korean relations in serious disarray in 1998, Bill Perry, Clinton's former secretary of defense, was called in to lead a broad review U.S. policy toward the DPRK. By May 1999, Perry had forged a policy approach that enjoyed interagency support within the executive branch, reflected the considered views of key Asian allies, and appeared generally acceptable to many leaders of the Congress. Reduced to its essentials, the approach Perry recommended was designed to confront Pyongyang with a clear choice: either cooperate in dismantling its nuclear and missile activities in return for substantial economic and security concessions, or persist in its proliferation program at the expense of greater isolation, economic sanctions, and perhaps worse.

Perry and his team presented its proposals to the North Koreans in Pyongyang in May 1999. For fifteen months, Pyongyang did not provide a clear authoritative response. But with the U.S. presidential election only weeks away, Kim Jong Il unexpectedly proposed to send Vice Marshal Jo Myong Rok, the number-two man in the DPRK military, to Washington.

One can only speculate on what prompted this decision. Perhaps it was a belated recognition that George W. Bush—whose party had been consistently critical of the Agreed Framework, and which cited North Korea's nuclear activities as a prime motive for its national missile defense proposals—stood a genuine chance of winning the presidency. Perhaps it was the result of energetic lobbying by South Korean president Kim Dae Jung with his North Korean counterpart. Perhaps it merely reflected the peculiar rhythm of policy making in Pyongyang.

Whatever the reason for delay, Jo's visit took place at an awkward moment. The administration's tenure was nearly up, and Jo did not explicitly address Perry's proposals. Rather, he brought an invitation for President Clinton to visit Pyongyang, arguing that if Clinton and Kim Jong Il could meet, "we will be able to find the solutions to all problems."[47]

Clinton parried the invitation without rejecting the possibility of a visit. He promised to study the proposal, while further discussions between Washington and Pyongyang explored prospects for the success of such a visit.[48] He offered to send Secretary Albright promptly to Pyongyang to prepare the ground and test the prospects. Marshal Jo agreed to Albright's trip, all the time offering vague hints of flexibility on the missile issue.

When Secretary Albright appeared in Pyongyang less than two weeks later, the ground was scarcely well prepared. Protocolary traps surfaced immediately (e.g., a visit to Kim Il Sung's tomb, and a massive cultural exhibition at May Day Stadium where flip cards celebrated North Korea's firing of a Taepodong ballistic missile). Established relationships with key North Koreans were virtually nonexistent. Albright dismissed suggestions that she devote some effort to cultivating personal relations with DPRK leaders. She characterized this advice as "fine for careerists," but noted that "I would be out of Pyongyang in two days and out of office in three months." So Instead, she "cut to the chase," offering assurances about benign American intentions, and then raising the main subject—a Clinton trip to Pyongyang. Noting that she had not yet decided what recommendation to make to the president, she emphasized that she could not promote a summit, "without a satisfactory agreement on missiles."[49]

Kim declared that his missile development program was entirely peaceful, and that he could close it down if someone else would launch North Korean satellites for them. As for missile exports, he claimed that he supplied the Syrians, Iranians, and others only in order to earn hard currency; such exports could be suspended if the United States would provide alternative sources of compensation.

He did not deny that his missile program had a national security dimension, but he also expressed a willingness to stop new production if South Korea agreed not to produce any missiles with a range exceeding three hundred miles.

Kim balked on verification arrangements. He noted that this issue would require further discussion, and he rejected intrusive inspections "because North Korea was neither an outlaw state nor a defendant on trial."[50] But he also expressed readiness to send a delegation to Malaysia promptly to work on the details of a missile agreement.

Albright, eager to wrap up an agreement on the president's watch, was impressed by what she perceived as Kim's candor and his decisiveness. She felt that the "dear leader" was someone with whom one could "do business" and was enthusiastic about the possibilities of a Clinton visit to Pyongyang.

The bar having been set for a Clinton visit—that is, assurance of a mutually acceptable missile agreement—attention turned to follow-on talks in Kuala Lumpur that were scheduled for the same week as the U.S. presidential election. Administration leaders recognized that there would not be time to negotiate a detailed agreement on missiles, so they set as their summit objective "a joint statement of mutual obligations, coupled with the exchange of confidential letters spelling out the details."[51]

More specifically, they sought a DPRK commitment to refrain from "production, testing, deployment, and export of whole classes of missiles (including those threatening Japan) in return for U.S. agreement to arrange for civilian North Korean satellite launches under safeguards outside the country."[52] The U.S. side also wanted the DPRK to phase out missiles already deployed; adequate verification principles, accompanied by a commitment to work out means for their implementation; a DPRK declaration of its acceptance of our troops deployed on the peninsula; and a reaffirmation of its readiness to honor the Agreed Framework and to bar all unauthorized nuclear activities. In return the United States would be prepared to normalize diplomatic relations with North Korea—a long coveted objective of Kim Jong Il.[53]

This was an extraordinarily broad and complicated agenda to be negotiated within a few weeks. Albright and her team considered these commitments negotiable, while acknowledging that the devil, as always, was in the details. In Malaysia, however, Kim Jong Il's negotiators were not willing to resolve all doubts, especially on the critical subject of verification.

What did the North expect to gain from a last minute visit by the U.S. president? They presumably hoped to nail down generous economic concessions in return for at least a temporary suspension of their missile activities. Of greater consequence, they probably viewed a visit by President Clinton as providing a major boost to the legitimacy of Kim's regime, thereby enhancing its prospects for survival. Statements of "nonhostile intent" of the sort signed when Marshal Jo visited Washington were fine, but a visit by the president of the United States to the North Korean capital would "go far beyond words to create a new fact of great importance."[54]

While Kim Jong Il showed some ankle in his discussions with the Albright delegation, he did so much too late, as the election signaled the impending end of Clinton's time in office. Arms control agreements are notoriously complicated. They require time for gestation. Congress was under the control of Republicans who harbored contempt for Kim's regime and had consistently trashed the Agreed Framework—the 1994 agreement the Clinton administration had concluded with the North Koreans. By the time Bush's victory in the election was confirmed, too little time remained to wrap up any meaningful agreement. Indeed, key members of the Bush team regarded even the effort to do so unseemly, if not craven.

While Bush, who was asked for his views on the project, expressed a noncommittal attitude, in private his aides were more forthright and clearly negative. And with violence breaking out with renewed intensity in the Middle East, Clinton accorded priority to an ambitious and ultimately abortive effort to midwife an Israeli–Palestinian agreement.

In both cases, last-ditch attempts to broker major deals as time ran out left a sour taste in the mouth of Clinton's successor. Consistent with the aforementioned disposition to reverse major elements of his predecessor's approach to foreign policy, President Bush resolved to shift course in both the Middle East and the Korean Peninsula. He resisted suggestions that he sustain an active role in fostering a Middle East peace process; he rejected suggestions that he seek to "buy out" Pyongyang's nuclear program with major economic concessions.[55]

President George W. Bush encountered a somewhat different policy dilemma after his successor, Barack Obama, was elected in November 2008. Nearly a year earlier, Nuri al-Maliki had indicated that the annual UN mandate for U.S. troops in Iraq that was to expire on December 31, 2008, would be the last. If it ran out without an alternative in place, U.S. troops remaining in Iraq would be on treacherous legal ground just as a new administration took office.

Bush and his secretary of defense, Robert Gates, consequently sought to negotiate some variation of a standard Status of Forces Agreement (SOFA) and a longer-term Strategic Framework Agreement with Iraq. They saw these agreements as a way to avoid a fixed timetable for U.S. troop withdrawals and hoped an American presence would remain there for a quite extended period of time—seven or eight years—to temper sectarian strife, deter Iranian meddling, reassure other friends in the region, train Iraqi troops, and buy time for a fledgling government in Baghdad. In their view, the accords preserved policy options for the next administration by providing legal protections for American troops and property that remained in Iraq along with a basis for continuing economic and political cooperation with its government.

Many Democrats dismissed the agreements as a crude attempt to lock his successor into Bush's policy. Barack Obama had campaigned against this "war of choice" as a misguided and costly failure. He had pledged a complete withdrawal of all U.S. troops by a date well before he faced reelection. Democrats, having acquired majorities in the House and Senate in 2010, were pressing hard to bring all American troops in Iraq home promptly.

The election result robbed Bush of diplomatic leverage, and in the end the Iraqi president possessed the decisive vote. He was wary of a SOFA, which many Iraqis regarded as acquiescence in a protracted foreign occupation. Maliki seized on the preferences of the next U.S. administration to accomplish his own objective, and he pushed successfully for the inclusion in the SOFA of a timetable for both the removal of U.S. combat forces from Iraqi cities—July 1, 2009—and the ultimate withdrawal of all U.S. forces from the country by December 31, 2011. An agreement incorporating such provisions was signed by George W. Bush on December 14, 2008, in Baghdad. For his trouble, he suffered the indignity of having shoes hurled at him by an Iraqi journalist during a press conference announcing the understanding.

Like his predecessor, President Bush also discovered the perils of last-ditch negotiations with the North Koreans. The unraveling of the Clinton administration's Agreed Framework with the North in 2002, following discovery of the DPRK's clandestine uranium-enrichment program, left Pyongyang's nuclear activities subject to no international restrictions. In his second term, with encouragement from Secretary of State Condoleezza Rice, Bush authorized Christopher Hill to embark on a renewed effort to regulate—in fact terminate—the North's nuclear program. The negotiations unfolded in the Six Party Talks format, which provided "political cover" for bilateral discussions between Hill and a North Korean counterpart, Kim Gye Wan.

The negotiations experienced ups and downs, but as the 2008 presidential election loomed, the core of a potential deal emerged. It involved a trade-off between North Korea's agreement to reimpose a cap on its plutonium program, disable its Yongbyon nuclear reactor, and provide a comprehensive list of its nuclear facilities in return for the delivery by the United States of 1 million tons of heavy fuel oil, and the removal of the DPRK from the State Department's list of states that supported terrorism.

There was no shortage of critics of the negotiations. Democrats complained that GOP mismanagement of the nuclear issue left Pyongyang with nuclear capabilities that it would have been unable to acquire had the Agreed Framework remained in place. Neoconservatives found any dealings with Kim Jong Il's regime distasteful. The Japanese government was unhappy with the quality and timeliness of Ambassador Hill's consultations with them. Knowledgeable observers considered persistent North Korean denials of any uranium-enrichment activities deceitful. Its refusal to acknowledge involvement in the construction of a nuclear reactor in Syria compounded the perception of its treachery. To add insult to injury, the list of nuclear facilities provided by the North was neither complete nor verifiable, and the document it turned over to U.S. negotiators contained traces of enriched uranium.

In response to widespread criticism and with time running out on the administration, Hill made a last-ditch attempt to resolve at least some of the outstanding differences. He sought what was termed an "action for action" bargain, which evidently stipulated that Pyongyang would be removed from the State Department terrorism list in return for adding a protocol allowing verification of the North's disablement of nuclear facilities through, among other methods, scientific procedures, including sampling and forensic activities.

Differences swiftly surfaced over the interpretation of what had been agreed. This prompted additional talks from December 8 to December 11, 2008. The U.S. priority was to confirm satisfactory verification arrangements in a Six Party document; the North Koreans' aim was a firm timetable for the delivery of 450,000 tons of heavy fuel oil. Agreement was reached on a schedule of oil deliveries, but DPRK representatives refused to confirm written verification arrangements in a manner that satisfied the United States and its allies.

Hill sought to keep the process alive, but negotiations were left in suspense until the arrival of Bush's successor. By the time President Obama was inaugurated, Pyongyang had renounced the cap on its plutonium activities and was preparing to resume testing of longer ranged missiles and another nuclear device. It seemed increasingly apparent that rather than securing a lucrative buyout of its nuclear program, the North's objective was to obtain international acknowledgement of its nuclear status. Widespread reports that Kim Jong Il had suffered a stroke in August 2008 now raised questions as to whether nuclear policy was being driven by internal concerns about the political succession.

Whatever the motivations, instead of playing for time in hopes of getting a more accommodating deal from the Obama administration, the North reverted to its familiar tactic of adopting a confrontational posture to raise the stakes for its future return to talks. The Six Party Talks have not reconvened since 2008.

TAKEAWAYS

Incumbent presidents confront a variety of policy dilemmas during the political transition following the election of their successors. They retain the duties and perquisites of their office. But their days are numbered, their power is ebbing swiftly away, and their successor now possesses the stronger political mandate.

A key decision is whether to sprint for the finish line in hopes of bolstering one's record, or adopt a more leisurely pace in performing what amount to custodial duties as one's tenure runs out. Some presidents remain active during the transition in hopes of adding luster to their record or making their policies harder to reverse. Others limit their activities largely to tidying up.

The rituals of transition are now well established. The public expects the transfer of power to unfold in an orderly way and with a measure of grace. Outgoing presidents eagerly brief their successors in hopes of fostering the continuity of foreign policy and amending the incoming president's strategic priorities. Successors dutifully listen, but their national security plans and diplomatic priorities are rarely adjusted in line with a predecessor's admonitions.

An incumbent's final ten weeks in office may provide opportunities to bolster his record, but he is wise to pursue a modest agenda. Since his political interests and those of his successor are not naturally aligned, controversial initiatives are unlikely to fly. Negotiating leverage slips away fast; hence, complex international deals are difficult to wrap up. Even offers from an incumbent to accelerate pending decisions to relieve his successor from taking the heat for a tough call are likely to be resisted by his successor. More limited efforts to enlist a successor's help in reinforcing a negotiating demand, or in keeping a future policy option open, have better chances of succeeding.

Quite often, incumbents facing the end of their tenure simply kick tough decisions down the road. They may not want to limit a successor's options, or they may simply wish to duck a controversial decision on their watch. They may even derive pleasure in putting the next president on the spot or feel they have can best exercise their responsibility by passing along contingency plans, while leaving a formal or final decision to one with a fresh political mandate. But if contingency plans are highly developed, they can generate momentum that is difficult for a successor to arrest.

Cooperation may be arranged between an outgoing and an incoming president in response to an urgent international crisis. But success requires converging perceptions of the costs, benefits, and risks of a proposed course of presidential action, limits on its scope and duration, a focus on results, and a readiness to share the credit for success or the blame for failure.

Last-minute, beat-the-clock negotiating initiatives undertaken by incumbents are rarely welcomed by successors and are readily frustrated by foreigners simply by letting that clock run out.

Despite the miscues transitions can produce, catastrophic problems have been rare. They seem likelier to occur early in the life of a new administration than during the closing days of an outgoing president. For incoming presidents, the transition period is an integral part of the liftoff of a new administration. And it is to these start-up problems that we now turn.

6 LAUNCHING A PRESIDENTIAL TERM

CAMPAIGNS ARE LONG ON ASPIRATION AND INSPIRATION; governing puts a premium on priorities and execution. Arguably, the most important quality that a new president can bring to his work is "knowing the difference between what sells and what works. Both are necessary," as Samuel Popkin has observed; "knowing the difference is critical."[1]

The campaign is prologue; when the victor enters the Oval Office, it is "game on." A new president inherits the huge, complex machinery of the federal government. Persuading it to adopt a new set of policy priorities reflecting the interests of a new coalition of political constituencies is no simple task. As many have noted, the American ship of state is more like a gigantic barge than a sleek sailing sloop: it does not turn on a dime. Changing course is daunting and time consuming.

It is hardly surprising, therefore, that the start-up phase of every new administration produces many a rude awakening for those entering the Oval Office. This is particularly the case in the field of foreign policy. Most new presidents bring with them substantial experience in dealing with domestic issues; few know intimately how the world works beyond America's territorial domain and legal jurisdiction.

All new presidents bring to their new duties a rough agenda and a multitude of campaign promises. They do not, however, enjoy the luxury of writing on a blank slate. Each inherits the policy legacy of his predecessor. Each must cope with events over which his control is limited. Each must work with large bureaucracies, which have strong policy reflexes of their own. Each must come to terms with the central challenge of government: aims are legion; resources are scarce; priorities must be asserted; tough choices made. Little wonder that early miscues are frequent.

This chapter focuses on the early months of new administrations and explores examples of such difficulties and the collateral damage they sometimes inflict. Of course, new administrations are not foreordained to commit foreign policy blunders right off the bat. Some get off to a surprisingly smooth start. We also look at how several administrations managed to launch early national security initiatives smoothly, implement them with impressive flair, and achieve noteworthy results abroad while eliciting enhanced respect at home. The chapter also examines the difficulties of the start-up phase of an administration's conduct of foreign policy and focuses primarily on the first six months of a new administration.[2] The choice of this time frame is, of course, arbitrary. One could just as easily choose nine months or a year.

But six months is longer than "one hundred days"—the standard often applied by the press—yet short enough to highlight the unique challenges a president faces in getting his foreign policy up and running. For a newly elected president, the start-up phase begins immediately after Election Day. He cannot act officially for another two and a half months, but the choices he makes during the transition—particularly the personnel decisions—will shape, often decisively, the trajectory of his first term.

PRESSURES TO GET OFF TO A FAST START

Newly elected presidents are under tremendous pressure to make their marks swiftly. Having campaigned for months, even years, to secure the presidency, winning candidates are eager to promptly put their stamps on policy. Campaign promises have been reduced to sound bites; they roll easily off a new president's tongue. This may deceive them into imagining they can be easily translated into policy, executive orders, laws, or international agreements.

A new president is naturally eager to get out of the blocks quickly. There are many reasons. He knows that first impressions tend to stick, and he yearns to impress voters with his decisiveness. He understands that power is evanescent. "Use it or lose it" is the politician's watchword. He readily assumes that his chance to make a mark on policy is greatest when his political mandate is fresh. And most new presidents presume that the public, and particularly the media, are more favorably impressed by dramatic actions than by protracted policy reviews.

It is natural for newly elected presidents to seek early implementation of the key promises that helped get them elected. Beyond their commitment to the substance of specific initiatives, prompt action helps establish their authority, confirm their reliability, and remind competing centers of influence in Washington just who is in charge.

Incoming presidents deny responsibility for the conditions of the world they inherit. Their campaigns provide them with an irresistible incentive to blame their predecessor for those conditions. As Stephen Sestanovich has observed, "Almost every new occupant of the Oval Office thought the world had changed in some fundamental way that his predecessor either totally misunderstood or failed to manage effectively."[3] He is thus obliged to move swiftly to display his own ability to set things aright.

Pro-active instincts are also reinforced by a new chief executive's political base, whose members, eager for payback are impatient to cash in the chits acquired through devoted precinct work or generous campaign contributions. New members of a president's policy-making team generally press proposals for bold substantive action as a way of impressing the new chief executive with their energy and resourcefulness.

The national press and media are also relentless cheerleaders for a quick start. They invariably measure new residents of the White House against the "one-hundred-day" standard set by Franklin D. Roosevelt, conveniently ignoring the fact that FDR took office in the midst of an unprecedented domestic economic crisis.

There are other insistent pressures to act quickly and decisively. During a lengthy campaign, many foreign policy issues are put on the back burner. Once the election is over, the bureaucracy, as well as key members of Congress and special interest groups, clamor to get their favorite issues back on the agenda.

Foreign friends and adversaries also look for ingenious ways of placing their concerns before a new president, preferably by securing an early invitation to visit Washington. Some can also act in ways that put American interests at risk if attention is not paid.

In the aggregate, these various incentives often prompt new presidents to unveil foreign policy initiatives before the full implications of the proposed actions are subjected to thorough and thoughtful review. To be sure, many new presidents concentrate first on domestic rather than foreign policy issues: they are more familiar to them, and there are generally larger and more predictable political rewards. But events abroad have a way of altering the settled priorities of even those new incumbents who intend primarily to be "domestic presidents."

Within a few weeks or months of assuming office, President Carter killed the B-1 bomber program and announced the withdrawal of ground troops from Korea; President Reagan terminated an embargo that his predecessor had imposed on grain exports to Russia; President Clinton issued an executive order linking most-favored-nation treatment for China to its performance on human rights; President George W. Bush reversed a wide range of actions pursued by his predecessor; and President Barack Obama commenced a major augmentation of U.S. troop deployments to Afghanistan and vowed to close the Guantanamo Bay prison where many captured terrorists were held.

Many of these decisions, announced with great flourish, were implemented without sufficient attention to technical details, or how they could or should be effectively related to ongoing negotiations or the management of other issues. For example, Jimmy Carter terminated the B-1 bomber program without seeking any Soviet concessions in return, without indicating that the administration planned to design a more sophisticated substitute, and without deferring action until he and his colleagues had a clearer understanding of the impact of this decision on the SALT agenda. His secretary of state, Cyrus Vance, later acknowledged that "this correct and courageous decision became a millstone around the administration's neck and hurt us in the [SALT Treaty] ratification debate."[4]

Bill Clinton's linkage of Beijing's human rights performance to its access to the U.S. market not just alienated the Chinese but also irritated key elements of the American business community before it was abandoned little more than a year later. George W. Bush's wholesale reversal of Clinton administration policies convinced many that he, Bush, was a bull in a China shop and inattentive to the concerns of friends, particularly in Europe. Within months of his inauguration, Barack Obama, having expanded U.S. troop levels in Afghanistan, began to harbor second thoughts, and before the year was out he initiated a major policy review, which linked a temporary troop surge with the announcement of a date certain for commencing a troop drawdown. The prison at Guantanamo Bay remains open.

OBSTACLES TO A SMOOTH LIFTOFF

Unfortunately, the pressures to undertake quick policy adjustments are often greatest when a new administration's capacity to launch them thoughtfully and effectively is perhaps most limited. There are various reasons for this, but they boil down to the fact that it takes time for a new president to get his team in place, his decision-making structure fine-tuned, his support network in Washington mobilized, and his policy priorities settled—in short, to get his ducks in a row.

Bill Clinton's retrospective reflections on his early months in office are telling. "We didn't know enough about how the system worked. . . . I think in the beginning, . . . I was pushing a lot of rocks up the hill, . . . I was trying to learn on the job, . . . how to get the White House functioning."[5]

Putting a National Security Team in Place

Recruiting a foreign policy team takes time. Cabinet members are generally confirmed within days of a new president's inauguration. Six months or more often pass, however, before many subcabinet officials are securely in place. Regrettably, the time required to settle in is getting longer and longer. During presidential transitions in 1981 and 1989, I served as acting assistant secretary of state for East Asia, and as acting undersecretary of state for political affairs while awaiting the confirmation of a successor. The division of labor during this awkward interval was clear: the nominees to replace me participated—albeit without fanfare—in policy-making deliberations with the new secretary of state; I signed out the cables.

Such interim arrangements have lengthened considerably. President George W. Bush's secretary of defense, Donald Rumsfeld, complained that he was still—four months into his tenure—the only confirmed political appointee in the entire Pentagon. Nine months into President Obama's first term, only half of the foreign policy slots requiring Senate confirmation were filled.

With each presidential-election cycle, the number of political appointees expands, the vetting requirements in both the executive branch and congressional committees become more complex and intrusive, and the time required to confirm senior officials gets longer and longer. Often senators place "holds" on candidates with the express purpose of taking hostages to trade for concessions on completely unrelated policy or personnel matters.

The results are sometimes perverse. President Obama promised to pursue his national security policy with a wider range of instruments and greater emphasis on diplomacy and development. Yet it took him a full year to get a director for U.S. Agency for International Development (USAID) nominated and confirmed, and this was accomplished only after one early favorite for the position, thoroughly disgusted with the tortuous process, withdrew his name from consideration.

Selecting a national security team is among the most consequential decisions a president makes. Putting together a strong team is complicated by a number of factors. Many presidents enter the White House without a firsthand knowledge of the outside world, or even a wide range of close acquaintances in the foreign policy establishment.[6]

Many new presidents select members of their national security team from a roster of unfamiliar individuals with strong résumés but no prior acquaintanceship with the chief executive. Kennedy's cabinet was dubbed "Nine strangers and a brother." He picked secretaries of state and defense on the recommendations of others, and met Dean Rusk and Robert McNamara for the first time when interviewing them for those jobs. Richard Nixon knew Henry Kissinger primarily by reputation when he tapped him as his national security adviser. Cy Vance had met Jimmy Carter only twice before being asked to serve as his secretary of state.

Ronald Reagan tapped Al Haig as his secretary of state largely on the recommendation of Richard Nixon; he had spent less than three hours with him before his inauguration. Reagan had enjoyed considerably longer personal associations with Bill Casey and Casper Weinberger (whom he appointed to direct the CIA and Pentagon, respectively), but in each case, their previous interactions had been focused essentially on domestic issues or campaign activities.

In recruiting their teams, presidents are naturally preoccupied with finding people who satisfy certain domestic political considerations. Robert Dallek noted that John Kennedy wished to assemble a "ministry of talent," but the 1960 election was so close that he felt "he had to choose appointees who would be considered bipartisan or would not intensify national political divisions."[7] The men he selected to be secretary of defense (Robert McNamara), secretary of the Treasury (Douglas Dillon), and national security adviser (McGeorge Bundy) were all Republicans.

Other presidents have sought to broaden public support for their policies by recruiting members of the opposition to serve in key positions. Lyndon Johnson picked a Republican, Henry Cabot Lodge, to fill the highly sensitive post of U.S. ambassador to South Vietnam. Nixon offered critical assignments to Hubert Humphrey, Henry "Scoop" Jackson, and Sargent Shriver during his first term, though each of them demurred.

Since then, this practice has waned, though Bill Clinton sounded out Colin Powell about serving as secretary of state (perhaps in order to remove him from contention for the presidency in 1996) and tapped William Cohen, a GOP senator from Maine, to serve as his secretary of defense. President Obama retained Robert Gates, a relatively nonpartisan public servant who had worked mostly in Republican administrations, as his secretary of defense; chose a promising GOP politician, Governor Jon Huntsman of Utah, as his ambassador to China; and later recruited a maverick former Republican senator, Chuck Hagel, to head the Pentagon.

It is noteworthy that Dwight Eisenhower, who sought to put containment beyond partisan politics in the 1950s, felt no compelling need to enlist prominent Democrats for his foreign policy team. Why? Because Ike was a relatively nonpartisan figure, and the major domestic rift on foreign policy at the time was between internationalists and isolationists within his own Republican Party.

In recent decades, presidents have tended to include within their foreign policy teams individuals from rival wings of their own party. This was not a prominent feature of administrations until the 1970s. "Internationalists" and "political centrists" dominated the key foreign policy slots under Truman, Eisenhower, Kennedy, Johnson, and Nixon.

Jimmy Carter, however, either knew or quickly discovered that on East–West policy issues, Zbigniew Brzezinski, his NSC adviser, and Cyrus Vance, his secretary of state, were on decidedly different wavelengths. President Reagan's early national security teams were fraught with bitter rivalries. George W. Bush's national security team initially seemed free of ideological divisions, but intense turf fights swiftly emerged between Colin Powell, on the one hand, and Dick Cheney and Don Rumsfeld, on the other.

Adjusting Policy-Making Procedures

In addition to the difficulties of getting a cohesive team in place, the procedures of policy making are normally in flux during the early months of a new administration's tenure. The NSC structure is regularly tweaked to suit the style of a new incumbent in the Oval Office. During the inaugural parade on January 20, 1969, Henry Kissinger managed to secure Secretary of State William Rogers's unwitting acquiescence in a Presidential Decision Memorandum, which effectively ceded domination over the interagency policy-making process to the NSC.[8]

Zbigniew Brzezinski got a comparably quick start, albeit a somewhat less contentious or dominant one, in refining Nixon's NSC structure for President Carter. Al Haig attempted to reclaim a preeminent role for the secretary of state in 1981 by presenting a preemptive draft Presidential Directive to the Reagan White House. His tactic was foiled by the White House counselor, Ed Meese, who allowed Haig's proposal to languish for months in his briefcase.

The NSC machinery is, in many respects, the "lengthened shadow" of the president. Some arrangements obviously work better than others. Eisenhower's NSC system produced an orderly staff process, which conformed to his prior experience in the military. His White House, like Truman's, was staffed largely by civil servants, who managed interagency planning and oversaw the coordination and execution of policy with a "passion for anonymity." Critics regarded it as cumbersome, and stifling to creativity, but it worked well for someone of Eisenhower's military background and experience.

Kennedy dismantled this structure, considering it too bureaucratic. He and McGeorge Bundy "shifted the focus of the NSC staff from being a group of career officials serving the presidency to a personal staff, serving the incumbent."[9] He placed intelligent and highly assertive individuals in competition with one another, used rivalry among key advisers to maximize his personal authority, and routinely bypassed the usual channels in seeking information and ideas.

While Lyndon Johnson retained most of the features of Kennedy's structure, he personalized it over time through his heavy reliance on regular, if somewhat informal, Tuesday lunches. Attendance at these was generally limited to a few principals—the president, his secretaries of state and defense, the national security adviser, the CIA director, and the chairman of the Joint Chiefs of Staff. The record of decisions and responsibility for their implementation was informal and, at times, erratic.

Richard Nixon altered the NSC system fundamentally in order to centralize both the conceptualization and the operational conduct of foreign policy in the White House. Henry Kissinger and his NSC staff utilized the interagency system to generate policy analyses, define options, examine the consequences of choices, and facilitate crisis management. The president and his NSC adviser also exploited it systematically to exclude the Departments of State and Defense from key decisions, to conduct sensitive negotiations through back channels, and occasionally to direct military operations outside the normal command chain.

The Carter administration was eager to reshape the content of foreign policy, but the president and his national security adviser, Zbigniew Brzezinski, despite astringent criticism of their predecessor's policies, were reluctant to abandon those features of the Nixon/Kissinger policy-making structure that enhanced the White House role. Brzezinski recruited more outsiders to the NSC staff and downgraded its involvement in secret negotiations. But he used the NSC to compete relentlessly, and rather successfully, with the State Department for preeminence in policy making. In this quest, he had not only the advantage of proximity to the Oval Office but also, on many occasions, Secretary of Defense Harold Brown's "swing vote" at regular "BVB lunches"—attended by Brzezinski, Cyrus Vance (State), and Harold Brown (Defense).

Ronald Reagan chose initially to downgrade the NSC's role by subordinating his national security adviser, Richard Allen, to Ed Meese, the White House counselor; populating the NSC staff with a number of academics with little prior experience in government; and deliberately downgrading foreign policy in the administration's priorities during his early months in office. Reagan also went through six national security advisers in eight years.

George H. W. Bush's policy-making system was arguably the most efficient and effective since World War II. Bush inherited Reagan's NSC structure, as modified by the Tower Commission report, whose author, Brent Scowcroft, became Bush's national security adviser. The president appointed a team, whose other key members—James Baker, Dick Cheney, Colin Powell, Bob Gates, and William Webster—all possessed pragmatic policy instincts, collegial temperaments, and significant respect for the foreign policy bureaucracy (though they were never prisoners of the bureaucracy's policy reflexes). The president consistently played the lead role himself.

Bill Clinton initially devoted little attention to the NSC system, intending to delegate national security responsibilities to Tony Lake (NSC), Warren Christopher (State), and Les Aspin (Defense). These three made modest claims on the president's time, and the interagency system initially proved to be long on discussion, short on decisions, and bereft of the paper trail required for orderly policy implementation. Colin Powell, the holdover JCS chairman, compared some NSC meetings to "graduate student bull sessions." But Clinton did introduce one timely innovation: the establishment of the National Economic Council, one of whose senior staff members handled international economic issues, while serving concurrently on the NSC staff.

George W. Bush's first term policy-making system was unique in the dominance achieved by Vice President Cheney and his burgeoning staff; the constrained role played by Condoleezza Rice, Bush's national security adviser, in adjudicating interagency disputes; and the success enjoyed by Secretary of Defense Rumsfeld (with help from Dick Cheney) in neutralizing the bureaucratic clout and personal prestige of Secretary of State Colin Powell.

President Obama maintained a fair amount of continuity with his predecessor's NSC system, while seeking to take into account the need to integrate energy policy, environmental concerns, and homeland security more fully into the organizational structure. His initial national security team was long on experience and political clout. Yet, to the surprise of many, the president, despite his own lack of deep experience on national security issues, established a White House–dominated foreign policy–making process whose most influential members had previously served on the president's 2008 campaign staff. The NSC staff also expanded dramatically in size.

Establishing Cooperative Ties Between Political Appointees and the Bureaucracy

A further noteworthy obstacle to smooth and orderly policy making in the early months of new administrations arises from the mutual suspicions that political appointees and senior bureaucrats initially harbor toward one another. "Grand designs" and "visionary schemes" are in ample supply among the political appointees of any new administration. Less readily available at the outset are people skilled at transforming broad concepts into operational plans, which is, of course, the normal work of the bureaucracy. Senior bureaucrats who are already in place tend to be viewed with suspicion by their new political bosses. Their competence is not highly regarded, and their loyalty is often suspect—particularly foreign service personnel at the State Department. Dean Acheson put the matter bluntly:

All presidents I have known have had uneasy doubts about the State Department. They extend to the White House staff, and in fact often originate there. They are strongest at the beginning of presidential terms, when the incumbent and his new associates in the White House believe that foreign affairs are simpler than they in fact are and that they can be confidently approached under the guidance of principles (liberal, conservative, idealistic or moral) even without much knowledge or experience. Foreign Service officers seem to them cynical, unimaginative, and negative.[10]

Suspicion of the bureaucracy is typically greater among Republicans than among Democrats, perhaps because the former assume that government servants are rarely afflicted with conservative views. In 1968, Nixon urged his cabinet "to move quickly to replace holdover bureaucrats with people who believed in what we were trying to do." He added, "If we don't get rid of these people, they will either sabotage us from within, or they'll just sit back on their well-paid asses and wait for the next election to bring back their old bosses."[11] His suspicions were perhaps extreme, but they were scarcely unique. If the Right harbors deep reservations about the bureaucrats at State, the Left is perhaps more paranoid about the uniformed officers either working at the Pentagon or serving temporary duty assignments (TDY) in the White House.

Forging Policy Priorities

There is an additional obstacle to thoughtful policy making in the early months of a new president's first term. Presidential campaigns place a premium on tabling detailed policy proposals to cope with every conceivable problem. The test of most such proposals is simple—that is, whether they attract votes. The practicality of these ideas, the compatibility among them, and their fiscal costs are rarely debated in earnest prior to the election.

After elections, new and more operational tests assume central importance—whether policy proposals can achieve the advertised results at a reasonable strategic, financial and political cost, and a tolerable impact on other priorities. These considerations must be weighed carefully in winnowing from a welter of campaign promises a few practicable initiatives worthy of execution.

Establishing priorities is particularly tough in the field of foreign policy, since many of the factors affecting results are beyond a president's control. In estimating the likely impact of policy initiatives, a substantial element of conjecture is involved. Some call this "guesswork"; others consider it prudential judgment.

A new president, however, often has little basis for knowing who among his closest advisers will offer the most reliable judgments on tough external policy issues. Professional foreign policy experience was not abundantly to be found among the Georgians around Carter, the Californians around Reagan, the Arkansans around Clinton, the Texans around George W. Bush, or the Chicagoans around Obama. All, certainly, had individuals on their staffs who possessed some expertise or experience in the field. Still, time is required for a new president to determine whether he can confidently rely on the political instincts and policy reflexes of his cabinet colleagues, senior officials, and White House aides.

The White House is easier to staff quickly than are the various departments, since its officials do not require Senate confirmation. Consequently, power initially tends to flow to the White House and NSC staffs, where there is inevitably a high premium on political loyalty. Smaller, and with fewer bureaucratic encumbrances, they are generally able to move with greater agility.

They have their own liabilities though. With occasional exceptions, the membership of the NSC staff changes with each new administration. However personally well informed its new members may be, they start with no records in their files, since outgoing presidents immediately transfer White House records to the National Archives or their own presidential libraries. Thus new appointees are often bereft of institutional memory regarding the issues for which they now bear responsibility. It is no surprise that each new NSC staff floods the bureaucracy with study requests. They need such analyses as quickly as possible in order to evaluate existing policies and to design plausible alternatives to them.

And, of course, there is intense competition for an incoming president's time and attention. At the outset, most new incumbents are likely to be primarily preoccupied with domestic issues. And, too, a new president must perform a variety of Washington rituals during the transition and his early months in office. Forging an executive branch team and shaping its policymaking procedures takes precedence, but the need to build effective working relationships with congressional leaders is also critical. Making a favorable impression on Washington society and enlisting support from the nation's media are also demanding preoccupations. If properly managed, these tasks enhance a president's ability to launch successful policy initiatives at home and abroad. If they are poorly handled, official business can rapidly become a lot more difficult.

These, then, are among the obstacles to getting off to a good start as opposed to a fast start on foreign policy issues: the necessity and difficulties of putting a national security team in place, the uncertainties associated with the establishment of orderly interagency procedures for policy making, the residue of distrust that normally shapes initial relations between political appointees and bureaucrats, and the need for a new administration to sort out its policy priorities clearly before embarking on major initiatives.

All constitute good reasons for a new president not to operate against artificial deadlines or to subdue second thoughts before launching policy initiatives or major course corrections. They also suggest that "do no harm" may be more appropriate as an early operational guideline than "make a splash."

HANDING OFF FOREIGN POLICIES WHEN POLITICAL CONTROL OF THE WHITE HOUSE CHANGES HANDS

When one administration hands off power to another, major policy adjustments are to be expected. Our national interests do not change with each election cycle, but those who get to define those interests often do. Elections, after all, are supposed to open the door for changes of policy. In the realm of foreign affairs, neither continuity nor discontinuity of policy is intrinsically good or bad. It depends on the circumstances.

The pressures on a new administration to get off to a brisk start are most intense, however, when the challenge of getting a new administration up and running is most acute, and early foreign policy miscues at this point are not particularly surprising. Some foreign policy handoffs go awry due to the sheer inexperience of the incoming president. Some result from unwarranted confidence by the new incumbent in the practicality and timeliness of policy promises he announced during the campaign. Some emerge from the botched execution of misconceived plans passed along by a predecessor. Some reflect major disjunctions between the policy priorities of an outgoing administration and its successor.

Early Policy Miscues

JOHN KENNEDY AND THE BAY OF PIGS DEBACLE IN 1961

The Kennedy administration experienced a particularly traumatic baptism of fire when a botched covert action designed to overthrow the Castro government in Cuba blew up in its face at the Bay of Pigs in mid-April 1961. This fiasco was scarcely inevitable. But as McGeorge Bundy, Kennedy's national security adviser, retrospectively observed, when JFK took office, it "was just sitting there, ready to go off." Kennedy and his senior advisers approached the choice of whether to launch a covert exile invasion—an inheritance from the Eisenhower administration—as one that would not "keep" that "had to be decided."[12] But going forward with a flawed plan was not the only policy option available.

We saw in chapter 5 that the Eisenhower administration accelerated planning for a major covert action against Castro's regime even as its time in office was running out. Kennedy was briefed several times on Project Zapata (as it was then dubbed), between Election Day and his inauguration. He neither nixed the plan, sought to slow down the planning process, nor subjected its premises to a detached, comprehensive review. He did authorize the CIA to continue preparing for the operation, without formally endorsing its proposed plan.

Why did Kennedy not subject the premises and details of the plan to a more serious, critical analysis? Explanations abound. He had criticized Eisenhower sharply during his campaign for failing to prevent Fidel Castro's growing reliance on Moscow, and he had publicly championed the kind of strong actions against Cuba that the CIA was proposing. [13] This surely encouraged CIA leaders to believe that Kennedy was sympathetic to the aims of their evolving covert operation.

The president-elect's early decision to keep Allen Dulles as CIA director inadvertently reduced his freedom of maneuver. Intending to signal a measure of continuity in the management of national security policy, this decision effectively eliminated the likelihood that Project Zapata would get a fresh, detached, or critical look within the intelligence community.

So, too, did the high regard that Kennedy and key members of his team had for Richard Bissell, the key architect of the CIA's proposed operation. McGeorge Bundy later acknowledged that one reason he had been "inefficient" in reviewing Project Zapata was that "his favorite college teacher, Dickie Bissell, was in charge."[14]

When Allen Dulles organized a dinner in Georgetown in early February 1961 to introduce senior officials of the CIA to their new counterparts in the White House, Bissell was the "star of the evening." He characterized himself as a "man-eating shark" in what Evan Thomas aptly described as "just the right mix of bravado and self-mockery to charm the New Frontiersmen."[15] Whatever skepticism JFK may have harbored toward some features of the CIA's plan was thus balanced against his high esteem for those putting the plan together—especially Bissell.

Nor was the policy-making system the new president put in place well equipped to perform the due diligence, which an inherently risky covert action plan deserved. Impressed by Richard Neustadt's analysis of presidential power and how an incumbent could maximize it, Kennedy swiftly dismantled Eisenhower's thorough, if cumbersome, NSC staff apparatus. He intended to replace it with a more free-wheeling arrangement designed to foster intellectual and policy agility at the possible expense of orderly procedure and bureaucratic rigor. But such a transformation took time, and the new president assumed office bereft of White House associates sufficiently familiar with the proposed covert action to spot the flaws in the agency's proposal or to suggest appropriate fixes.

Tough political calculations also confronted the new president. He was squeamish about endorsing a visible U.S. role in covert operations against a neighbor. But he recognized that if he rejected the CIA's plan, he would be portrayed as a wimp. His brother Bobby Kennedy later stated, "If we hadn't gone ahead with it, everybody would have said it showed that he [Kennedy] had no courage. Eisenhower's people said it would succeed—and we turned it down."[16]

Thus at the time Kennedy took office, bureaucratic momentum was impelling the planning process toward a decision, and the pressures to authorize the plan promptly intensified. By early spring, the operation envisaged an amphibious landing of roughly 1,500 Cuban exiles at the Bay of Pigs. Their objective was to hold ground in an isolated area while a provisional government, to which the United States would then provide material support, was brought in and set up.

Factors hastening a decision were of several kinds. The intelligence community argued insistently that Castro was rapidly consolidating his regime, upgrading its military capabilities, tightening links with Moscow, and fostering unrest elsewhere in the hemisphere. Thus, they warned, the "window of opportunity" for the mission would soon close.

There was also a worrisome "disposal problem." The Guatemalan government wanted to rid itself of the Cubans whose training activities on their soil were beginning to leak. In addition, CIA operatives worried that if their plan were aborted, the exiles would drift back to Miami full of tales of the administration's perfidy in calling off a promising effort to take down a Communist regime just ninety miles off our coast.

The political consequences of this further increased President Kennedy's apprehensions. He told Arthur Schlesinger on April 7, 1961, "If we have to get rid of those 800 men, it is much better to 'dump them in Cuba than in the United States.'"[17] The president's misestimate of the number of exile troops—there were actually around 1,500—also suggests that he may have not thoroughly familiarized himself with key details of the operation just one week before it was launched.

Factionalism within the exile force also increased as time passed, and its cohesion suffered. It experienced a mutiny of sorts in January 1961. Rather than reassessing the risks of the plan, however, Richard Bissell and his colleagues treated this as an additional reason to move as quickly as possible, lest the force fall completely apart.[18] Even Bissell later conceded that the Kennedy administration inherited a military organization "that would have been difficult . . . and embarrassing to dispose of in any way other than by allowing it to go into action."[19]

Meanwhile, agency representatives continued to characterize the project as posing manageable risks and promising a high probability of success. The force was to be entirely manned by Cuban exiles, and would augment indigenous resistance to Castro's regime. Its covert nature, CIA operatives affirmed, would obscure the U.S. "hand." The operation offered the administration a chance to take down a leftist government in the Caribbean before it posed "a clear and present danger" to American security. And, the operators argued, the Cuban rainy season, which started in April, would soon make an amphibious operation even more hazardous.

Still, during his early months in office, the new president remained highly ambivalent about the CIA plan. McGeorge Bundy passed two papers on the subject to Kennedy in early February 1961. One, from Richard Bissell, urged its prompt execution; another, from Thomas Mann, Eisenhower's holdover assistant secretary of state for Latin America, expressed skepticism about its feasibility. But these alternatives were not systematically reviewed, and a new assignment for Mann as U.S. ambassador to Mexico, soon attenuated his involvement in policy making on the issue.

Ted Sorensen later claimed, "The advice of every member of the Executive Branch brought in to advise was unanimous—and the advice was wrong."[20] Perhaps Sorensen was referring only to cabinet members.

There were certainly doubters and critics. Sherman Kent, chairman of National Intelligence Estimates, believed that Castro was firmly in control and that his authority was growing, not declining—a view directly at odds with a central premise of the CIA plan. Dean Acheson, to whom Kennedy confided the outlines of the venture, dismissed it with scorn. "It doesn't take Price Waterhouse to figure out that fifteen hundred Cubans aren't as good as twenty five thousand," he observed archly.[21] White House staffers, especially Arthur Schlesinger Jr. and Richard Goodwin, were consistent and outspoken critics, though some senior officials dismissed them as "bit players" on the issue.[22]

Chester Bowles and Paul Nitze, senior officials at State and Defense, also expressed doubts about the wisdom or feasibility of the plan. Bowles's reservations were not, however, shared by his boss, Dean Rusk, and Nitze squandered an opportunity to express his misgivings directly to the president. In a meeting of senior executive branch officials to which Kennedy was quite surprisingly accompanied by Senator J. William Fulbright, Nitze devoted his remarks to challenging Fulbright's assertion that an invasion of Cuba would be immoral—a decision that Nitze later regretted because it prompted him to neglect his own principal worry that the operation, as planned, might not work.[23]

Even the military high command rated the prospects for the plan's success as only "fair"—not exactly a ringing endorsement. In fact, the JCS was bureaucratically wary of dissecting another agency's cherished enterprise too critically. And, in any event, it did not feel obliged to do so, since in the event of failure, the CIA would catch the blame. Unfortunately, the White House did not seem to understand that because the Pentagon was not in charge of the mission, its review of CIA plans was at best perfunctory.

The chairman of the Senate Foreign Relations Committee, J. William Fulbright, who had been informed by President Kennedy of the covert plan, gave JFK a lengthy memo on March 30 arguing that its implementation would do incalculable harm to U.S. interests in Latin America even if it succeeded. He maintained that Castro posed at worst a "thorn in our side," rather than "a dagger in the heart." A successful invasion, he maintained, would damage America's reputation while leaving us with the unpalatable task of governing Cuba.[24] Fulbright's memo evoked a noncommittal response from President Kennedy, and his conclusions elicited little resonance within the upper reaches of the administration.

Whatever their private misgivings, the responsible cabinet-level officials—Secretary of State Rusk, Secretary of Defense McNamara, National Security Adviser Bundy, CIA Director Allen Dulles, and Chairman of the JCS Lyman Lemnitzer—all supported moving forward with the covert operation.

Unfortunately, the decision-making process, which McGeorge Bundy oversaw, was surprisingly casual and woefully deficient. In the run-up to the mid-April invasion, no regular meeting of NSC principals was convened on the subject. No National Intelligence Estimate on the issue was requested. No settled NSC structure for crisis management even existed. The operation was so highly classified that a number of experienced experts were excluded from the deliberations. Meanwhile, several key figures—Allen Dulles and Lyman Lemnitzer—were holdovers from the Eisenhower administration and were highly unlikely to criticize a plan, which their staffs had either conceived or endorsed.

President Kennedy consulted with a number of advisers one-on-one or in small groups. But he never organized a discussion among all his senior advisers in order to formulate systematically his own personal judgment of the pros and cons of the proposed project.

As a result, the president's support for action vis-à-vis Cuba and his reservations about specific features of the CIA's plan were never effectively reconciled. Kennedy did not want the American hand to be visible. But the plan he inherited was formulated, organized, financed, and supported by the U.S. government.

The president made decision after decision designed to diminish the visibility of the U.S. role, to "reduce its noise level," to "make it less spectacular." At his insistence, the location of the landing was changed from Trinidad to the Bay of Pigs, where there was a local airfield from which air strikes could be launched to increase the appearance of a wholly indigenous operation. Since the new location was surrounded by a huge swamp, however, it eliminated a line of retreat to the Escambray Mountains—which was a major fall-back alternative if the invasion ran into trouble. Since few people lived close to the Bay of Pigs area, moreover, action there was unlikely to inspire a major uprising, which was another presumed fallback option.

The timing of the invasion was also changed from a daytime affair to a nocturnal amphibious operation to accommodate presidential reservations.

This adjustment made already challenging logistic requirements even more hazardous.

The air-strike components of the strategic plan were also altered at the president's request. He initially limited their authorized number. He then reduced, and later scrapped, follow-on missions without evidently recognizing that this undermined a fundamental premise of the plan—the need to establish clear control of the skies over the invasion site and to knock out Castro's communications systems.

All these adjustments reduced the plan's operational feasibility without concealing America's involvement. Richard Bissell repeatedly accepted proposed modifications in the plan to "make it more Cuban in its essentials."[25] But he did so on the supposition, shared by other officials, that if push came to shove, the president would do whatever was necessary to ensure the success of the mission, including more substantial and visible U.S. support. Instead, JFK used a press conference on April 12 to make the limitations on the operation explicit and public by declaring, "There will not be under any conditions, an intervention in Cuba by the United States Armed Forces."

This signaled that a key presumption underlying the CIA plan was no longer valid without, however, proposing that the plan's execution be called off. Indeed, Kennedy then authorized moving forward with the plan in mid-April. In the event, Murphy's Law—"Anything that can go wrong, will"—marked every stage of its execution.

The initial air strikes did not take out Castro's air force. The cover story that the strikes were launched from within Cuba did not hold up to press scrutiny. A follow-up exile aerial assault on the air base at Santiago de Cuba flopped completely. Adlai Stevenson, the U.S. representative to the UN, was not provided timely information on the operation and initially misrepresented the U.S. role, much to the administration's embarrassment and Stevenson's consternation.

Follow-on strikes by Cuban exiles flying B-26s planned for D-day were called off by the president with the concurrence of Dean Rusk and Mc-George Bundy; all wished to delay further strikes until they could be conducted from an airstrip from within the exile beachhead. That, unfortunately, required that the invasion be launched with no assurance of air superiority over the battlefield. Bissell sought Rusk's help in reversing the president's decision, but to no avail.

The night landing at the Bay of Pigs was slowed by coral reefs, which the CIA had not identified in advance. Nor was surprise achieved on the beach at Playa Girón—another by-product of faulty intelligence. Without control of the air, several supply ships were sunk by the Cuban air force at first light, while others headed out to sea for safety.

When the seriousness of the trouble became evident, the president flatly rejected requests for an expanded U.S. role. Aside from his persistent misgivings about the scope and visibility of the operation, there was another reason for his caution—concern about Soviet reactions, particularly in Berlin. It did not take long for Nikita Khrushchev to weigh in with a message, which arrived on April 18. In it he warned that a "little war" could precipitate a chain reaction "in all parts of the globe," and he added ominously, "There should be no mistake about our position. We will render the Cuban people and their government all necessary help to repel armed attack against Cuba."[26]

Although Kennedy sent Khrushchev a stiff rejoinder, he remained generally unresponsive to subsequent calls for more direct U.S. involvement. Bissell and Admiral Arleigh Burke pressed for limited U.S. air cover for the exile planes. But the president affirmed again that he was not going to get involved in the conflict. Burke persisted, bluntly noting that the United States was already involved. The president relented slightly, agreeing to permit six unmarked U.S. jets to protect the Cuban exiles' B-26s for one hour as they dropped supplies and ammunition to troops on the ground. Unfortunately, the bombers arrived well before the air cover, because the operators forgot that there was a time difference of one hour between Nicaragua (where the escorts embarked) and Cuba (where the B-26s were attempting to drop equipment and ammo). The exiles consequently got no re-supply. The Cubans downed two of the escort planes whose pilots were Americans. And the surviving members of the exile force were quickly and unceremoniously mopped up by Castro's troops.

Kennedy evidently persuaded himself that he was signing off on a clandestine plan that stood some chance of success. Yet the plan he approved "was too large to be clandestine, and too small to be successful."[27] When things went awry, the president confronted a vexing dilemma the plan had not openly confronted: whether to utilize U.S. power to save the exile force at the risk of a wider conflict, or to cut U.S. losses at the price of a humiliating defeat. When forced to choose, Kennedy picked the latter alternative.

Some members of the administration sought—not without some justice—to lay the blame for the plan's failure on the CIA and Joint Chiefs. Their performance certainly warranted acute criticism and stern rebuke.

The CIA had accommodated presidential adjustments to the plan, which undermined its efficacy. The JCS gave the plan only a perfunctory review and failed to voice their professional misgivings about it clearly to the president. The president was eager to preserve "plausible deniability" about the operation. Yet as prospects of an exile invasion began leaking to the press in late November 1960, no one insistently asked how American involvement could conceivably be denied with any credibility.

Whatever the failings of others, Kennedy and his closest advisers could not escape their share of accountability. The president and his White House team acquiesced in what Ted Sorensen later characterized as a perverse role reversal between politicians and policy experts. Instead of making a presidential determination that action was required against Cuba, and asking the bureaucracy for a plan, holdovers from the previous administration persuaded a new president that "action was necessary and the means were already fashioned . . . [while] making his approval . . . appear to be a test of his mettle."[28]

The president did not recognize the momentum contingency plans initiated by a predecessor could acquire. Thus he launched an operation that was poorly planned and haphazardly executed with disastrous results.

There are lessons beyond the obvious one that transitions are often prelude to serious policy miscues. Letting those operationally responsible for a covert mission provide the intelligence supporting it is always foolhardy. Failure to subject a risky plan to rigorous review by skeptics is dangerous. Modifying salient features of a complex operation without revisiting its premises is unprofessional. Executing plans the operators know are flawed on the supposition that when push comes to shove, the president will ignore the restrictions he himself imposed is treacherous.[29] Changing the policy-making process without understanding clearly the functions that the established procedures had performed is imprudent.

In the wake of the fiasco, there were several consolations for President Kennedy. While he doubted that any British prime minister could have survived such a policy debacle, he acknowledged the advantage he derived from a fixed term: "Well, at least I've got three more years—nobody can take that away from me."[30]

Although the Bay of Pigs incursion failed ignominiously, Kennedy's personal popularity actually increased, prompting his sardonic ex post remark, "The worse you do, the better they like you."[31] And with McGeorge Bundy's help, JFK subsequently removed some of the kinks in the interagency policy coordination system, as his management of the 1962 Cuban missile crisis confirmed.

Other consequences were far less salutary. In March 1961, President Kennedy sent Nikita Khrushchev an invitation to meet at a neutral site later in the spring. Despite the Cuban debacle, he decided to go through with the summit in June. Unfortunately, the deeply flawed Bay of Pigs operation signaled weakness to Khrushchev, and the Soviet leader resolved to test the new president further by bullying him in Vienna, and subsequently precipitating a renewed clash over Berlin. The aborted Bay of Pigs invasion may even have encouraged the Soviet leader later to dispatch strategic missiles to Cuba—thereby setting off the most dangerous crisis of the Cold War.

To display U.S. resolve in the East–West struggle, Kennedy directed the Pentagon to establish a Presidential Task Force on Vietnam, headed by Deputy Secretary Roswell Gilpatric, to develop a program of actions to prevent Communist domination of South Vietnam.[32] This helped transform a Southeast Asian sideshow into a central item on the U.S. foreign policy agenda. And Cuba remained an obsession for the president and his brother Bobby. They ordered the Pentagon to develop a plan for overthrowing Castro with conventional U.S. forces, and redoubled previously initiated covert CIA efforts to eliminate Fidel Castro, possibly through what was euphemistically termed "executive action."

BILL CLINTON AND "MISSION CREEP" IN SOMALIA IN 1993

If Kennedy's early trouble arose from a misguided effort to implemented a flawed covert operations plan inherited from the Eisenhower administration, Clinton experienced grief when a humanitarian intervention to which he gave his assent during the transition morphed unwittingly into a virtual counterinsurgency effort in Somalia—a country in which the United States had no clear-cut security interest.

The food delivery operation the George H. W. Bush administration designed was limited in scope and duration. But by the time Clinton took office, U.S. efforts to ensure a "secure environment" for food deliveries in Somalia remained incomplete. Supplies were being delivered on the ground, but tribal clans were occasionally interfering in their distribution.

Within the Clinton administration, there was a general predisposition to tackle an enlarged U.S. role within the UN, and the Somali intervention was not particularly controversial at home. Congress had challenged neither the propriety nor the legality of the mission, although it never got around to formally approving it until February 1993, by which time a decision had been made to reduce U.S. forces from a high of slightly more than 25,000 in January to 4,200 in late spring 1993.

Meanwhile, the policy initiative for managing the enterprise was migrating from Washington to the UN. There, Secretary General Boutros Boutros-Ghali was actively recruiting military units from a variety of countries for deployment in Somalia to implement a Chapter 7 enforcement action to maintain peace. He expected to rely primarily on Pakistani troops.

Even as U.S. forces were being drawn down, Clinton was pressed by Boutros-Ghali to shoulder the broader mission that Bush had steadfastly resisted "to assist the people of Somalia to create and maintain order and new institutions for their own governance."[33] The Security Council, with Washington's concurrence, commended the secretary-general for his plan and essentially endorsed it—a major decision casually assumed without much reflection on its implications. Since the operation was proceeding rather smoothly, the new administration evidently saw no need for an NSC review of the premises or possible consequences of the UN resolution.

Despite some reservations in the Pentagon, the new administration had a higher comfort level than its predecessor with the secretary-general's expansive mission in Somalia.[34] Bill Clinton had championed "assertive multilateralism" during his campaign. The administration was not opposed to the use of force, as long as it was authorized by the UN and undertaken in concert with others. Nation-building was not regarded as anathema.

The Somali mission evolved incrementally in response to events. It unfolded largely in accordance with Boutros-Ghali's agenda. In May 1993, leadership of the troops deployed there was turned over to Turkish general Çevik Bikr, the UN force commander for the United Nations Operation in Somalia (UNOSOM). American logistic units were placed under his command, though Quick Reaction Force personnel remained under exclusive U.S. control. Their mission now included pacification, political reconciliation, and rehabilitation. Madeleine Albright, the U.S. ambassador to the UN, welcomed the broadened mandate of the force enthusiastically: "With this resolution we will embark on an unprecedented enterprise aimed at nothing less than the reconstruction of an entire country as a proud, functioning and viable member of the community of nations."[35]

Such enthusiasm proved to be short-lived. That spring, factional infighting in Somalia intensified ominously. When twenty-five Pakistani troops were killed in June, it became crystal clear that powerful Somali clans did not accept and would not tolerate the UN mission. Boutros-Ghali and his representative in Mogadishu, Jonathan Howe, decided that if the UN mission were to succeed, it would be necessary to put the most powerful Somali clan leader, Mohamed Farah Aidid, out of business.

The corollary was a presidential decision, this time with General Colin Powell's reluctant concurrence, to undertake a parallel effort by U.S. Army Rangers to capture Aidid—a course that engaged American troops in what amounted to counterinsurgency operations. A few months later, a tactical operation in Mogadishu resulted in American casualties—eighteen American soldiers were killed and scores wounded. This shocked the American people and exposed the fragility of domestic political support for the expanded Somali mission.[36]

The battle, and the casualties it produced, seemed inconsistent with a humanitarian food-delivery operation. Some in Congress reacted with alarm when they were reminded that command and control of some U.S. forces in Somalia had been transferred to the UN. Many more questioned why Americans were involved in pacification operations in a remote African country of scant relevance to the security of the United States. At this point, U.S. policy appeared confused and adrift. And in this context, the political pressures to disengage proved irresistible, though President Clinton refused to authorize an immediate withdrawal.

President Clinton claimed retrospectively to have felt "let down" by his national security team, one of whom—Defense Secretary Les Aspin—paid for the episode with his job. But the president also acknowledged that he had approved a mission that he understood in general, but not in its particulars, and that he allowed the United States to get caught up "in a vengeful obsession—UN Secretary-General Boutros Boutros-Ghali's determination following the attack on Pakistani UN troops to capture the clan leader Aidid, and put him on trial."[37] Neither Clinton nor members of his national security team asked insistently how U.S. national interests justified the involvement of American troops in a shooting war in a remote African nation bereft of effective governing authorities.

By the summer of 1993, a disaster was waiting to happen in Somalia. In October, "creeping multilateralism" died on the streets of Mogadishu. President Clinton subsequently conceded that he had invested relatively little time during his early months in office schooling himself in the intricacies of foreign policy. For this he also paid a price. He later conceded, "I would have handled it in a different way if I'd had more experience."[38]

Unfortunately, the costs of failure in this Somali misadventure were significant. It confirmed a widespread impression at home and abroad that the Clinton administration's foreign policy was adrift. More seriously, America's retreat from Mogadishu in the face of trouble evidently reinforced Osama bin Laden's conviction that the United States was a "paper tiger," which he could taunt and attack with relative impunity.

In the Bay of Pigs fiasco, President Kennedy modified details of an operational plan in the vain hope that he could preserve its "plausible deniability." The limitations he imposed further diminished the plan's remote chance of success. Yet he failed adequately to review the premises of the undertaking or to consider thoughtfully the consequences of its possible failure. In the Somali case, though, President Clinton provided general approval for an expansion in the mission of what began as a food-distribution operation. When the unanticipated consequences began to unfold on the ground, he appeared unfamiliar with the operation's details until those shortcomings were clear for all to see.

In each case, the political concepts underlying operational activities were flawed. In both, the policy-making process broke down, and there was a failure of political oversight. For that matter, it was not entirely clear who was in charge. In both cases, the NSC system was in transition, and it malfunctioned. In neither instance did the White House undertake a careful and comprehensive review of proposed changes in operational plans. In both cases the president's political equities were inadvertently placed in jeopardy.

Both Kennedy and Clinton took away lessons from their early "on-the-job" training. Kennedy resolved not to rely so heavily on the advice of experts in the intelligence community and military establishment, and he tightened up the procedures for interagency coordination. Clinton recognized that he would have to devote more personal attention to foreign policy issues, and resolved to put the White House into better working order. Both learned from painful experience, but it did not come quickly enough to spare them consequential mistakes.

Resisting Inherited Policies

RONALD REAGAN AND THE MX/MPS BASING-MODE DECISION IN 1981

New presidents are not compelled to accept the policies handed off to them. They can be rejected or ignored, and they often are. An illustrative example emerged in the transition from Jimmy Carter to Ronald Reagan. In the late 1970s, the Carter administration was increasingly apprehensive about the survivability of the U.S. nuclear deterrent. American bombers were aging; U.S. submarine-based missiles were readily survivable but less accurate than other elements of the strategic triad. Most worrisome, America's land-based missiles remained housed in fixed silos whose location Moscow could presumably identify.

Before leaving office, President Carter settled on using a combination of dispersion and mobility to defend the land-based missile component of the U.S. deterrent. The MX/MPS basing mode system (Missile-experimental/ Multiple Protective Shelter), which Carter approved, envisaged an elaborate shell game. Two hundred MX missiles were to shuttle between 4,600 shelters that were to be located in the southwestern United States. Carter's term in office, however, ran out before he had a chance to implement this basing-mode decision.

When Ronald Reagan took office, he was enthusiastic about the robust production decision that Carter had approved for the MX missile. He was not, however, keen on the basing-mode plan that he inherited. He dismissed it as an unworkable "Rube Goldberg scheme." Since Carter had favored it, Reagan, egged on by his secretary of defense, Casper Weinberger, was inclined to reject it. He was put off by its technical complexity and was unprepared to impose its political burdens and financial costs on senators and governors from the Southwest, most of whom were fellow Republicans.

Some Reagan appointees—among them Bill Casey, Jeane Kirkpatrick, and Al Haig—were, however, more sympathetic to the MS/MPS Plan, and a study group, the Towne Committee, was reassembled to take a fresh look at the options. It proposed another technically dubious solution— called "Dense Pack"—that had little chance of accommodating the political interests of the Reagan White House or, for that matter, the Democratic House and Republican Senate, whose support would also be essential.

In the face of the president's reservations, persistent disagreements among his national security experts, and the intense hostility between the White House and the Hill, decisions were deferred, and a new study commission—this one led by Brent Scowcroft—was formed in January 1983. Its members were distinguished, its composition was bipartisan, and its task was daunting: to find a basing mode that was modest in cost, yet capable of resisting even the most determined Soviet attack, without infringing on the public spaces of the country.

The Scowcroft Commission proposed a package solution: a modest number of MX missiles in existing ICBM silos for near-term deterrence; the production of a smaller, mobile "Midgetman" missile to bolster and diversify the U.S. deterrent over the longer term; and an admonition to both Moscow and Washington to "move toward more survivable ICBMs" in order to promote a possible future arms control agreement.[39]

In the end, the package, which was approved by the president and Congress, did not produce swift or dramatic results. It did save the MX missile, though deployed in modest numbers in potentially vulnerable sites. And over time, it helped move the United States toward a more diversified and survivable deterrent system at a cost that was somewhat cheaper than that of the MX/MPS basing mode it replaced.

George W. Bush and Counterterrorism Policy in 2001

Anytime there is a change of party control of the White House, momentum is likely to be lost in implementing specific policies, even when the issues themselves do not excite great partisan controversy. In the wake of the September 11, 2001, attacks on the World Trade Center and the Pentagon, the George W. Bush administration was sharply criticized for its alleged lack of urgency in addressing the threat of international terrorism. A brief look at the trajectory of U.S. counterterrorism policy from late 2000 through mid-2001 does indeed suggest that the political transition had some affect on the momentum behind counterterrorist activities. Whether with a smoother transition the tragic events of September 11 could have been averted is another matter.

When President Bill Clinton met with George W. Bush shortly after the belated resolution of the 2000 election recount dispute in Florida, he urged his successor to consider Osama bin Laden and al-Qaeda the sources of America's greatest external threat. He had ample reasons for doing so. He and his national security team had weathered major terrorist attacks on the World Trade Center (1993), the Khobar Towers (1995), American embassies in Kenya and Tanzania (1998), and a naval vessel, the USS *Cole* (2000), in the Yemeni port of Aden just weeks before the election. Clinton had observed a major spike in intelligence reports on potential terrorist attacks around the turn of the century, and was aware of the possible existence of al-Qaeda "sleeper cells" inside the United States.

In response, his administration had begun to build a more robust human intelligence network in the Arab and Muslim world. It augmented the capabilities of the CIA's Counterterrorism Center. It put in place "findings" permitting the covert use of lethal force to capture bin Laden and his lieutenants. It established a more robust interagency process for coordinating responses to actionable intelligence. And in the fall and winter of 2000/2001, two senior "hold-over" appointees in the new Bush administration—Richard Clarke, Clinton's national coordinator for counterterrorism in the White House, and George Tenet, director of the CIA—were running around Washington as if "their hair was on fire" seeking to generate a sense of alarm about what they perceived as the growing menace of al-Qaeda.[40]

What then accounts for the deliberate, rather stately pace with which the George W. Bush administration tackled counterterrorism policy? For one thing, it was not the top priority issue on Bush's agenda when he took office. He had said little about it during his campaign. It merited only a brief mention in an article that Condoleezza Rice, who was to become his national security adviser, published in Foreign Affairs in the summer of 2000. Nor did the so-called Vulcans—key foreign policy advisers who secured key positions on Bush's national security team—consider counterterrorism the most urgent issue requiring early action.[41]

Bush and his advisers had focused on a different set of security policy priorities during the campaign. These included an accelerated development and deployment of National Missile Defense, modification of the Anti-Ballistic Missile (ABM) Treaty, a redesign of the Iraqi sanctions regime, expanding NATO and revitalizing other traditional alliances, "re-setting" relations with Russia and China, and scuttling various treaties—such as the Comprehensive Test Ban Treaty, the Kyoto Protocol, and an International Criminal Court Treaty—negotiated by the Clinton administration.

Beyond its different policy priorities, the Bush team did not regard the Clinton record on counterterrorism as especially worthy of emulation. Indeed, they considered it ineffectual. The Clinton administration had been unsuccessful in persuading the Taliban to give up Osama bin Laden. It had been reluctant to provide assistance to the anti-Taliban Northern Alliance in Afghanistan. It had been unwilling to dispatch armed Predator drones to South Asia for surveillance or operational missions against terrorist groups. And it had not retaliated at all following the October 2000 assault on the USS *Cole*, on grounds that the intelligence community had reached only a "preliminary judgment" that al-Qaeda was culpable.

Those pressing hardest for urgent action—Richard Clarke and George Tenet—were, as noted, "holdovers" from the Clinton administration. While their competence and loyalty were respected, they were not among the Bush inner circle, and their personalities were not a perfect fit with those for whom they now worked. In her memoir, *No Greater Honor*, Condoleezza Rice referred to Clarke as a "piledriver" whom she kept on "despite [his] awful reputation with many who'd worked with him."[42] She considered his office too large, and his activities too operational. She downgraded his position bureaucratically and perhaps suspected his early pressure to schedule an NSC principals meeting on counterterrorism was a turf-grabbing ploy. Tenet eventually developed a close rapport with President Bush, but that took time.

Rice and her deputy, Steve Hadley, also felt that their predecessor's counterterrorist strategy failed adequately to address the Afghanistan/Pakistan dimension of the challenge. They insisted that a more comprehensive review be undertaken and completed before specific recommendations for action were taken up. This review took several months.

By late spring and early summer of 2001, intelligence reporting on planned terrorist actions began again to surge, and the reports contained occasional references to possible terrorist "sleeper" cells in the United States. Most analysts, however, believed that further attacks were most likely to be directed against U.S. interests in the Middle East or elsewhere overseas, rather than on American soil.

More seriously, there was no clear consensus within the administration that al-Qaeda necessarily posed the most urgent threat. Secretary of Defense Donald Rumsfeld and his deputy, Paul Wolfowitz, expressed greater alarm about Iraq. The dispatch of Predator drones to South Asia was delayed by intramural struggles between the Pentagon and the CIA over which agency would bear responsibility for the operation and, hence, absorb the costs. Needless to add, systemic problems continued to hinder effective collaboration between the FBI and CIA in compiling and sharing operational intelligence related to terrorism.

Whatever the reasons or rationalizations, al Qaeda achieved strategic surprise with its attacks on September 11, and the impact was devastating. George W. Bush discovered his "mission and his moment." Counterterrorism immediately became the administration's central policy preoccupation. Whether the new president could have shifted decisively to a more proactive strategy without the jolt supplied by the attacks remains uncertain.

But some weaknesses in U.S. homeland defenses and some deficiencies in its deterrent posture could surely have been attenuated or mitigated. That, at least, was among the conclusions reached by the nonpartisan National Commission on Terrorist Attacks upon the United States (9/11 Commission). An item read by the president on August 6, 2001, in his Daily Intelligence Brief was headlined, "Bin Laden Determined to Strike in US." It mentioned bin Laden agents within the United States, the confirmed surveillance of federal buildings, and references to terrorist hopes of hijacking American aircraft. Who knows what would have happened if the president had responded by calling for an immediate NSC meeting, ordering stepped-up surveillance at airports, or placing security agencies on a higher alert.

What we know is that neither President Clinton, in the twilight of his tenure, nor President Bush, during his early months in office, displayed the strategic resolve and political will to retaliate in the wake of the terrorist attack on the USS *Cole*. This failure presumably reinforced Osama bin Laden's determination to pull off an even more dramatic and brutal attack on America's own soil. The devastation of September 11 was the result, and it had a gigantic, albeit belated, catalytic effect on U.S. national security policy.

FOLLOWING UP ON CAMPAIGN PROMISES

Campaigns put a premium on bold ideas designed to appeal to voters. Once a new president takes office, foreign policy promises confront more operational tests such as their efficacy abroad, their financial and opportunity costs, and their "fit" with other policy priorities. In this context some promises are abandoned, some are placed on the back burner, some are modified, and some are hastily implemented without the benefit of sober second thoughts.

Jimmy Carter and South Korea in 1977

Jimmy Carter took his promises dead seriously. During the 1976 campaign, he promised to withdraw U.S. ground troops from South Korea. Retrospectively, it is difficult to pinpoint where exactly this idea originated. In his memoirs, *Keeping Faith*, Carter made no reference to the subject at all. While researching his excellent book, *The Two Koreas*, Don Oberdorfer, the distinguished *Washington Post* journalist, asked the former president when he first got interested in the troop-withdrawal proposal. Carter could not recall, and none of his closest political or policy advisers subsequently illuminated that mystery.

Withdrawing some U.S. ground forces from South Korea was not an implausible concept in the mid-1970s. President Nixon had redeployed a division out of Korea in the late 1960s. In the wake of Vietnam, many policy makers were anxious to avoid "trip wires" that could drag the United States into other Asian wars. Even South Korean president Park Chung-hee hinted occasionally that his nation could manage its own ground defenses. Certainly there was support in the Congress for at least modest U.S. troop reductions. As a former naval officer, Carter perhaps found a strategy focused principally on bolstering American links to maritime Asia appealing. His disgruntlement with the South Korean government over its human rights performance doubtless contributed an additional motive.

Whatever the reason, Carter assumed this policy initiative, earnestly determined to implement it expeditiously once in office. Shortly before his inauguration Carter confirmed before a gathering at the Smithsonian Institution his intention to withdraw U.S. ground troops from Korea, though he also declared that American air power would remain.

Within weeks after he took office, the NSC issued a Policy Review Memorandum on Korea. Well before it was completed, the agencies involved were informed by the White House that it was not to include "the consequences of proceeding with partial or complete troop withdrawals, only the manner of implementing the policy of complete withdrawals already publicly enunciated by the President."[43]

When Vice President Walter Mondale was dispatched in early February 1977 for high-level talks with key European and Asian allies, his talking points for use with Prime Minister Takeo Fukuda of Japan, which were opened only after his plane departed from Andrews Air Force Base, included an explicit signal from the president that the United States planned to withdraw its ground forces from South Korea. The notion of "consulta-tions" implicit in his exchange with Japan was limited. It disclosed a deci-sion; it did not invite a discussion of the strategic concept or logic behind it. The message did not go down well with Fukuda, but his cool reaction did not dissuade the president from moving forward.

Mondale's instructions from the White House also called for him to urge Prime Minister Fukuda to find an occasion to encourage President Ferdi-nand Marcos of the Philippines to improve his human rights performance lest the United States withdraw some of its air force units from Clark Air Base. Mort Abramowitz, Dick Holbrooke, and I accompanied the vice pres-ident on this trip; we all considered this suggestion ill-advised and counter-productive. We urged Mondale strenuously not to raise this matter. Whether the vice president subsequently reviewed his talking points with the president or the national security adviser I never learned, but this sub-ject, happily, was not mentioned to Fukuda.

Foreign Minister Park Tong-jin of South Korea visited Washington in early March 1977. President Carter circulated handwritten policy guidance for key meetings with him. The instructions were terse and unequivocal: "(a) American forces will be withdrawn. Air cover will be continued; (b) U.S.-Korean relations as determined by Congress and American people are at an all time low ebb; (c) Present military aid support and my reticence on human rights issue will be temporary, unless [ROK] President Park vol-untarily adopts some open change re: political prisoners."[44]

These instructions were dutifully carried out. Foreign Minister Park was bluntly informed of the administration's plans to move forward with troop withdrawals with no ifs, ands, or buts. And on March 9, the president pub-licly announced his intention to implement the policy.

President Carter discovered, however, that it was easier to issue directives than to quell doubts among his senior advisers. He could force his military commanders and bureaucratic aides publicly to salute. But he was unable to convince them that his decision was prudent or timely. Early meetings on the Korean issue had revealed deep misgivings about the policy among key members of the National Security Council, not least those with respon-sibilities for arms control. The initiative provoked pervasive skepticism from the professionals in the State Department and from senior intelligence analysts, uniformed military leaders, and key civilians in the Pentagon.

One army general, John Singlaub, took his opposition public and paid for it with his job. The U.S. commander in the Republic of Korea, General

Jack Vessey, played a more subtle and patient game. So did the intelligence community, which surfaced new appraisals of North Korean strength designed to reinforce doubts about the timeliness of withdrawals. Secretary of Defense Harold Brown responded to efforts by the president to pull all U.S. nuclear weapons summarily out of Korea by arguing that such a decision should be taken up only in conjunction with the details of a troop withdrawal plan—a tactic that facilitated delay. When a senior Pentagon official, Mort Abramowitz, expressed doubts about the initiative to Vice President Mondale, he was reminded firmly, if good-naturedly, "Hey, Mort, there's been an election."[45] Nor did Carter's decision find much resonance on the Hill, where the troop-withdrawal proposal evoked skepticism from influential centrists like Senators Sam Nunn and John Glenn.

Thus President Carter not only short-circuited a review of policy toward Korea that he had personally authorized, but he did so in the face of strong reservations from key members of his national security team, acute fears among America's Asian allies, and the absence of clear and forthright support from the congressional leadership. He made no attempt to utilize a troop-reduction plan to obtain diplomatic concessions from North Korea, nor did he seek the collaboration of Moscow or Beijing in pressing Pyongyang for reciprocal arms-reduction measures. Instead, he appeared hopeful that the withdrawals would provide pressure with which to encourage President Park Chung-hee to improve his human rights record—an implausible expectation.

For his part, President Park chose not to confront Carter directly, preferring to use the occasion to press for a robust "compensation package" of military assistance ($1.9 billion), an expanded U.S. Air Force presence on the peninsula, generous technology transfers, and a slow pace for contemplated U.S. troop withdrawals.

Despite bureaucratic maneuvers to temporize, modify, and water down the president's initiative, Carter issued a Presidential Directive in May 1977 to withdraw at least one brigade of the Second Infantry Division by the end of 1978; a second brigade by June 30, 1980; and a gradual reduction of nuclear weapons and their final withdrawal along with ground troops.[46]

If most of the compensation package to the ROK was subsequently implemented, the troop withdrawals were not. A protracted bureaucratic struggle ensued, which first delayed then eventually killed the plan.

Had President Carter proposed limited ground troop withdrawals contingent on reciprocal North Korean military reductions, he would likely

have galvanized political support at home and among Asian allies. By insisting on the swift and unconditional implementation of a campaign
pledge, he dissipated scarce political capital at home, and spurred doubts
abroad about his policy judgment. In the end, he was persuaded reluctantly
to abandon the troop-withdrawal policy in 1979. Ironically, U.S. troop levels in Korea were higher at the end of the Carter administration than when
it began.

Yet by then, Washington enjoyed normal diplomatic relations with Beijing, had buttressed its alliance with Japan, signed a new base agreement
with the Philippines, and taken a leading role in mitigating a refugee crisis
on the Thai–Cambodian border.

Bill Clinton and China and Bosnia in 1993

Foreign policy pronouncements issued during his 1992 election campaign
also tripped up Bill Clinton in the early months of his first term. He experienced acute problems with China for implementing a campaign promise
in a problematic way. With respect to Bosnia, he promised actions, which
his administration was unable to implement.

At the Democratic Convention, Clinton offered a "New Covenant" for
"an America that will not coddle tyrants from Baghdad to Beijing."[47] He
promised a "values-based diplomacy," and described Chinese leaders as the
"butchers in Beijing." In a post–Cold War environment, the geopolitical
value of the China connection traded at a discount in the eyes of many
Democratic Party leaders.

Early in his tenure in the Oval Office, Clinton's national security adviser,
Tony Lake, pronounced the PRC a "rogue" state, and his assistant secretary
of state for Asia and Pacific affairs, Winston Lord, fashioned an executive
order that threatened to deprive China of Most Favored Nation (MFN)
trading rights in the United States if it did not ease its internal repression.
Both Lake and Lord were experienced and skilled diplomats. But the executive order the administration contrived, arguably a model of executive/
legislative branch cooperation at home, was scarcely an impressive methodology for advancing U.S. interests in China.

The PRC regime in Beijing governed a proud nation. It deeply resented
public instruction from Washington on its internal affairs. Undertaking
domestic reforms in order to sidestep threatened trade sanctions was predictably regarded by Chinese leaders as submission to foreign pressure, and
they were in no mood to acquiesce.

Nor did they see any necessity to do so. The trade weapon brandished in the U.S. executive order was not considered a genuine threat, since prominent American business leaders were openly opposed to its use. To make matters worse, congressional initiatives to oppose Beijing's bid to host the 2000 Olympics further alienated broad segments of the Chinese public. In addition, a U.S.-inspired inspection of a Chinese ship thought to be carrying chemical agents went badly awry. The Clinton administration's allegations challenged the credibility of China's leaders, but when neutral inspectors found nothing on the ship, it was the U.S. intelligence community that suffered embarrassment.

By the spring of 1994, the White House realized that its policy was alienating American business interests while souring U.S. relations with China. Secretary of State Warren Christopher's efforts to negotiate human rights adjustments with the PRC during a March visit to Beijing were sharply rebuffed, and the NSC staff and Robert Rubin, director of the National Economic Council, began looking for ways of abandoning the threatened trade sanctions with whatever grace could be mustered.

Although by then retired from the Foreign Service, I was invited to undertake a "secret mission" to Beijing to explore whether the Chinese might be willing to soften some of their human rights practices in return for abandonment of the executive order. I was prepared to make a confidential, private trip to China, but I had no interest in replicating the secretary of state's vain effort to negotiate a deal. I informed Tony Lake that I would make the trip only if it were clear that the administration was genuinely serious about dropping the effort directly to link the trade and human rights issues.

I asked to see President Clinton to confirm that he was indeed serious about the proposal. I was escorted to the Oval Office by Tony Lake and was surprised to see a gaggle of people there. With the exception of White House Counsel Lloyd Cutler, I did not recognize them. It was pretty clear that they were not along to discuss China policy. Tony and I waited just inside the Oval Office door, and in a few minutes the president disengaged himself from the crowd around his desk and walked over to confer with Tony and me.

He acknowledged the downsides of the existing policy and indicated a clear readiness to look for a fresh start. It was evident that this would be facilitated by some political gestures from the Chinese. On that basis I agreed to make the trip, though I resisted a State Department offer to send a small delegation to accompany me.[48]

I traveled to China soon thereafter. With Stape Roy, our distinguished ambassador to China, I visited key PRC leaders, including President Jiang Zemin. I expressed the personal expectation that Washington was prepared to drop the executive order, and I urged the Chinese to take some concrete steps that might politically facilitate the Clinton administration's adjustment of policy. The Chinese were courteous but not especially accommodating. They subsequently announced a few modest gestures. The administration, as anticipated, backed off the executive order, extended MFN trade privileges to China, and abandoned the tight and explicit linkage between human rights and trade sanctions.

I neither presumed nor claimed any credit for the policy change that ensued. Indeed, my trip remained secret and went essentially unreported. Win Lord's own analysis of negative Asian reactions to contemporary U.S. policy in the region did leak to the press. Concerns about North Korea's accelerated drive for nuclear capabilities were growing in Washington, and the administration recognized that effective countermeasures would require greater cooperation among the United States, China, Japan, and South Korea. The course correction with Beijing was prompted by strategic concerns and was accompanied by efforts to put relations with both Tokyo and Seoul back on a more even keel. A campaign pledge had been quietly and unceremoniously jettisoned.

The administration's follow-through on the Bosnia-related "lift and strike" policy it had embraced during the campaign, proved equally vexing to carry out. The Europeans had put troops on the ground in Bosnia as peacekeepers under UN auspices. Unfortunately, there were too few of them, and they possessed insufficient military capacity to protect either the local civilian population or themselves. By providing Serbian leader Slobodan Milosevic with potential hostages, moreover, their presence essentially neutralized American airpower.

During the transition following the 1992 election, Secretary of State Larry Eagleburger traveled to the Continent in hopes of persuading European leaders to adopt the lift-and-strike option. But, as David Halberstam later observed, "His trip changed neither hearts nor minds."[49] President Clinton's support for this policy option was sustained during the early months of his administration, evidently without awareness of Eagleburger's failed mission.

A plan authored by Cyrus Vance, President Carter's secretary of state, and former British foreign minister David Owen was also on the table. It called essentially for the "cantonization" of Bosnia. While President George H. W. Bush had quietly acquiesced in the plan without formally endorsing it, Clinton was reluctant to embrace an arrangement he feared would reward aggression, imply partition, and mock the principle of self-determination. Some Democrats were prepared to brandish force in the service of humanitarian causes. But Clinton was not interested in becoming the "cop on the Balkans beat." He intended to focus his attention mainly on domestic issues.

Clinton and his advisers consequently played for time and hoped for the breaks. The administration appointed a new Balkans negotiator and contemplated stronger sanctions, more rigorous enforcement of a "no fly zone," and a new international war crimes tribunal. But it authorized no bombing, pledged no intervention, extended no endorsement to the Vance/Owens plan and left the arms embargo in place. It did commence an interagency policy review of the Bosnian situation.

In April 1993, the Srebrenica massacre, which mocked the new administration's humanitarian impulses, galvanized it into the appearance of action. The national security team belatedly took up the lift-and-strike option but only on the still dubious condition that the Europeans were prepared to go along. The consensus within the administration on this course of action was, at best, fragile.

The holdover chairman of the JCS, General Colin Powell, who enjoyed extraordinary prestige within the Clinton administration in its early months, expressed major doubts about the lift-and-strike option. The Europeans, it turned out, still possessed a veto and were ready and willing to use it.

Secretary of State Christopher was dispatched to Europe to consult, and consult he did. Instead of telling the allies forcefully what the United States planned to do, and expressing a firm expectation that they should fall in line, he conveyed American intentions in a rather tentative way. The American approach appeared irresolute. The Europeans stiffed Christopher's advances, as they had refused Eagleburger's. Richard Perle, chairman of the Defense Policy Board, applied a harsh epitaph to the secretary of state's consultations: " It was an exchange all right. Warren Christopher went to Europe with an American policy, and he came back with a European one."[50] Meanwhile, the president went wobbly, and the enterprise collapsed.

It proved an inauspicious start for the administration. The gap between campaign rhetoric and governing decisions on Bosnia was evident for all to see. The administration looked weak; the policy appeared contradictory; its presentation to allies lacked conviction; and the president, when challenged by the Europeans, backed off without putting up a fight.

Many later concluded that inaction in early 1993 was a tragedy. But a new administration was fearful that intervention in the tar pit of the Balkans would put its domestic priorities at risk. Eventually, Clinton adopted a more robust approach to the Bosnian issue, though only when its reappearance in 1995 threatened to put his reelection at serious risk.

The episode serves as a reminder that initial mistakes, however damaging their consequences may be at the time, are not necessarily irretrievable. But neither are the costs necessarily inconsequential.

WHOLESALE POLICY REVERSALS SIGNALED BY "ANYTHING BUT . . ." CAMPAIGNS

New incumbents often declare their intent to undertake wholesale adjustments in the policies of a predecessor. Occasionally they proceed to do so. In 1981 and 2001, Ronald Reagan and George W. Bush took office resolved to abandon major features of the foreign policies they inherited.

President Reagan regarded Jimmy Carter's external policy legacy with a certain scorn. His differences with his predecessor's approach to the Soviet Union were scarcely tactical. Nor was he inclined to return to Nixon's policy of détente.

When Reagan assumed office in 1981, his broad policy priorities were clear from the campaign: build up American defenses, reduce marginal tax rates, balance the budget, and diminish the weight of regulation on the economy. He lost no time augmenting the defense budget. Otherwise, he devoted his initial efforts primarily to his domestic priorities.

This was a conscious choice. Reagan was persuaded by President Richard Nixon to devote his first six months in office primarily to economic policy. This, Nixon argued, would permit him to get his national security team in place and develop solid working relations with Congress while devoting his primary attention to battling inflation. If he did these things well, he would create a strong base for an effective foreign policy. If he didn't, he would be destined to play a weak hand abroad.

The advice proved to be useful.[51] It allowed him to buy time before launching East–West initiatives. And he used the time to improve U.S. industrial and military power, permitting him later to engage Soviet leaders from a position of greater strength. In the meantime, he directed more confrontational rhetoric toward the Soviets and made no major effort to meet with their leaders, although he did seek from his earliest days in office to commence a personal correspondence with Leonid Brezhnev and his successors.

This approach evoked much criticism—especially from the American and European press. Nonetheless, it produced no crises, and on one aspect of East–West policy there was a fair amount of continuity. The Reagan national security team enthusiastically embraced and extended the covert actions the Carter administration had initiated to counter the Soviet Union's occupation of Afghanistan.

Although George W. Bush focused his 2000 campaign primarily on domestic issues, once in office he lost no time reversing many elements of Bill Clinton's foreign policy. He foreswore a proactive U.S. mediating role in the Middle East, withdrew support for Kim Dae Jung's "Sunshine Policy" toward North Korea, buried Clinton's "strategic partnership" with China, modified sanctions directed against Iraq, extricated the United States from the ABM Treaty with Moscow, accelerated development and deployment of a national missile defense system, and withdrew a host of treaties that President Clinton had sent to the Senate for ratification at the end of his term.

These adjustments reflected the Bush administration's general disdain for President Clinton's foreign policy legacy, the special role carved out by Vice President Dick Cheney during Bush's first term, and his success in concert with Secretary of Defense Donald Rumsfeld in countering the influence of Secretary of State Colin Powell on policy.

So even before the September 11 terrorist attacks gave Bush "his mission and his moment," his administration appeared well launched on an "anything-but-Clinton" course adjustment. Whether one regards this as a series of early miscues or timely policy adjustments depends on one's point of view. But generally they reflected neither unseemly haste in getting out of the blocks nor slavish determination to follow through on campaign promises. There were instances of deficient policy coordination. For example, Vice President Cheney essentially ignored the State Department and Environmental Protection Agency in altering previous U.S. obligations to the Kyoto Protocol. But most of the early policy adjustments reflected the shared convictions of senior foreign policy officials eager to abandon the policy legacy of the Clinton administration.

SMOOTHER "PASSES" OF THE BATON

Neither Jimmy Carter nor Bill Clinton got off to a particularly smooth launch in the field of foreign policy, but each successfully concluded with noteworthy dexterity and dispatch a negotiation handed off by a predecessor. In Carter's case it was the Panama Canal negotiations; in Clinton's the NAFTA Accord.

When Carter took office, U.S. administrations had been negotiating adjustments in the Panama Canal Treaty for more than a decade. Although progress had been achieved, an agreement proved elusive. Lyndon Johnson and Richard Nixon chose to "slow-ball" ongoing talks during the election campaigns of 1968 and 1972, as did Gerald Ford in 1976. When Ford lost, the Panamanians were in no mood to brook further delay. They were determined to move forward immediately. With President-elect Jimmy Carter's concurrence, therefore, Ford authorized the U.S. negotiator, Ellsworth Bunker, to reopen the discussions promptly during the transition.

President Carter agreed that something needed to be done. He believed, as Secretary of Defense Harold Brown put it, that the canal could best be kept in operation "by a cooperative effort with a friendly Panama," rather than by "an American garrison amid hostile surroundings."[52] He acknowledged that the foundation for an agreement had been well laid by his predecessors. He recognized that only a bipartisan approach had any chance of reaching an agreement that could be approved by the Senate.

Carter surprised many by according this issue a high priority on his foreign policy agenda. It was decidedly unpopular, especially among conservatives and southerners. Many of the special interest lobbies, which fiercely opposed a new treaty, were dug in and eager for a fight. Carter was convinced of the need to "correct an injustice,"[53] he knew that backsliding on the Panama Canal negotiations would have a negative impact on U.S. relations with other hemispheric nations, and he understood that any attempt to conclude a Panama Canal Treaty would be more difficult in 1978 when midterm elections would be pending. Thus he chose to move swiftly, while his popularity was high.

The trick was to preserve U.S. strategic interests in the canal while accommodating Panamanian demands for eventual control of their country's most important asset. Fortuitously, within the Pentagon and among the uniformed military there was support for a deal. There was also heightened pressure within the Western Hemisphere to modernize the Panama Canal arrangement. Centrist Democrats and moderate Republicans understood that a new treaty would improve the U.S. image not only within Latin America but throughout the developing world.

A quick start was essential, and Carter provided the political impetus. His first Policy Review Memorandum was directed at this subject. By keeping Ellsworth Bunker on the job, while adding Sol Linowitz as co-negotiator, no time was lost bringing the new U.S. negotiating team up to speed. Instead of appointing Linowitz to a position requiring a possibly contentious and prolonged Senate confirmation, he made him a Special Representative with a tenure of just six months. August 10, 1977—the end of Linowitz's term—proved to be a useful deadline for completing the negotiation.[54]

Expeditious agreement was also facilitated by the Carter administration's decision to divide the negotiation into two parts. One focused on the arrangements for joint operation of the canal until the end of the century, at which time the Panamanians would assume total control. The other guaranteed the permanent neutrality of the canal, and the right of the United States to defend it.

The bargaining was promptly resumed, and the sticky points were overcome. Bipartisan efforts were skillfully organized to secure Senate ratification. The White House ran an "all hands on deck" exercise to nail down the support of Democratic senators; Gerald Ford, Howard Baker, and Henry Kissinger were among the prominent Republicans mobilized to get GOP senators on board. It was a cliff-hanger, but the needed votes were obtained and the treaties ratified. The baton passed smoothly without a major hitch.

The NAFTA agreement, which George H. W. Bush signed during the 1992 campaign, was his bequest to Bill Clinton. It promised the establishment of the world's largest free-trade region, and major reductions on tariffs and the modification of nontariff barriers to trade between the United States, Mexico, and Canada. Enabling legislation was passed during the Bush–Clinton transition, but the agreement itself had not yet been ratified by the Democratic Congress when Clinton assumed office.

Ross Perot, the third-party candidate in the 1992 presidential sweepstakes, made NAFTA a hot political issue with his assertion that it produced "a giant sucking sound" of jobs leaving the United States for neighboring countries. Bill Clinton had waffled on the matter during the campaign. A free-trader by conviction, he expressed only "lukewarm" support for the treaty, while adding what one biographer characterized as "a thick mayonnaise of qualifications that rendered his commitment almost meaningless."[55]

In setting plans for his first year in office, Clinton weighed the effort necessary to secure a congressional stamp of approval on NAFTA against other priorities. Hillary Clinton was pressing for health care reform; Al Gore for "Reinventing Government." The president was initially inclined to push first for congressional passage of a fiscal stimulus package.

Key aides to Clinton, including his political adviser, George Stephanopoulos, warned him about the political risks of tackling NAFTA early in his tenure. The agreement, after all, had been negotiated and signed by a Republican president; it was despised by the AFL-CIO; its passage in the House appeared at best a long shot; and a defeat would scar Clinton's first year in office.

Secretary of the Treasury Lloyd Bentsen—a genuine political heavyweight in Clinton's first cabinet—insisted, however, that the agreement represented good policy and would be a test of the president's own principles.[56] Public-opinion polls showed surprisingly strong support for it. Mobilizing bipartisan backing for NAFTA had some attraction for Clinton, because it would position him more firmly in the political center. And there were strong geopolitical and strategic arguments for fostering closer ties with America's neighbors.

Whatever the precise mix of motivations—stemming the tide of immigrants from Mexico was certainly one of them—Clinton decided to invest serious political capital in the ratification of NAFTA. He picked Bill Daley to coordinate legislative strategy. He nailed down "side deals" with Canada and Mexico on labor and environmental issues. This permitted him to honor campaign pledges and mollify elements of his political base. In a widely viewed television debate on this subject, Vice President Gore demolished Ross Perot's arguments against the treaty, and, coincidentally, finished him as a political force in the country. And Clinton enlisted strong GOP support for the agreement in Congress, particularly in the House.

The president contributed personally to the campaign for Democratic congressional support through his own considerable talents for wheeling and dealing. Even some of his supporters were reportedly offended by the horse-trading. But he got the job done, and as he later put it, "It's not like we were giving them backrubs or whorehouses or money, or things like that. We were trying to make policy accommodations in exchange for enough votes, and they were trying to look out for the folks back home. That's what the voters hired us to do."[57] The final House tally in favor of the agreement—234 to 200—included 132 Republicans and 102 Democrats. This was sufficient to give both parties a stake in the effective implementation of the accord. NAFTA thus became one of the new president's most tangible and widely lauded achievements during his first year in office.

SMOOTH FOREIGN POLICY LAUNCHES
BY NEW ADMINISTRATIONS

Some presidents obviously get off to a stronger start on foreign policy than others. This may be attributable to relevant experience, painstaking preparation, a healthy measure of good luck, or some admixture of all the aforementioned.

Among the presidents that experienced a relatively smooth start-up, three stand out: Dwight Eisenhower, Richard Nixon, and George H. W. Bush. Each successfully tackled the most urgent diplomatic challenge he confronted, and each adjusted U.S. grand strategy thoughtfully in the light of changing circumstances.

When Eisenhower became president, he was no stranger to high-level command. As the leader of a great wartime alliance, his duties had demanded diplomatic dexterity as well as strategic insight. After the war, he maintained a wide range of contacts with a global network of political leaders. His approach to decision making relied heavily on orderly staff work. And he had kept foreign policy options open during the 1952 campaign by avoiding precise commitments to particular courses of action.

His early months as president were marked by two noteworthy accomplishments—the successful negotiation of an armistice agreement in Korea, and a comprehensive review of grand strategic options, which resulted in putting a Republican stamp of approval on Truman's containment strategy, while giving it a "New Look."

Eisenhower's promise to "go to Korea" played a critical role in his 1952 electoral victory, and he acquitted his campaign promise within weeks of the election. His visit to Korea lasted only three days and produced no dramatic policy announcements. He intended, however, that this trip remind Moscow, Beijing, and Pyongyang that he was reviewing his options. And he was confident that any subsequent threat to widen the war would have greater credibility coming from a former general who had personally reviewed developments on the ground.

As expected, Ike found the available strategic options in Korea to be as limited and daunting as had his predecessor. America's allies were unwilling to join in any broadening of the theater of conflict. Neither Eisenhower nor his key advisers were inclined to "soften" the U.S. negotiating position. Yet waiting for the other side to make a conciliatory gesture risked further prolonging the stalemate.

While in Korea, Ike listened to Generals Mark Clark and James Van Fleet, who favored intensifying offensive operations, but he gave short shrift to their views. He also rejected the advice of his nominee for secretary of state, John Foster Dulles, who urged that the United States threaten to scrap what had previously been agreed on in the truce talks unless the Communists moved the military demarcation line to the narrow waist of the peninsula and concurred in an agreeable formulation for unifying the peninsula. The trip to Korea fortified Eisenhower's conviction that the situation on the ground would not be easily or cheaply improved, and that a political settlement was essential. Upon assuming office, Ike left the U.S. negotiator in place in Panmunjom and sanctioned no break in the talks.

Recognizing that a negotiated truce would require expanded U.S. diplomatic leverage, he immediately sought to mobilize it. He promptly disclosed plans to expand the ROK army, re-equip U.S. Air Force squadrons in South Korea with Saber jets, add a Marine division to American forces on the peninsula, dispatch atomic weapons to Okinawa, and pull the Seventh Fleet out of the Taiwan Straits. The last move unleashed Chiang Kai-Shek (at least symbolically), thereby complicating Beijing's strategic calculus, while tossing some "red meat" to GOP conservatives.

Eisenhower also authorized Secretary Dulles to convey to the Chinese (through a conversation with the Indian prime minister) a threat that the United States might bomb Communist sanctuaries north of the Yalu River—possibly with atomic weapons—if the stalemate in Korea was not swiftly resolved.

At a minimum, these moves got Beijing's attention and induced the Chinese to return to the peace talks in Panmunjom. Perhaps they had more consequential effects. Eisenhower certainly thought they did. He later claimed to his chief of staff, Sherman Adams, that it was the "danger of atomic war" that brought the Communists into line.[58] Alexis Johnson, the senior State Department truce negotiator, was more inclined to believe that the PRC decided to settle when it recognized that America was unwilling to yield on the POW issue, referring to the "voluntary repatriation" principle.[59] The two hypotheses are not, of course, mutually exclusive.

By March 1953, the Chinese began to float some interesting ideas as to how to deal with POWs who did not want to go home. They suggested, for example, handing them over to a neutral state after the armistice was signed and allowing them to remain there until their future was resolved. Whatever prompted this display of flexibility, it certainly helped break the negotiating logjam.

Still, it was Stalin's death in the same month that removed the most significant obstacle to a truce agreement. Mao Zedong and Kim Il Sung, for whom the stalemate had become extremely costly, could now more readily settle because they no longer had Stalin "egging them on."[60]

Even then, it took several months to consummate a deal. Not the least of the problems was getting South Korea's president, Syngman Rhee, on board. He initially refused to sign the truce, and he acted preemptively to release all POWs before the armistice was formally concluded. Eventually, Washington bought him off with a combination of warnings (e.g., the United States would not expand the war to achieve Korea's unification) and inducements (including a major aid package, the continued deployment of U.S. troops on the peninsula, and a mutual security treaty).

What, then, can be said about the effect of the 1952 election on the Korean War? It brought to office a new administration whose first order of business was ending the war. Its success may have reflected its apparent readiness, by contrast with its predecessor, to threaten a wider war. The terms on which Ike settled were not, however, materially different from those Truman had offered. Still, in Eisenhower, America had a new leader whose popularity and prestige permitted him to accept the kind of inconclusive truce that Truman was politically unable to sell. And Stalin's timely death reminds us that lucky breaks are occasionally an important ingredient of diplomatic success.

With Stalin gone and the Korean War resolved, President Eisenhower turned his attention to wider strategic concerns. He had sought the presidency to sustain America's commitment to collective security in Europe. Yet many of the leaders of his party clung to isolationist sentiments. He was a "Europe-firster," while many Republicans were more preoccupied with Asia. The Taft wing of the GOP was determined to roll back Soviet influence in Eastern Europe—a policy whose efficacy and prudence Ike questioned.

Eisenhower deliberately chose not to try to resolve such intraparty differences during the 1952 campaign. He was reluctant to politicize foreign policy choices in a partisan way, fearing this would expose deep fissures within the GOP and complicate the task of forging a bipartisan consensus later. He thought it wiser to defer serious deliberation about grand strategy until he had assembled a national security team and could work through the issues in an atmosphere free of electioneering.

During the campaign, Ike was careful to leave the platform drafting to John Foster Dulles, the heavy partisan attacks on President Truman to Richard Nixon, and reactions to Senator Joseph McCarthy's scurrilous innuendos against General George C. Marshall to others. Ike benefited politically from a nonpartisan stance, and with respect to policy, his intent, after all, was not to replace Truman's strategic handiwork but to modify and refine it.

During the latter years of Truman's administration, a major military buildup was launched in accordance with the conclusions of National Security Council Report 68.[61] The need for balance between the military and economic requirements of containment, however, was a prominent feature of Eisenhower's campaign, and this concern was on his mind when he took office. He was not inclined to prepare defenses for a specific "moment of maximum danger," fearing that this would expose the nation to the risk of "feast-and-famine" defense budgets and imprudent fiscal policies.[62] He was determined to review carefully certain alternative strategies for dealing with Moscow and, in this connection, to examine what to do about NSC-68 and its recommendations for much higher levels of defense spending.

Hence, in the summer of 1953, Eisenhower initiated what came to be known as the Solarium Project. Panels were carefully selected to examine three alternative grand strategies:

- Consolidation of the basic containment policy set forth by the Truman administration
- A more assertive declaratory policy designed to increase Soviet perceptions of the risks of nuclear war if they sought political victories or pursued subversion in areas beyond their existing sphere of influence
- A strategy combining psychological operations and covert measures to erode unity within the Sino-Soviet bloc (i.e., a relatively risk-averse version of a "rollback" strategy for Central Europe)[63]

Principals in the administration participated in the exercise, alongside experienced professional experts and career officials. The discussions were carefully prepared, and they continued at the National War College through the summer. Candor was encouraged. When the deliberations were completed, the participants met at the White House where Ike, after listening to their discussion, summed up the results.

The settled strategy that emerged confirmed the broad outlines of Truman's containment policy, implemented with heavier reliance on air power and atomic weapons, a more assertive declaratory policy, greater emphasis on Continental defense, and a more robust use of psychological warfare and covert action measures to weaken the Soviet bloc and ward off Soviet inroads in the Third World.

According to Robert Bowie, the fundamental elements of the strategy that emerged "so closely paralleled [Eisenhower's] pre-presidential views that one could argue that he would have adopted similar policies without the Solarium exercise, the numerous commissions, panels of consultants, staff studies, Planning Board papers, and even the vigorous NSC debates."[64]

The formal exercise was, however, highly useful. It exposed strategic alternatives, provided an orderly process of discussion, encouraged senior officials in the administration candidly to critique existing policy and the leading alternatives to it, sharpened the president's own thinking, and got the key members of the national security team "on board" behind a consensus view, which Ike articulated at the wrap-up session. For all practical purposes, it finessed, in fact interred, the preference of the Taft faction of the GOP for "liberating" Eastern Europe. As Andrew Goodpaster put it later, "The notion of a rollback with either military action or the threat of military action sank without a trace at that time."[65]

George Kennan, the distinguished diplomat for whom Secretary Dulles could find no appropriate job at the State Department, proved to be a central player in the Solarium Project. As Kennan recalled in his memoirs:

> I was chosen, on the President's orders, as director of one of the three teams by whose competitive efforts the exercise was to be carried through.... When it was completed it was the concept propounded by my team that received the presidential approval. This had the ironic consequence that I found myself ... standing at a podium ... in the White House basement, briefing the entire cabinet and other senior officials of the government on the rationale and the intricacies of the

policy toward Russia which, it was decided, the government should now pursue. At my feet, in the first row, silent and humble but outwardly respectful, sat Foster Dulles, and allowed himself to be thus instructed. If he, in March, had triumphed by disembarrassing himself of my person, I, in August, had my revenge by saddling him, inescapably, with my policy.[66]

In fact, it was the president who orchestrated the exercise. And through it, Eisenhower managed to fine-tune America's grand strategy while lending Truman's internationalist policy greater durability by giving it bipartisan support.

Like Eisenhower, Richard Nixon inherited, along with the Oval Office, an Asian war, a public deeply divided, rapidly expanding foreign policy commitments, and growing concerns about the resources necessary to sustain them. Though Nixon did not swiftly extricate the United States from the war in Vietnam, he did move deliberately to adjust American strategy in Southeast Asia, initiate fundamental changes in America's policy toward the major powers, and rely more heavily on diplomatic maneuverability than the sheer weight of our resources to advance U.S. objectives overseas.

Prior to entering the White House, Nixon had traveled widely and acquired, as Eisenhower's vice president, substantial foreign policy experience. In picking Henry Kissinger as his national security adviser, he recruited a brilliant practitioner of realpolitik and a savvy bureaucratic infighter.

The president's initial policy focus was naturally on Vietnam. He took office as a supporter of established war aims but with fundamental misgivings about the Johnson administration's strategy for attaining them. He and Kissinger recognized that their options were limited.

They presumed that a military victory was not in the cards, but neither was inclined simply to blame the war on the Democrats and bug out. Having ruled out major military escalation and a quick, complete troop withdrawal, they were left essentially with the quest for a negotiated solution.

The key to successful negotiations, they believed, was hanging tough in the field while holding the home front. Neither was simple. They were convinced that to have any chance of mustering the requisite bargaining leverage for a successful negotiation, they would have to use more brutal military tactics in the field to deny victory to Hanoi, accelerate the training and equipping of South Vietnamese forces in order to shift the burdens of combat to them, and bolster ties with Moscow and establish a connection with Beijing to diminish their material support for Hanoi. They quickly learned that any chance of a negotiated outcome with Hanoi would also demand the identification of more modest negotiating objectives, and that mustering broader public support for U.S. foreign policy would require regular troop withdrawals and limits on America's role as a "global policeman."

Through the early policy adjustments Nixon and Kissinger introduced, they believed that a negotiated resolution of the conflict might be swiftly found.[67] This seriously underestimated the patience, tenacity, and perseverance of Hanoi, but they did reposition the United States more effectively in the global balance of forces and thus put America's foreign policy on a more promising track.

"Vietnamization" commenced: troop withdrawals were announced and secret negotiations with Hanoi launched. An effort to link Washington's approach to arms control with Soviet readiness to rein in support for Vietnam was tested. A variety of channels—the French, Poles, Romanians, and Pakistanis—were used to signal interest in engaging China diplomatically. The administration also initiated the secret bombing of supply routes in Cambodia in hopes of providing protection to declining U.S. troop levels, bolstering the confidence of the South Vietnamese and encouraging Hanoi to contemplate the possibility that Nixon was an unpredictable "madman" determined to use any means available to avert a military defeat.

By the spring of 1969, the key element of Nixon's policy toward Vietnam were in place. By August, general limits for American intervention in Asia were articulated in the so-called Guam Doctrine, which morphed into the Nixon Doctrine. It provided a concept with which to explain the U.S. troop withdrawals from Vietnam, a prophylactic against reflexive American interventionism in other Asian disputes, a marketing device for promoting a new division of labor between the United States and its allies in the Pacific, and, above all, a means of reassuring the American public that the administration did not intend to be a "Lone Ranger" but a "Reluctant Sheriff," more reliant on its deputies.[68]

These course corrections were substantial but did not yield swift results. The adjustments that Nixon and Kissinger introduced in America's relations with the great powers reflected careful planning and skillful improvisation, and they eventually paid major dividends. They expanded America's diplomatic flexibility, redefined Washington's foreign policy agenda, and deflected attention away from the war in Indochina.

If Eisenhower and Nixon took office in the midst of war after winning elections marked by bitter partisanship, George H. W. Bush secured what some regarded as "Reagan's third term" in a political environment of relatively good feeling. Since Bush had served as Reagan's vice president for eight years, one might have anticipated seamless continuity in the field of foreign policy. Yet Bush was also determined to be his own man, and much of his effort in the early months of 1989 was invested in differentiating his policy priorities from those of his former boss.

President Bush's personal knowledge and experience in foreign affairs was one key to the successful launch of his administration's diplomacy. Determined to play a large role in managing national security policy, he devoted much of his time during his early months in office to cultivating foreign leaders through visits and phone calls. He understood that while personal relationships may not overcome tough issues dividing states, "they can provide enough goodwill to avoid some misunderstandings."[69] Equally important, Bush put together a first-rate national security team composed of competent, experienced, and collegial individuals.

Like Eisenhower, George H. W. Bush tackled his most politically contentious policy challenge—Nicaragua—up front, with a sense of urgency and noteworthy pragmatism. He also took the time needed deliberately to review and modify grand strategy in light of the dramatic changes that were then reshaping the international environment.

No foreign policy issue had polarized feelings between Republicans and Democrats or left such a residue of mistrust between the executive and legislative branches during the late 1980s than the U.S. policy toward Nicaragua. President Bush and his secretary of state, James Baker, were determined to attenuate this partisan divide by escaping from this Central American policy cul-de-sac.

In his 1988 campaign, Bush played to the GOP's base by pledging additional military aid to the Contras. There was virtually no chance that he could deliver on this promise. The Democrats retained a solid majority in the House and Senate, and were dead set against further security assistance to the rebels. Baker's courtesy calls on members of Congress during the transition period underlined the urgent need for policy adjustments that could enlist bipartisan support.

Instead of fighting a futile battle over military aid to the Contras, the administration organized a diplomatic effort around an existing regional arrangement—the Central American Peace Process, which had been proposed in 1987 by Costa Rican president Óscar Arias Sánchez. Its most significant provisions called for a cease-fire between the Sandinista government and the Contras, and for free and fair elections in all signatory countries: Costa Rica, Guatemala, El Salvador, Honduras, and Nicaragua.

With a signal of stronger U.S. interest in their initiative, the Arias group gathered in El Salvador in February 1989 and announced that the Sandinistas were prepared to hold a presidential election within a year; in addition, the five Central American presidents would formulate a plan within three months to demobilize the Contras.[70] This set the stage for unusually intense, complicated, and ultimately fruitful diplomatic and political maneuvering by the administration.

Bush and Baker now offered Congress a bargain. The administration would tacitly agree to stop trying to overthrow the Sandinistas by force and accept the results of a free election in Nicaragua if Congress would extend the Contras sufficient humanitarian aid to keep them intact in Honduras for at least eight months. This provided a source of leverage on the Sandinistas. In return, the administration agreed to utilize the aid for "voluntary political reintegration" or "voluntary regional relocation," and to give four separate committees of the Congress a potential veto on the release of the authorized funds. The deal enabled the administration to claim the high moral ground on the issue, and it provided a solid basis for mobilizing bipartisan support.

Next, the administration chose to put Mikhail Gorbachev's "new thinking" on foreign policy to the test. In effect, it offered the Soviet Union a modest diplomatic role in the Western Hemisphere and a U.S. pledge to respect the outcome of free elections in Nicaragua in return for Moscow's support for efforts to facilitate democratic political change in Central America. Specifically, it challenged Gorbachev to respond to Washington's shift of course by terminating the delivery of major military equipment to Nicaragua, persuading the Cubans to follow suit, and urging Daniel Ortega to entrust his political fate to his people by holding a free and fair election.

The administration also developed an elaborate methodology for rewarding Nicaraguan cooperation or penalizing its backsliding on the road to elections. It encouraged the Nicaraguan opposition to overcome debilitating factional rivalries and unite behind a single candidate. It pressed the international community to send election monitors to raise the price for cheating. And in the end, it got the Congress to provide technical support for the election through the National Endowment for Democracy.

The Democratic leadership on the Hill provided solid political support for the administration's change of course. The Soviet Union took the bait and played a generally helpful role by reducing its subsidies and admonishing its ally to countenance free elections. The opposition in Nicaragua managed to unite behind an impressive candidate, Violetta Chomorro, and won a decisive victory. Daniel Ortega, who ran for reelection and lost, grudgingly accepted that outcome.

This creative effort to escape a debilitating policy legacy unfolded over the course of more than a year. But the outlines of the deal were clearly visible by the spring of 1989, and it launched the administration's foreign policy on a high note.

This success in turn lent impetus to a broader effort to fine-tune U.S. policy toward the Soviet Union. George H. W. Bush inherited a strategy toward Moscow that he did not wish to repudiate but intended to amend. A drastic change of policy was not necessary. East–West relations were in good shape, and no crisis loomed on the horizon.

But President Bush and Brent Scowcroft harbored major reservations about President Reagan's bid for an agreement at Reykjavik to abolish nuclear weapons. They perceived new policy opportunities—especially in Central Europe—in the political and economic vulnerabilities of the Soviet system.

Bush, Baker, and Scowcroft believed they would be in a better position to launch new initiatives once their team was firmly in place, their interagency policy-making system was up and running, their control of the bureaucracy was more secure, and their relations with Congress and the press were better established. In mid-February 1989, President Bush authorized a basic review of East–West relations.

The draft policy proposal turned up on the president's desk in mid-March. Authored mainly by officials held over from the previous administration, it was dismissed by the secretary of state as "mush," and the responsibility for developing another draft migrated to the NSC staff.

While the administration struggled to shape its own "new thinking," Gorbachev dominated headlines in the spring of 1989 by throwing out a variety of self-serving arms control proposals, which attracted much favorable comment in the international media. This provoked critics in the United States to complain that the new administration lacked vision and offered no new strategic ideas.

Baker's early travels to European capitals highlighted the need for a greater sense of shared purpose with America's allies. Gorbachev's offer to promote equal East–West reductions of short-range missile forces had stirred widespread public support in some NATO capitals, particularly Bonn, and strong resistance in others, especially London. This focused Washington on the need for a dramatic initiative to bolster NATO unity, counter Gorbachev's proposals, and establish the president's credentials as a strong leader.

Fortunately, Gorbachev's initiatives confirmed Moscow's readiness to consider broad reductions in conventional arms and ground troops on the Continent. This was intrinsically appealing to the Bush administration. Reciprocal arms reduction proposals could be used to thin out Soviet forces in Eastern Europe and thus give Central Europeans wider political latitude to pursue their own plans for political and economic reform. With greatly reduced tensions on the Continent, moreover, growing nationalist resistance to U.S. military deployments there could be anticipated. In this context, a reduction of American forces could serve American political interests without exposing it to greater strategic risks. A major conventional force reduction agreement could provide a means of finessing rival intra-NATO perspectives on short-range nuclear forces (SNF) modernization.

Gradually, the president's goading, and the interagency debates it precipitated, generated a comprehensive new East–West agenda and a set of specific policy initiatives, which the president outlined in four separate speeches in May and June 1989. The outcome was not unlike that of Ike's Solarium Project—that is, significant refinements in Reagan's approach to East–West issues without rejecting the core elements of a predecessor's approach.

Nor were these the only foreign policy building blocks the administration put in place during its early months in office:

- It positioned America to play a less assertive, more "even-handed" role on Arab–Israeli issues by signaling that deeper U.S. diplomatic engagement in the Middle East would come only when the parties directly concerned were prepared to make significant moves of their own.
- It adapted U.S. policy toward South Africa by increasing exchanges with prominent black leaders, and spelling out for Pretoria the

policy adjustments it would need to take if it wanted closer ties with Washington.

- It responded to Deng Xiaoping's brutal crackdown on Chinese dissidents—the Tiananmen Incident—by applying sanctions in concert with G-7 allies, while keeping direct channels of communication to China's leaders open.

This was an impressive opening act. It enhanced the administration's political and diplomatic flexibility, and redefined policy priorities with subtlety. It suggested a deft touch in managing political and military challenges—qualities that served the administration well as it worked with the Soviet Union to bring the Cold War to an end and to manage its aftermath.

In short, new presidents, equipped with the right experience, advised by prudent colleagues, and content to begin deliberately rather than hastily, have managed to get their administrations' foreign policies off to a smooth start.

A number of common threads link the favorable foreign policy start-ups of Presidents Eisenhower, Nixon, and George H. W. Bush. Each had extensive experience in dealing with foreign policy and had cultivated close relationships with a wide range of foreign leaders. Each preserved a healthy measure of policy flexibility by avoiding specific campaign promises for adjusting America's conduct overseas. None attempted to accomplish too much too soon. All recognized not just the virtues of careful preparation but also the advantages of getting a team in place and policy priorities sorted out before launching major initiatives. All swiftly tackled the most urgent issue draining America's fiscal coffers or alienating public support. Each recognized the need for a clear concept of grand strategy to guide their relationships with the major powers, and they defined this concept in a way that yielded broader support from the establishment, the press, and the public.

TAKEAWAYS

Launching a new president's foreign policy is challenging. Few bring deep overseas experience to the job. Lengthy campaigns impel them to spend many months prior to their election primarily with people who are more useful in getting them elected than helping them subsequently to govern.

Pressures to act swiftly and decisively are very intense early in a president's tenure before his team is fully in place, before the procedures of policy making have been firmly established, and before policy priorities are clearly settled. Early miscues, again, are scarcely surprising. The test of governance is not whether a foreign policy proposal has domestic appeal, but whether it promises at reasonable cost and risk to advance the interests of the country abroad.

Presidents make the tough calls, and indeed the buck stops in the Oval Office. To mobilize bureaucratic and political support for a significant foreign policy decision, however, a president must provide a more compelling logic than the mere fact that he promised it during his campaign.

Some early foreign policy miscues are almost inevitable. Some reflect the inexperience of a new chief executive on external matters. Some are a result of hasty efforts to acquit campaign pledges without careful review of their efficacy, timeliness, and fit with other policy priorities. Some are by-products of deficient interagency policy coordination within a new team. Some are due to overzealous determination to repudiate the policy legacy of a predecessor.

Fortunately, few early mistakes are politically or diplomatically fatal. Foreign policy errors, however costly, are rarely irretrievable. Major start-up errors are avoidable, and in that connection hands-on experience with the outside world obviously helps, as does a disposition to prepare carefully before launching complicated, controversial initiatives.

CONCLUSION

THE U.S. PRESIDENTIAL ELECTION SYSTEM WAS NOT DESIGNED for the efficient pursuit of foreign policy objectives. It was established to safeguard the freedom of Americans by limiting the power and authority of government. Despite the complications this system injects into the management of foreign policy, the Republic has survived quite comfortably, and the United States has compiled a creditable, albeit uneven, record of accomplishment in its engagement with the world.

The preceding chapters illustrate a variety of ways in which the modalities of our presidential election system influence the content and conduct of American foreign policy for better or for worse.

- If a president's diplomatic role may be complicated by the distractions of a reelection campaign, the "accountability moment" that elections provide forces incumbents to be highly attentive to the domestic costs and risks of their policies overseas. This keeps the chief executive's feet firmly grounded in the political fray at home, where a reelection bid will provide a referendum on his record. Thus, politics can trump strategy in election years.

- By giving voters a periodic chance to "throw the rascals out," our system provides regular opportunities to put the spotlight on troubling foreign policy problems, and supplies an incentive to consider course corrections for costly, inconclusive foreign as well as domestic policies, or offers a chance to select new management to fix them.

- Presidential election campaigns interject regular pauses or "time-outs" into the management of American diplomacy, and impart a certain stop-and-start quality to our foreign policy. Increasingly lengthy campaigns extend these interludes, particularly when an incumbent president faces a serious challenge for his own party's nomination. These lulls can deprive policy of momentum, forestall timely initiatives, or push promising ventures off track.

- Presidential elections tend to focus attention on the shortcomings of policy. Contenders invariably highlight difficulties in America's engagement with the world and seek to affix blame for them on the incumbent. Many new presidents assume that their predecessor's foreign policy reflected a misreading of global conditions and failed to advance U.S. interests. Their campaign criticisms of the incumbent's inadequacies, and their own promises to ensure remedies, supply the predicates for a change of course.

- Campaigns encourage incumbents to oversell their achievements abroad, contenders to exaggerate the mess left by incumbents, and all candidates to embrace democracy promotion as a magic solvent for most of the world's ills. During campaigns, the rhetoric is more aspirational than strategic, tough policy trade-offs are rarely addressed, and the costs of highly touted initiatives are generally ignored. Campaign speeches and debates do little to clarify foreign policy priorities, since the candidates generally prefer to keep their options open, their commitments ambiguous, and their pledges flexible to avoid offending significant voting blocs.

- The election system does give many groups, regions, and constituencies a periodic opportunity to shape the foreign policy thinking of those who seek the Oval Office. Westerners may be preoccupied with Asia; easterners with Europe; southwesterners with Mexico and Central America. In general, southerners seem particularly inclined to boost the defense budget; midwesterners to crack overseas markets to sell food, energy, and manufactured products; northeasterners to press for protection from sources of "unfair" competition. Floridians are particularly absorbed by events in

Cuba and the Caribbean. But in the aggregate, presidential elections give them all some chance to register substantive concerns and geopolitical priorities with the candidates.

• When party control of the White House changes hands, transitions are frequently awkward. Some are managed with grace; some with barely concealed animosity. Collaboration between outgoing and incoming presidents is possible but, at times, vexing. For the former, the main challenge is to restrain the impulse to attempt to add too much to his legacy as time runs out; for the latter, the challenge is to avoid launching controversial new initiatives before adequate preparations have been laid. Confusion and drift are frequent by-products of transitions, but foreign policy crises have been mercifully rare.

• In the start-up phase of a new president's term, policy continuity is rarely the order of the day. The emphasis is on change. Few new presidents bring substantial foreign policy experience with them to the Oval Office. Hence, there are heightened risks of foreign policy miscues, not least because our patronage system sweeps most senior policy makers from office when political control of the White House changes hands, and political pressures to undertake bold actions are most intense when a new incumbent is least prepared to launch complex or controversial initiatives.

• Our two-term limit can swiftly transform a second-term president into a lame duck whose ebbing tenure diminishes his effective authority. But a chief executive who is reelected has the advantage of experience obtained on the job; he may consequently be prepared to fix previously committed mistakes and better equipped to exploit policy opportunities presented by events.

THE VIRTUES OF THE U.S. SYSTEM

While our presidential election system has its adverse side effects on foreign policy, it also possesses noteworthy virtues. Elections challenge the continuity of policy, and policy adjustments are often timely and useful. They also expose the policy process to fresh thinking, timely criticism, and new perspectives. Incumbents who are reelected often undertake welcome course corrections. When party control of the White House changes hands, a new president, having no political commitment to policy continuity, is free to undertake fresh initiatives.

Regular Political Incentives to Fix Foreign Policy Problems

One virtue of our election system, then, is that it regularly allows America to fix costly and persistent foreign policy problems by putting new management in charge. This is especially salutary when the United States is bogged down in prolonged, costly wars, which incumbents have been unable either to win or settle.

Harry Truman and Lyndon Johnson paid the political price for such stalemates in Korea and Vietnam. Jimmy Carter did not engage the nation in war, but his failure to secure the timely return of American hostages from Iran or anticipate Moscow's invasion of Afghanistan helped deprive him of a second term.

Deteriorating security conditions in Afghanistan seven years after President George W. Bush ousted its Taliban government certainly buoyed Barack Obama's electoral prospects in 2008, even though his own campaign characterization of the Afghan conflict as a "war of necessity" virtually ensured that his administration would feel obliged to expand the U.S. commitment there—at least for a while.[1]

A stalemated war can kill a president's reelection chances, but a military victory does not guarantee a second term. George H. W. Bush's triumph over Saddam Hussein in the First Gulf War was swift and sure, and he persuaded American allies and friends to pick up most of the tab. He lost his bid for a second term, mainly because the end of the Cold War turned voters' attention decisively back to domestic concerns. Al Gore, Clinton's vice president, was unable to translate the administration's low-casualty victory over Kosovo in 1999 into a successful campaign for the Oval Office in 2000. Bill Clinton and George W. Bush prevailed in 1992 and 2000, respectively, by highlighting their plans for domestic reforms.

The mere prospect of a reelection campaign can bestir an incumbent president into productive action or timely course-corrections overseas. With reelection bids looming, Ronald Reagan signaled plans for a more conciliatory approach toward Moscow in January 1984. In mid-1995, Bill Clinton embarked on more energetic efforts to tackle the Bosnian issue and to enlarge NATO—the former belatedly to redeem a major 1992 campaign pledge; the latter in part perhaps to harvest political gains in states where voters of Polish, Hungarian, and Czech heritage were numerous. In late 2003, George W. Bush altered the time lines for returning sovereignty to Iraq in order to provide retroactively a more plausible rationale for a war he had initiated to terminate Saddam Hussein's nuclear program. Some described these latter policy adjustments as "putting lipstick on a pig." In each case, policy adjustments were driven by events and substantive concerns as well as electoral political calculations. The latter, obviously, were clearly present.

As the second term of a president's tenure nears its end, incumbents generally seek to burnish their foreign policy legacy, and they only rarely succeed. As Dick Cheney once noted, "The president's ability to do big things diminishes on an almost weekly basis in the final year of his presidency."[2] Attempts by the administrations of Ronald Reagan, Bill Clinton, and George W. Bush to midwife Israeli–Palestinian agreements late in their second terms fell short. The reasons are clear: the issues were complex, the antagonisms deep, and those who were reluctant to conclude an agreement had merely to run out the clock.

But there are exceptions. Despite the Iran-Contra scandal in late 1986, President Reagan completed his second term on a high note through the negotiation of historic arms control agreements with the Soviet Union. President Clinton managed a successful humanitarian intervention in Kosovo and sealed a trade pact with China during his last two years in office. President George W. Bush managed to conclude free-trade agreements with Panama, Colombia, and South Korea during the final quarter of his eight-year tenure, and his 2007 "surge" of U.S. troops in Iraq (combined with the belated embrace of counterinsurgency tactics and the Great Sunni Awakening) reversed rapidly deteriorating security conditions there and averted a military defeat—though it scarcely ensured enduring stability, let alone victory—in the signature mission of his administration.

Efforts to tackle major foreign policy challenges following the election of a successor are generally vain. Not only is the authority of the incumbent diminished, but the president-elect will usually harbor reservations about the effect such initiatives may have on his own future options.

When George W. Bush sought to establish a sustainable legal base for continued U.S. force deployments in Iraq following the 2008 election, Democratic Party critics claimed he was seeking to constrain President-elect Obama's options and expressed reservations about the terms of a proposed U.S.-Iraqi Status of Forces Agreement. Iraqi president Nuri al-Maliki had objections of his own to an extended U.S. military presence and appeared comfortable with the time frame for withdrawal, which Barack Obama had proposed during the campaign. In the end, an understanding was reached, which accomplished Bush's legal objective, generally within the limits of President-elect Obama's preferred time table.[3]

Adjusting the Balance Between the Ends and Means of Foreign Policy

Presidential elections are also the mechanism through which the United States periodically adjusts the balance between overseas commitments and the resources needed to achieve them. Historians have long noted that U.S. foreign policy alternates between phases of "soaring self-assertion" and "sober retrenchment."

These alternating phases reflect enduring tensions between the idealistic impulses of the United States and the imperatives of realism inspired by threatening security conditions or the high costs of foreign exertions. This tension between American "values" and American "interests" is discernible in the country's two most cherished documents: the Declaration of Independence and the Constitution. The former proclaims the nation's fidelity to universal principles, and the Preamble to the latter outlines its enduring purposes, only one of which—"the maintenance of a suitable establishment for the common defense"—refers to interests beyond our shores.

Since World War II, the United States has consistently pursued a global role, but the tempo of its engagement with the world has been repeatedly adjusted to reflect external circumstances and domestic moods. During periods of self-assertion, presidents have extended the range of our foreign commitments and bolstered the instruments through which we pursue them. Such self-assertion has been regularly accompanied by sizable increases in the national security budget, growth in the power of the executive branch, and limits on congressional foreign policy prerogatives. In his splendid history of post-1945 U.S. foreign policy, Stephen Sestanovich described these phases as "maximalism," and characterized Presidents Truman, Kennedy, Johnson, Reagan, and George W. Bush as its practitioners.[4]

Periods of consolidation or retrenchment have been marked by more modest definitions of U.S. national interests, reduced expenditures for foreign entanglements, a stronger preoccupation with domestic issues, a reassertion of limits on executive branch power, and greater respect for congressional prerogatives. Presidents Eisenhower, Nixon, Ford, Carter, and Obama comprise the "minimalists" or "retrenchers."

George II. W. Bush and Bill Clinton are, as Sestanovich notes, more difficult to categorize. During his first several years in office, Bush was very active tidying up matters left in the wake of the Cold War. This enlightened assertiveness (e.g., promotion of the unification of Germany and the expulsion of Saddam Hussein's forces from Kuwait) capitalized on and extended America's global role. But as the 1992 election neared, he kicked major external initiatives down the road and turned his attention to domestic matters in response to an evident shift in the public mood.

Clinton's policy interests and political experience inclined him to focus initially on domestic economic and social issues. So did early foreign policy miscues in Somalia, Haiti, and Bosnia. He did, however, manage to secure ratification of the North American Free Trade Agreement and the General Agreement on Tariffs and Trade. Only with the success of a renewed effort to secure a negotiated resolution of the Bosnian issue in late 1995 did Clinton begin actively to expand America's global role anew.[5]

These pendulum swings reflect the natural tendency of Americans to set uniquely ambitious goals, and the equally understandable disposition to curb commitments when their attainment proves elusive or their political and financial costs become too burdensome to sustain. As Gideon Rose observed, "For more than half a century over-enthusiastic idealists of one variety or another have gotten themselves and the country into trouble abroad and had to be bailed out by prudent successors brought in to clean up the mess. When the crisis passes, however, the realists' message about the need to act carefully in a fallen world ends up clashing with . . . Americans' loftier impulses."[6]

When aims and means are out of balance, the nation risks insolvency. To overcome a disequilibrium between objectives and resources, presidents must either define external aims more modestly or persuade Congress to pony up additional resources.[7] When presidents fail to make such choices in a timely way, they implicitly invite the voters to make them.

These alternating cycles of policy are not difficult to identify. The Truman Doctrine, Marshall Plan, NATO alliance, Point Four Program, Bretton Woods institutions, and UN-authorized intervention in Korea were tangible expressions of President Truman's robust response to Moscow's post-1945 challenge. As time passed, the financial costs of these initiatives, the frustrations provoked by the Communist's victory in the Chinese civil war, the casualties incurred in the Korean stalemate, and the bitter domestic divisions stirred by Senator Joseph McCarthy took their toll. Dwight

Eisenhower was elected, among other reasons, to relieve those costs without abandoning an active international role.

While Eisenhower was supportive of the general contours of Truman's containment policy, he tailored American external obligations to a more limited view of what the United States could prudently afford. He secured a truce to end the fighting in Korea. He maintained the containment doctrine but adapted it to the fiscal priorities of the Republican Party. He ignored calls for U.S. intervention in Indochina, resisted a major buildup of the army, relied on relatively cheap and deniable covert methods to compete with Moscow in the Third World, and explored a relaxation of tensions with a post-Stalinist Soviet Union. His administration presided over a period of relative tranquility in foreign policy.[8] Nonetheless, it did not keep the public's adrenalin flowing, and by 1960 many Americans felt that we were losing ground to the Soviets in space, defense, and political influence around the world—not least in our own hemisphere.

President Kennedy articulated American idealism by promising to "pay any price, bear any burden, meet any hardship, support any friend, oppose any foe to assure the survival and success of liberty." He upgraded U.S. strategic capabilities to overcome an alleged—though nonexistent—"missile gap"; he expanded the army and augmented U.S. Special Forces to broaden conventional military options. He put the U.S. Information Agency "on steroids" and established a variety of new foreign policy instruments, including the Alliance for Progress, the Peace Corps, and the Arms Control and Disarmament Agency.

During his administration and that of his successor, Lyndon Johnson, the United States also drifted into a growing conflict in Indochina. During his three years in office, Kennedy increased U.S. military advisers in South Vietnam from several hundred to more than 16,000. Throughout the 1964 presidential campaign, LBJ resisted pressures from his key advisers to intervene more directly in Vietnam. His motives were political as well as strategic, but he authorized the dispatch of combat troops in 1965, and by 1968 the war, which Johnson was reluctant to finance on a "pay as you go" basis, had turned into a quagmire. It dissipated American strength, tarnished its prestige, divided its society, and alienated it from friends and allies around the globe—and it presented the GOP a chance to reclaim the White House.

Richard Nixon inherited the task of reestablishing a more affordable equilibrium between U.S. commitments and the resources required to sustain them. He and Henry Kissinger, his national security adviser, sought to accomplish this by gradually extricating U.S. forces from Vietnam, opening relations with China, and pursuing détente with the Soviet Union. In addition, Nixon shut down the so-called gold window to preserve U.S. freedom of action in international finance, and he enunciated the Guam Doctrine to delimit American commitments in future wars in Asia. He withdrew an army division from Korea, reduced the Pentagon budget, and ended the draft. He also accepted "sufficiency" as a substitute for "superiority," or even "parity" to guide strategic arms control efforts vis-à-vis Moscow. He diluted, though he did not terminate, the U.S. defense commitment to Taiwan. He energetically defended American interests, but in doing so he relied less on the sheer weight of U.S. power, and more on the flexibility and resourcefulness of American diplomacy. Gerald Ford inherited this portfolio when Nixon resigned and hewed to much the same course.[9]

Unfortunately for the Republicans, détente lacked resonance with key elements of both major parties. To Reagan Republicans and to "Scoop" Jackson Democrats, it betrayed weakness, masked retreat, sounded European, concentrated too heavily on realpolitik, and seemed to foreswear the pursuit of American values. Critics described it as a "one-way street" and argued that the United States was constantly making concessions without getting much in return.

Jimmy Carter exploited this mood in the 1976 election, championing more idealistic impulses felt by voters in the aftermath of Watergate and the fall of Saigon. He acknowledged the need for some policy continuity, especially in the field of arms control. But he also was determined to differentiate himself from his predecessors and did so particularly by affirming the importance of human rights as a core element in his foreign policy. He also shared the public's desire for a "peace dividend," and he accommodated the determination of the Congress to impose sharp restrictions on the intelligence community's covert activities.

Jimmy Carter by no means shunned ambitious foreign policy initiatives. On the contrary, he concluded the Panama Canal Treaties, mediated the Camp David Agreement between Egypt and Israel, and normalized U.S. diplomatic relations with Beijing—policies whose substantial benefits have stood the test of time. But in the late 1970s, many regarded these signature achievements of his administration as meek accommodations to the interests of others rather than bold expressions of American self-assertion.

Carter's response to the Soviet invasion of Afghanistan was reasonably robust—particularly the enunciation of the Carter Doctrine[10] and the covert assistance the United States supplied to the mujahedeen. Covert actions were not, of course, publicly acknowledged, and many considered other measures too little, too late. Above all, failure to secure the return of the hostages being held in Tehran conveyed an impression of weakness. This contributed to his failed bid for reelection in 1980, and it ended another period of retrenchment in U.S. foreign policy.

President Reagan promoted a reassertion of American power and purpose. He did not mince words, and his recipe for ending the Cold War was simple and concise: "We win; they lose." His language was often combative. He characterized the Soviet Union as an "evil empire" and challenged its leader to tear down the Berlin Wall. He was prepared to confront adversaries, and he drove a hard bargain.

He also dramatically increased the defense budget and commenced what he termed the Strategic Defense Initiative (SDI) and his critics derided as "Star Wars." Confident that Moscow's refusal of a reasonable deal would leave it no alternative to an arms race it could not win, Reagan negotiated from a position of strength on arms control. He proposed an ambitious "zero option" for intermediate-range ballistic missile (IRBM) reductions and provided a major incentive for Soviet agreement by building up American missiles on the Continent, despite Western European doubts and massive protests. To get rid of these, Moscow was eventually persuaded to dismantle its own SS-20 missiles—all five hundred of them.

Reagan also enthusiastically provided assistance to anti-Soviet groups in Central Europe and the Third World (e.g., Poland, Afghanistan, Nicaragua, Angola, and Cambodia) among others. He broadened public support for this by demonstrating that he was also prepared to help local proponents of democratic reform supplant non-Communist, authoritarian regimes in places like the Philippines, South Korea, and Chile. The nature of the assistance Washington provided varied, but it gave the cause of democracy promotion public appeal on both the Left and the Right.

While Reagan was prepared occasionally to authorize direct U.S. military intervention—as he did by sending U.S. armed forces to Lebanon and Grenada, advisers to Central America, and planes to bomb Libya—relatively few troops were involved, and when they encountered trouble, as they did in Beirut, he pulled them out.

Over all, U.S. foreign policy commitments proliferated under President Reagan, and the resources needed to sustain them expanded. Yet the Cold War thawed, and the West prevailed. While Reagan succeeded in tempering Soviet assertiveness, it was on his successor's watch that the Cold War ended, the Warsaw Pact dissolved, and the Soviet Union disintegrated.

America remained the sole global superpower. Changing global conditions opened the door to significant adjustments in U.S. security policy.

President George H. W. Bush displayed noteworthy prudence and restraint in responding to this changing world order. He negotiated significant agreements with Moscow and offered technical assistance to encourage Russia's modernization and democratization. He helped reunify Germany while keeping it within NATO. He reversed Iraq's conquest of Kuwait without occupying Baghdad. He joined in G-7 sanctions against China after the Tiananmen Incident without foreswearing high-level diplomatic contacts with Beijing. He launched a broad diplomatic effort to foster peace in the Middle East, though his failed bid for reelection denied him a chance to exploit this opening.

Beyond defining U.S. interests in a disciplined fashion, Bush also imposed budget rules to constrain the fiscal deficit, initiated a review and modest reduction of American bases and force deployments in Europe and Asia, pushed hard for more reciprocal access to the markets of allies, and resisted pressures to intervene in trouble spots like the Balkans. He also violated his own pledge not to raise taxes in order to cope with a growing fiscal deficit. In short, the George H. W. Bush administration managed to reduce the risks associated with America's global commitments, and in the process fortified American primacy without provoking a counter-coalition.

Early on, Bill Clinton cut defense spending, foreign assistance funds, U.S. troops deployed overseas, and American diplomatic and intelligence establishments in order to provide the American public an added "peace dividend." Early foreign policy miscues reinforced Clinton's disposition to concentrate on domestic preoccupations. He opted out of his campaign pledges regarding Bosnia when the Europeans balked. When the Chinese stiffed his pressures for human rights reforms, he backed off the linkage of human rights to trade. And when the intervention in Somalia took an ugly turn and yielded American casualties, he resisted congressional requests for the immediate withdrawal of U.S. troops but just for a few months.

Only when the 1996 election loomed did the administration bestir itself anew on the Bosnian issue. This time, it applied military muscle against the protagonists and displayed diplomatic resourcefulness in the Dayton negotiations. Clinton also brandished American power more actively in his second term. He responded to China's military exercises off Taiwan's coast by dispatching two carrier battle groups to the Taiwan Strait. He expanded

NATO, adopted "regime change" as the U.S. objective in Iraq, and forged an activist policy toward al-Qaeda.[11] He also went to war to thwart the Serbs in Kosovo and embraced a more robust diplomatic style in seeking to mediate or mitigate conflicts in Northern Ireland, Cyprus, South Asia, the Middle East, and the Korean Peninsula. This activity notwithstanding, Bill Clinton left office with a sizable fiscal surplus. Thus, as Stephen Sestanovich aptly observed, "American foreign policy in the decade after the end of the cold war was the story of a widely anticipated pullback that didn't materialize."[12]

George W. Bush sought election as a "domestic president" who promised a "more modest and less arrogant" foreign policy. But in response to the September 11 terrorist attacks, he dramatically extended American overseas commitments. He undertook a punitive attack on Afghanistan, launched a preventive war against Iraq, and mobilized a global counterterrorism coalition to combat al-Qaeda and other Islamic extremist groups that had or were acquiring global reach.

He unleashed unprecedented increases in the defense budget, expanded the size and broadened the activities of the intelligence community, created the Department of Homeland Security, augmented funding for economic assistance programs, and loosened legal constraints on the handling of enemy combatants. In addition, he sought to make his counterterrorist strategy more palatable by embracing a democracy promoting "Freedom Agenda," launching a multibillion fund to battle AIDS in Africa, creating a new policy instrument—the New Millennium Fund—for encouraging good governance in emerging states, and attempting through negotiations to reverse or slow the spread of nuclear weapons in North Korea, Iran, and Libya.

With modest course adjustments to U.S. policy in Iraq in 2004, he managed to earn a second term. But chaos spread in Iraq, the struggle against the Taliban lost momentum in Afghanistan, and the president appeared unable decisively to fix these problems, until the public signaled its frustration by delivering a devastating defeat to Republicans in the 2006 midterm elections. Only then did Bush fire his secretary of defense, change field commanders, approve a troop surge, alter U.S. strategy to focus on local population protection to ward off defeat, and secure a measure of stability in Iraq before leaving office. He was unable to stave off a major financial crisis in 2008, and his administration set the stage for yet another attempt to bring external commitments back into balance with available resources.

Barack Obama, like Eisenhower and Nixon before him, inherited a stark disequilibrium between expansive overseas commitments and highly constrained means to pursue them. He brought to the Oval Office a distinct skepticism about the efficacy of nation-building, a campaign promise to shift U.S. priorities away from a "war of choice" in Iraq, to a "war of necessity" in Afghanistan, and major fiscal incentives to reduce external obligations.[13]

Improving security conditions in Iraq permitted the steady withdrawal of U.S. forces, and negotiations with Iraqi authorities revealed President Obama's reluctance to leave even a modest residual force there. Nor did his initial embrace of the Bush/Petraeus Counter-Insurgency (COIN) doctrine in Afghanistan last long. The Joint Chiefs of Staff and American field commanders got a temporary surge of 30,000 troops (augmented by additional allied contributions), and the Democratic Party's base got a date certain for the commencement of a force drawdown—July 2011. In the 2012 election campaign, Obama pledged to get all American combat troops out of Afghanistan by 2014.

Aside from extricating the United States from costly wars in the Middle East and South Asia, President Obama improvised a "light footprint" strategy for dealing with Islamic terrorism. To reduce American "boots on the ground," he relied more heavily on improved intelligence, expanded law-enforcement cooperation, and the use of Special Forces and drones for the targeted killing of al-Qaeda leaders—not only in Iraq and Afghanistan but in weak or failing states like Pakistan, Yemen, and Somalia. The COIN doctrine was officially abandoned.

To be sure, President Obama did support a multilateral "free-fly zone" designed to protect civilians in Libya—a mission that gradually morphed into bringing down Muammar Gaddafi's regime. But he authorized American participation only in response to heavy pressure from NATO allies, an Arab League endorsement, and the UN's authorization of the intervention. While the United States dominated the early air sorties, and provided much of the intelligence, logistic support, and firepower for the mission, Washington ultimately turned over the leadership to others. This was belittled by critics as "leading from behind," but it did impose limits on the size of America's military, financial, and political role.

For a time, retrenchment played well to war-weary Americans. But in 2014, new dangers emerged in the Middle East, central Europe, East Asia, and Africa. Meanwhile, public approval of President Obama's handling of foreign policy dropped precipitously.

The reasons seem clear. Major policies failed to yield the outcomes sought. American troops were completely withdrawn from Iraq, but sectarian strife intensified. We intervened with others to oust Colonel Gaddafi from Libya, but chaos rather than order filled the resulting political vacuum. The administration stood aside from the Syrian civil war, but the results included not only a humanitarian disaster, but the occupation of large swaths of Syria and Iraq by an even more virulent strain of Islamist extremism—that is, Sunni terrorists identifying themselves as the Islamic State or Caliphate.

President Obama's failure to enforce his own "red-line" against Bashar al-Assad's use of chemical weapons diminished the credibility of the president's word and American threats. Sanctions imposed by the United States and others did not dissuade Vladimir Putin from intimidating Russia's neighbors or reclaiming the Crimea. America's "pivot back to Asia" did not deter Beijing from pursuing its territorial claims in the East and South China Seas with increasingly muscular and implicitly coercive tactics. Secretary of State John Kerry's effort to revive the Israeli–Palestinian peace process proved abortive. And the U.S. air campaign against the Islamic State in Syria and Iraq appeared scarcely adequate, even with the collaboration of Kurdish Iraqi ground troops, "to degrade, and eventually destroy," ISIS, without the implicit and awkward collaboration of Iranian militias and the Assad regime. Efforts to regulate a nuclear accord with Tehran persist, but in the face of outright Israeli opposition.

These developments not only bred frustration in Washington, but prompted many Americans to consider "retrenchment" as a synonym for weakness and retreat. Anxious allies encouraged the United States to deepen its engagement with the world and to more actively counter the growing aggressiveness of Islamic extremists, the increased pugnacity of Putin's Russia, the expanding power of Xi Jinping's China, and the wily tactics of Iran.

As the Obama administration scrambled to formulate and implement a more coherent strategy for responding to emerging sources of turmoil abroad, the public, the Congress, and the press did not constrain Washington from assuming a more active global role. If anything, critics appear more worried that America was responding too timidly rather than too truculently.

Thus retrenchment appears to be giving way again to greater assertiveness. This is spurred by a heightened sense of foreign dangers. And public support for policy adjustments is arguably reinforced by an up-tick in U.S.

economic growth, a bonanza in the production of natural gas and light oil, and the improved efficiency of American manufacturing. Nonetheless, fiscal realities will continue to temper our external ambitions.

POLICY CONTINUITY DESPITE REGULAR ELECTIONS

If presidential elections are often the forerunner of major course corrections in U.S. foreign policy, they have not impeded a healthy measure of continuity in America's engagement with the world.

Alexis de Tocqueville famously observed that "a democracy can only with great difficulty regulate the details of an important undertaking, persevere in a fixed design, and work out its execution in spite of serious obstacles."[14] However, although Harry Truman's containment doctrine was characterized in the 1952 Republican platform as an "immoral, ineffective, and cowardly policy," Dwight Eisenhower, once ensconced in the White House, embraced an adjusted version of that policy, which, with further variations, retained substantial public support throughout the balance of the Cold War. "Great difficulties" were experienced from time to time in sustaining the policy or adapting it to changing circumstances. Yet Washington persevered, and eventually the Soviet Union succumbed to its internal contradictions, as George Kennan, the architect of the original policy, had anticipated.[15]

For decades, the United States extended security guarantees to valued allies while encouraging them to shoulder more equitably the burdens of collective defense. It bolstered Israel's security while attempting to broker agreements between Tel Aviv and its Arab neighbors. It sought to arrest the spread of nuclear weapons by offering "extended deterrence" to allies and imposing sanctions on aspiring nuclear proliferators.[16] It engaged the People's Republic of China without abandoning "unofficial" links with Taiwan. It fostered the freer movement of goods, services, capital, and technology across borders through multilateral, regional, and bilateral trade agreements. And it consistently promoted democracy either by example or by more active interventionism.

The United States also consistently underwrote a disproportionate share of the costs of international public goods. It patrolled the oceans to safeguard the sea lanes through which commerce flowed. It provided the world's chief reserve currency—the dollar. It fueled global economic growth by serving, at least until recently, as the "consumer of last resort." It regularly took the lead in attempting—with some notable successes (Germany, Japan, South Korea, Taiwan, Libya) and some noteworthy failures (India, Pakistan, North Korea)—to arrest the spread of weapons of mass destruction and their means of delivery. The jury remains out on Iran.

Presidents of both parties have built and sustained a capacity to project force throughout the world; they have preserved a global base system and deployed forces in Europe, Asia, and the Middle East. And they have on occasion utilized military power—sometimes wisely, sometimes fecklessly—to defend or advance U.S. interests or values. Andrew Bacevich has even argued that our major parties "exchange portfolios at regular intervals" without altering the "Washington rules" by which national security is managed.[17]

In the early post–Cold War world, America persistently attempted to preserve its primacy and to extend the unipolar moment without provoking the formation of a counter coalition. President George H. W. Bush pursued this aim with prudence; President Bill Clinton with hints of triumphalism.

After September 11, George W. Bush initiated striking changes in America's grand strategy, including a shift in its geopolitical focus from Europe and the Far East to the Middle East and South Asia, preemptive interventions or preventive wars against states supplying safe haven and support for terrorists, and harsh interrogation and incarceration procedures on captured enemy combatants.

Barack Obama promised in his 2008 campaign "a sweeping overhaul of the Bush administration's war on terror." Yet, once in the Oval Office, he wound up preserving many Bush legacies. As Peter Baker later observed, "Obama essentially ran against Bush's first term but inherited his second."[18] By the time President Obama took responsibility for the war against Islamist extremism, the secret prisons had already been emptied, waterboarding stopped, and Congress had authorized vastly expanded surveillance.

President Obama pursued a counterinsurgency strategy in Afghanistan; relied on drones and Special Forces to go after terrorists in Pakistan, Yemen, and Somalia; retained the Patriot Act; kept the Guantanamo Bay prison open; and prosecuted terrorists primarily in military courts. One might even say that President Obama strengthened many of those policies by converting them from conservative initiatives into policies enjoying wider political support. Needless to add, nation-building and the counterinsurgency strategy were gradually abandoned.

Both Democratic and Republican presidents have supported some nonpartisan aims and sustained some nonpartisan policies. Both have achieved successes and suffered setbacks in their pursuit. Some presidents have exhibited greater aptitude for these tasks than others. But the sheer continuity of effort is impressive. Many central precepts of American foreign policy have demonstrated impressive staying power, and policy adjustments have frequently appeared on the margins of well-established policy traditions.

How can one explain this impressive degree of policy continuity despite the uncertainty and diplomatic volatility that is widely associated with our presidential election system? The paramount reason is perhaps self-evident. In America, elections decide who gets the right to define our national interests, but the interests themselves are rather durable. They are not in constant flux. They abide, and presidents are not free to ignore them or redefine them too radically.

Beyond this, newly elected presidents do not commence their terms writing on a blank slate. When they assume office, they almost invariably promise big-time change. Although they belittle the foreign policy legacy of their predecessors, they inherit a substantial endowment of enduring commitments. These inevitably constrain the range of their own strategic and diplomatic choices. They also acquire a national security bureaucracy that possesses its own policy reflexes. Major and sustained efforts are required to overcome inertia.

When policies yield favorable results, moreover, they acquire political support, which lends them staying power. Political leaders, whichever party they represent, naturally wish to associate themselves with successful ventures, and powerful special interests tend to coalesce behind policies that pay off. Needless to add, some measures acquire durability even though they lead into a blind alley, such as the Cuban trade embargo. Other policy initiatives surface, if tentatively, with some regularity—for example, periodic attempts to dissuade Israel from building additional settlements in the West Bank—only to be discarded in the face of resolute opposition.

Differences in the foreign policy DNA of the Democrats and Republicans persist. But these differences can be overstated, encouraged by our presidential campaigns. Rival candidates often present their differences on foreign affairs as if they were fundamental. They rarely are. In general elections, the candidates usually compete vigorously for the votes of centrists and independents upon whose support victory depends. This forces them to focus at least to some degree on what unites rather than divides the public—especially on matters beyond America's shores.[19]

In the end, of course, neither continuity nor discontinuity in foreign policy is intrinsically virtuous. It all depends on the international context, the content of policies, and the response of the public. Since World War II, the U.S. foreign policy record is certainly not free of blunders, but Washington has successfully defended the nation's territorial integrity, safeguarded its institutions, maintained its key alliances, developed a workable modus vivendi with many of its adversaries, and generously supported international public goods. It is a record that is far from perfect, but by any comparative standard, it is certainly creditworthy.

DID THE END OF THE COLD WAR CHANGE THE PARADIGM?

Many of the major continuities in U.S. foreign policy were doubtless by-products of the prolonged bipolar struggle for geopolitical and ideological supremacy with the Soviet Union. When that contest ended, the security conditions that shaped American foreign policy changed fundamentally. And that was not all. A new generation of American political leaders—three presidents in a row—emerged who were born after World War II. Each took over the presidency more limited in his exposure to the military and generally inexperienced in foreign affairs. Meanwhile, American politics drifted toward increasingly intense partisanship and polarization, while American governance displayed growing dysfunction. Whether developments such as these alter the story line of this book is another question.

As we have seen, the end of the Cold War altered the global balance of forces and America's position in it. Bipolarity disappeared; the existential threat the Soviet Union had presented receded. America recovered the healthy margins of safety that it had traditionally enjoyed as a result of vast oceans to the east and west, friendly neighbors to the north and south, abundant supplies of natural resources, and the military potential inherent in its industrial prowess. Our strategic choices expanded, even as containment—the central organizing principle of American foreign policy for four decades—lost relevance.

The Cold War's end was swiftly followed, moreover, by a series of developments that further augmented America's enhanced security position—the liberation of central Europe, the dissolution of the Warsaw Pact, the disintegration of the Soviet Union, the unification of Germany without forfeiting its membership in NATO, China's preoccupation with internal reform and economic growth, and the swift routing of Iraqi forces from Kuwait. These developments left America as the sole global superpower, enjoying what Charles Krauthammer characterized as a "unipolar moment."

But if this emerging balance of power was extremely favorable, the need to play a balancing game remained an inescapable Washington preoccupation. Its requirements, however, continue periodically to change. A challenge that our last four presidents faced was how to sustain the salutary conditions victory in the Cold War presented—an open global economic system, peace among the great powers, and the ascendancy of liberal values. This challenge will become even more daunting if America's relative power declines further, and that of a liberal world order's foes increases.

George H. W. Bush tidied up issues left by the Cold War and consolidated new gains that its victory yielded. It fell to Bush and his successor, Bill Clinton, to manage American primacy in a manner that did not provoke the other major powers to "gang up against us." Bush performed this task with prudent restraint; Clinton with a certain carelessness.

The latter had his ups and downs with the Chinese and Russians. Serious run-ins with the China flared over human rights and trade in 1993 and 1994, over Taiwan in 1995 and 1996, and over an errant U.S. bomb that hit the Chinese embassy in Belgrade in 1999. The expansion of NATO, diffidence toward Russian interests in the Balkans, and America's pursuit of new concepts like "humanitarian intervention," "the responsibility to protect," and "the democratic peace" alienated Moscow and left it with grudges to nurse.

After September 11, the focus of American policy shifted. Washington sought primarily to enlist the help of other major powers in combating al-Qaeda and other terrorist groups with "a global reach." International support for the punitive attack on Afghanistan was broad and deep. The invasion of Iraq produced sharper, critical reactions well beyond the Muslim world. Over time, these costly wars—along with deep tax cuts, the 2008 financial crisis, and the global recession that followed—dissipated America's financial surplus, diminished its relative power, and ushered in a renewed period of sober retrenchment. The past teaches us that current policies of retrenchment will not go on indefinitely. Indeed, they are already being revised. And this course correction will likely become more evident as the 2016 election approaches.

As events in 1989 altered America's role abroad, voters naturally turned their attention to long-neglected issues at home. Three successive presidents were elected whose quest for the Oval Office focused predominantly on domestic matters. Bill Clinton promised to focus "like a laser" on the economy; George W. Bush to lower taxes and reform America's K-12 educational system; and Barack Obama to fix a deep financial crisis, while pushing for more universal health care.

None of them ran for the Oval Office claiming noteworthy diplomatic or military credentials. Their apprenticeship in politics had taken place mainly at the state or local level. Each possessed some life experience abroad, but none had a genuine familiarity with the operational aspects of foreign policy or a feel for the exercise of influence beyond America's shores. Once in office, each struggled with new strategic challenges, and in responding to them each was forced to rely heavily on the national security team they selected and their own on-the-job training.

Meanwhile, domestic politics in America has moved increasingly in the direction of edgy partisanship and bitter polarization. The absence of an overriding global threat diminished the incentives for domestic unity and political civility. For a brief period following September 11, such solidarity reappeared, but it faded rapidly after the invasion of Iraq.

Partisanship is certainly not new in America, nor is it unwelcome. It is, after all, a central ingredient of competitive politics. But it surely has intensified. In 1998, 41 percent of Republicans and 45 percent of Democrats considered themselves "strong partisans." By 2011, those figures had risen to 65 percent and 62 percent, respectively. The major parties sorted themselves out ideologically and geographically. Red states became redder, and blue states bluer.

In the post–Cold War world, presidential elections have been generally close. Barack Obama won the popular vote in 2008 with a higher margin than any Democrat since Lyndon Johnson, but he had the smallest share of votes from the other party in many decades.

Such polarization has encouraged candidates for the presidency to play more heavily and persistently to their base. In Washington, moreover, comity between the branches is now less evident, as they are controlled by different parties. Timely passage of important legislation is extraordinarily challenging. Government shutdowns have not become routine, but they have been frequently threatened and occasionally endured.

Still, one should not exaggerate the novelty of political polarization. Partisanship was comparably intense during the McCarthy era in the 1950s and during the Vietnam War in the 1960s and 1970s. Indeed, Harry Truman, Lyndon Johnson, Richard Nixon, Jimmy Carter, Bill Clinton, George W. Bush, and Barack Obama were all polarizing figures in their own ways. None approached politics as if they were playing bean bag. Politics only occasionally stopped "at the water's edge."

But the impact of intense partisanship on foreign policy has been muted even in the wake of the Cold War. Bill Clinton relied on Republican support to secure ratification of NAFTA and GATT. Bob Dole, Clinton's rival in the 1996 election, was a steadfast supporter of his "lift and strike" policy and the Dayton Agreement on Bosnia in 1995.

George W. Bush was the target of harsh vituperation when the Iraq War went sour, but leading Democratic figures in the Senate, like Hillary Clinton, Joe Biden, and John Kerry, all voted to authorize the use of force there. While Barack Obama ran against George W. Bush's record in 2008, his policies in 2009 and 2010, as we have seen, revealed a surprising degree of continuity with course adjustments that Bush had undertaken during his second term.

By 2012, President Obama had "outflanked the GOP from the right" sufficiently, so that in the campaign debate on foreign policy, Mitt Romney did not challenge Obama's time line for extricating U.S. combat troops from Afghanistan, his withdrawal of all U.S. forces from Iraq, his reluctance to involve the U.S. militarily in Syria, his search for alternatives to a military strike on Iranian nuclear facilities, or his plans to devote more attention and resources to shoring up America's position and presence in East Asia.

It is certainly unusual for the American people to elect three successive presidents as inexperienced in foreign and military affairs as Bill Clinton, George W. Bush, and Barack Obama. Fortunately, the effects were somewhat mitigated by the fact that all three got two terms in office. These presidents' early miscues were not irretrievable, and they were able to learn from their mistakes. Bill Clinton and George W. Bush displayed a greater aptitude for foreign policy in their second terms than in their first. That may be the historical verdict on President Obama as well, but the jury is still out.

Looking at postwar presidents, it seems apparent that experience with the world beyond our borders helps. But it does not guarantee a stellar foreign policy record. Harry Truman assumed the presidency with a somewhat insular, provincial background, and Franklin Roosevelt did not even bother to inform his vice president that the Manhattan Project to produce an atomic bomb was nearing completion. Yet Truman compiled a formidable foreign policy legacy. Few of our presidents assumed office with a more cosmopolitan background than John Kennedy, and he was a genuine war hero. But his early foreign policy miscues were among the worst experienced by any of our post-1945 chief executives.

Long, costly, and inconclusive wars in Afghanistan and Iraq cast a long shadow on the record of George W. Bush. Yet his national security team included two former secretaries of defense (Dick Cheney and Don Rumsfeld) and a secretary of state (Colin Powell) who had previously served as national security adviser and chairman of the Joint Chiefs of Staff.

Can one say that any of our post–Cold War presidents—other than George H. W. Bush—have compiled stellar foreign policy records? I think not. To be sure, some progress has been achieved in eliminating al-Qaeda leaders, disrupting its operations, and avoiding another major attack on the United States.

There were other credit-worthy achievements. Free-trade agreements were signed and ratified. North Korea's plutonium program was capped for eight years. America helped mediate dangerous disputes in Northern Ireland and elsewhere .The Millennium Fund, an interesting innovation in the field of development assistance, was created and a major anti-AIDS fund established for Africa. Wars in Iraq and Afghanistan have been wound down.

But in general, big problems have tended to fester rather than be resolved. Periodic attempts to broker an Israeli-Palestinian peace agreement have failed. India, Pakistan, and North Korea have joined the ranks of nuclear proliferators, and Iran is knocking on the door. The Doha multilateral trade round has sputtered to a standstill. Regional free-trade agreements with Asian and European powers are in the works, but no deals have yet been struck. Attempts to regulate other transnational problems like global climate change have fallen well short of major tangible achievements. Mullah Omar (the leader of the Afghan Taliban), Saddam Hussein, and Muammar Gaddafi were driven from power, but sectarian strife persists in the Middle East and South Asia; neither Iraq nor Afghanistan boasts anything approximating stable democratic governance; and we are now at war with an even more brutal terrorist organization: ISIS.

Meanwhile, fiscal realities and a war-weary public impel the United States to operate as a more frugal superpower at a time when potent regional powers like Russia, China, and Iran appear eager to challenge the political or territorial status quo.

The trajectory of these developments notwithstanding, they do not appear to have fundamentally altered the ways in which our election system helps to shape American foreign policy. Presidential elections continue to bring new leaders and new ideas into the policy-making process. They provide opportunities to abandon policies that lead into blind alleys or costly, inconclusive conflicts; to redefine objectives with greater modesty or provide more adequate resources to implement ideas that evince promise; to inspire course corrections without disrupting the continuity of policies that produce visible results; and to provide firm deadlines, enabling negotiators occasionally to reach important deals.

Of course, there are the downsides that we have noted. Campaigns have gotten longer and more expensive, thus increasing the influence of special interests, and the role of political advisers of peripheral relevance to the conduct of foreign policy.

REFORMING THE PRESIDENTIAL ELECTION SYSTEM

Could we foster a steadier, less volatile, and more creative foreign policy by adjusting the American presidential election system? It is worthwhile to examine the possibilities.

Certain features of our system have been the subject of strong and repeated complaints—above all, the length and costs of campaigns, the sequencing of primaries, the fairness of the Electoral College, and the casual manner in which vice presidential nominees are selected. Yet these aspects of our system have proved particularly difficult to regulate.

• Campaign finance reforms have been implemented from time to time, but they have neither reduced the overall cost of presidential campaigns nor diminished the evident influence of special-interest groups on their financing. Recent Supreme Court decisions—above all, in the *Citizens United v. Federal Election Commission* decision in 2010, and the *McCarthy v. Federal Election Commission* verdict in 2014—have permitted gigantic increases in spending while diminishing the transparency of the donors.

• The schedule of primaries is subject to constant adjustment, as states compete to optimize the impact of their voters in determining the party's nominees. If anything, this has front-loaded the primaries, thereby increasing pressures to start presidential campaigns even earlier, thus assuring that they last longer.

• The Electoral College has been a persistent target for complaints—particularly among residents of the more populous states. But as long as we retain our federal system, the prospects for its elimination are negligible, though individual states continue to experiment with different methods of apportioning their votes.

• The selection of vice presidents remains decisively influenced by the political calculus of presidential candidates, who are mainly interested in a running mate who can help the most in securing their election. It is noteworthy that since 1976, most nominees of both major parties have sought running mates who possess some experience in the field of foreign affairs.[20]

Altering the fundamentals of the American presidential election system is inherently difficult. The basic rules are enshrined in the Constitution, whose amendment is appropriately challenging. Amendments have indeed been passed over the years requiring the vice presidential and presidential candidates to run on the same ticket, shortening the length of the transition between Election Day and Inauguration Day, and limiting presidents to two terms, for example. But the obstacles can be overcome only if there is a widespread consensus that a particular feature of the system is seriously flawed and also substantial agreement on how to fix it.

Several decades ago, many argued that a single, six-year term would result in a reduced level of policy volatility and a significant improvement in presidential performance. Cyrus Vance, a former secretary of state, was among the leading proponents of this reform. He put the case straightforwardly:

It takes each new president from six to nine months to learn his job and to feel comfortable in the formulation and execution of foreign policy. For the next eighteen months the president can operate with assurance. But during the last year or so, he is running for re-election and is forced to divert much of his attention to campaigning. As a result, many issues are ignored and important decisions are deferred. Sometimes bad decisions are made under the pressures of months of primary elections. And at home and overseas, we are frequently seen as inconsistent and unstable.[21]

As the analyses in this book suggest, the electoral calendar does impose some deleterious effects on the conduct of foreign policy. Yet changing to a single, six-year term would not provide a guaranteed remedy for the problems Vance described. It would create its own unique obstacles to the formulation and execution of effective strategy and diplomacy. And it remains of doubtful efficacy.

Elections enforce accountability. Often, as we have seen, the prospect of a reelection campaign may exert a salutary influence by forcing an incumbent to tackle foreign policy issues that have been neglected or to fix diplomatic initiatives that have gone off track. Limiting an incumbent to one term, moreover, will assuredly consign him to earlier lame duck status, thereby diminishing his power and weakening his ability to accomplish results. If the electorate chooses a chief executive who proves to be ineffectual, moreover, six years can be a very long time. Alternatively, if the president performs impressively, why deprive voters of a chance to extend his tenure?

The practicality of this proposal, which requires amending the Constitution, was tested in the 1980s when a number of public-interest advocacy groups promoted the idea. Neither politicians nor the public warmly embraced the concept then, and there is little perceptible interest in it today.

In any event, the shortcomings of a four-year term are mitigated by the fact that the "normal political cycle" is for presidents to serve two terms.[22] This arguably provides them enough time to learn the ropes, make necessary course corrections in response to mistakes, and still compile a substantial record. By most accounts, Ronald Reagan, Bill Clinton, and George W. Bush performed their foreign policy duties more effectively in their second terms than in their first.

Campaign debates have proliferated rapidly, particularly during the scramble for a party's nomination. Yet the greater visibility of the candidates has not thoughtfully illuminated the substantive differences between them, particularly on foreign policy issues. There is no magic formula. Participation in debates during the primary season is voluntary, and during the general election period the detailed arrangements are negotiated among the candidates, who do not approach the matter with objective detachment. They consistently attempt to shape the number, the subjects, and the format of debates to suit their political calculus. The result is inevitably a political compromise or alternatively the reflection of a failure to reach one.[23] Today there is a widespread expectation on the part of voters that at least one debate—and more likely three, plus one between the vice-presidential candidates—will take place. But the modalities remain up for grabs, and the voters, perhaps through public interest advocacy groups, deserve stronger representation in the negotiations over these.

Jim Steinberg and Kurt Campbell argued before the 2008 election that the transitions from one administration to another were becoming both more complex and potentially more dangerous.[24] Their arguments possess persuasive logic, and their recommendations for managing transitions more effectively have evident merit. Yet the Obama transition was comparatively smooth. Early foreign policy miscues were not extraordinarily numerous or damaging. No foreign country nor terrorist movement sought to exploit the transition by provoking a crisis or mounting an attack. Perhaps we were merely lucky.

I suspect, however, that more than luck was involved. Experience suggests that crises abroad stimulate unity at home. The public generally rallies around the flag—and the president—in an emergency. It is dangerous for foreigners to alienate a new president before he settles into the Oval Office. There is no political pressure at present to shorten the current ten-week transition and no self-evident reason to push for this.

The most vulnerable moments in a transition generally occur after a new president is inaugurated. Many make early mistakes, and this is attributable to the fact that it takes time to get an administration organized, staffed, and up to speed. Many have offered sensible suggestions for the wise management of this start-up period in a new administration. Hastening the confirmation process, making it more transparent, requiring up-or-down votes on political appointees within a prescribed time period, and eliminating the so-called secret holds on nominees are among the useful procedural suggestions that regularly circulate as new administrations take shape.

Such suggestions have merit, but the Senate, apparently considering them as challenges to its prerogatives, consistently ignores or opposes them. Without more comity between the branches, such recommendations are unlikely to be implemented. That is a shame, but it is nonetheless an objective reality. That, however, is no reason to cease denouncing dysfunctional practices.

Given current fiscal realities, it might be more realistic to strive to reduce the number of political appointees assigned to foreign policy departments and agencies. Their numbers have been steadily growing in recent decades. There are far too many of them already, and the increase in their numbers has almost inevitably been accompanied by an unseemly inflation in titles. A deputy associate undersecretary sounds like an oxymoron, and those occupying such positions generally add nothing to policy making except more required clearances, more confusion about lines of accountability, and more bureaucratic ballast.

A reduction in the number of such appointees could reduce the size of staffs to more manageable proportions, speed the pace of getting new administrations up and running, and possibly ease relations between political appointees and the foreign affairs bureaucracy. Promoting such limited adjustments in the system is, I believe, a worthy endeavor, even if the benefits may be relatively modest.

Promoting greater bipartisanship could also bolster U.S. foreign policy without altering the fundamentals of our presidential election system. It is a worthy aim, but the notion that "politics stops at the water's edge" on foreign policy matters has even less salience in Washington today than it once did.

The parties have sorted themselves out ideologically. There are fewer conservative southerners among Democrats in the House, and moderate Republicans appear to be a vanishing breed in Washington. Thus the anchors of bipartisanship are less weighty; habits of consultation and coordination between the parties have deteriorated; the civility of political rhetoric has declined; fewer members of Congress appear to cultivate personal friendships across the aisle (not least because there are more "safe seats," and the current congressional schedule now allows incumbents to return to their districts most weekends); and fewer individual senators aspire to play the kind of role that Arthur Vandenberg, a GOP senator from Michigan, did with the Truman administration, or Sam Nunn and John Glenn, Democratic senators from Georgia and Ohio respectively, did with the Reagan and George H. W. Bush administrations.

Still, significant policies have survived recent changes of political control of the White House. A minimal degree of bipartisanship remains essential to governance when party control of the branches or the Congress is divided. Palpable threats to the nation's security encourage concerted action in response, and the globalization of the economy enforces some measure of continuity on U.S. policies vis-à-vis trade, currency, and investment issues if the country is to thrive. In short, the necessity for some bipartisanship persists, though it is harder than in the past to attain.

In short, a search for adjustments in the presidential election system is unlikely to offer major improvements in the quality of the nation's foreign policy. In the end, such improvements will depend on the quality of the candidates selected by our two major parties and on the wisdom of the electorate in choosing between them.

Such choices involve an irreducible element of conjecture about how individuals with limited experience overseas will meet the daunting challenges presented by ever-changing international circumstances. Harry Truman, who took the helm in 1945 with scant foreign policy background, put the pillars of a durable containment policy in place. Ronald Reagan, widely regarded by the press in 1980 as a "cowboy," unencumbered by relevant overseas experience, managed, with the help of his secretary of state, George Shultz, to initiate transformative changes in East–West relations.

In short, some experience abroad counts. In the end judgment trumps experience. So does character. Selecting men or women possessing these qualities will best sustain the nation's ability to thrive in a dangerous world. A democracy like ours properly locates the responsibility for making those choices in the hands of its citizens, and within the peculiarities of our presidential election system the voters have acquitted their duties with generally laudable discernment. It does not hurt, as the German statesman Otto von Bismarck once ruefully remarked, that "a special Providence looks out for drunks, fools, and Americans."

NOTES

INTRODUCTION

1. Quoted in Alexander M. Haig Jr., *Caveat: Realism, Reagan, and Foreign Policy* (London: Weidenfeld and Nicolson), 80.

2. Zbigniew K. Brzezinski, *Power and Principle: Memoirs of the National Security Adviser, 1977–1981* (New York: Farrar, Straus and Giroux, 1983).

3. Ibid., 544.

4. Kenneth N. Waltz, *Foreign Policy and Democratic Politics: The American and British Experience* (Boston: Little, Brown, 1967).

5. William B. Quandt, *Camp David: Peacemaking and Politics* (Washington, D.C.: Brookings Institution Press, 1986).

6. Kurt M. Campbell and James B. Steinberg, *Difficult Transitions: Foreign Policy Troubles at the Outset of Presidential Power* (Washington, D.C.: Brookings Institution Press, 2008).

7. Richard E. Neustadt, *Presidential Power: The Politics of Leadership* (New York: Macmillan, 1960).

1. ELECTIONS, PARTIES, AND POLITICS

1. It was for this reason that Richard Cheney, a resident of Texas in 2000, was impelled to re-register to vote in Wyoming, where he was born, and which he had for several terms represented in the Congress.

2. There are two exceptions—Maine and Nebraska. There the candidate who wins a plurality of the popular vote receives two Electoral College votes; the other votes are assigned to candidates based on the popular vote in each congressional district. For a detailed enumeration of the changing laws, regulations, and practices that govern the U.S. electoral process, see Candice J. Nelson and Grant Park, *The Democratization of Presidential Elections, 1968–2008* (Washington, D.C.: Brookings Institution Press, 2011).

3. Originally, the transition continued into March of the year following the election—a practice reflecting the time required in the 1780s to make the rigorous journey to the nation's capitol, which was at that time in Philadelphia; it was subsequently moved to Washington.

4. Lawrence O'Brien, *No Final Victories* (New York: Doubleday, 1974), 324.

5. The Twelfth Amendment to the Constitution, published in 1804, prescribed that electors cast separate ballots for president and vice president. Previously, they cast only one, and the candidate receiving the most votes became president. The individual with the second largest total became vice president.

6. Joe Klein, *Politics Lost: How American Democracy Was Trivialized by People Who Think You're Stupid* (New York: Doubleday, 2006), 15.

7. Robert Merry, "Bring Back Smoke-Filled Rooms?" [op-ed], *Wall Street Journal*, December 1, 2011, A17.

8. As opposed to "super delegates," those members of the party's leadership that were given the right to choose among the candidates without regard for the results in state primaries or caucuses.

9. Quoted in Robert Merry, "Bring Back the Smoke Filled Rooms," *Wall Street Journal*, December 1, 2011, A17.

10. John W. Lederle, "Party Finance in a Presidential Election Year," in "Parties and Politics: 1948," special issue, *Annals of the American Academy of Political and Social Science* 259 (1948): 64.

11. Edward M. Kennedy, *True Compass* (New York: Twelve, 2009), 169.

12. Quoted in John Heilemann and Mark Halperin, *Game Change: Obama and the Clintons, McCain and Palin, and the Race of a Lifetime* (New York: Harper-Collins, 2009), 36.

13. For a thoughtful analysis of the sources of this polarization and its consequences, see Ronald Brownstein, *The Second Civil War: How Extreme Partisanship Has Paralyzed Washington and Polarized America* (New York: Penguin Press, 2007).

14. Gerald Seib, "Election Sharpens the Partisan Divide" [op-ed], *Wall Street Journal*, December 11, 2012, A6. While moderate Republicans are frequently portrayed as a vanishing breed in Washington, Republican voters in the blue states, while generally conservative, tend to be less religious, more urban, and more affluent and to put more stock in a candidate's electability than their counterparts in the red states. They do exert influence in their party's nomination fights, gener-

ally back establishment figures, and pose obstacles for those campaigning as dyed-in-the-wool right wingers.

15. Mark Halperin and John Heilemann, *The Way to Win: Taking the White House in 2008* (New York: Random House, 2006), 3–66.

16. Karl Rove, *Courage and Consequence: My Life as a Conservative in the Fight* (New York: Threshold, 2010), 71.

17. James Kitfield, "Mitt Romney's Neo-Con Puzzle," *National Interest*, September–October 2012, 29–39.

18. Henry Wallace, was a political force in the Democratic Party in the mid-1940s, but by the time Truman's term ended, Wallace Democrats were virtually extinct.

19. Klein, *Politics Lost*, 49.

20. Brownstein, *Second Civil War*, 195–200.

21. Peter Beinart, *The Good Fight: Why Liberals, and Only Liberals, Can Win the War on Terror* (New York: HarperCollins, 2006), 25.

22. Paraphrased from a quote by Richard Betts, cited in Derek Chollet and James Goldgeier, *America Between the Wars: From 11/9 to 9/11* (New York: Public Affairs, 2008), 326.

23. John Micklethwait and Adrian Wooldridge, *Right Nation: Conservative Power in America* (New York: Penguin Press, 2004), 139.

2. QUEST FOR THE NOMINATION

1. Presidents Eisenhower in 1956, Johnson in 1964, Nixon in 1972, Reagan in 1984, Clinton in 1996, and Bush in 2004 faced no serious challenge for renomination. Arguably, they may have adapted their foreign policies modestly to consolidate the support and enthusiasm of their base and head off other contenders for the nomination. But none had to pay obeisance to their "base" to avert an insurrection among party regulars.

2. In George Kennan's concise summary, in *Memoirs: 1950–1963* (Boston: Little, Brown, 1972), 94–95, quoted in Stephen Sestanovich, in *Maximalist: America in the World from Truman to Obama* (New York: Knopf, 2014), 63.

3. The characterization supplied by the chairman of the Joint Chiefs of Staff, General Omar Bradley.

4. Quoted in Sheila Miyoshi Jager, *Brothers at War: The Unending Conflict in Korea* (New York: Norton, 2013), 200–201.

5. Quoted in Gideon Rose, *How Wars End: Why We Always Fight the Last Battle* (New York: Simon & Schuster, 2010), 141.

6. The U.S. ambassador to South Korea was aware of these practices and reported extensively on them. See ibid., 147.

7. U. Alexis Johnson, *The Right Hand of Power: The Memoirs of an American Diplomat* (New York: Prentice Hall, 1984), 130.

8. Robert Dallek, *Lyndon B. Johnson: Portrait of a President* (Oxford: Oxford University Press, 2004), 318.

9. Ibid., 313.

10. Sestanovich, *Maximalist*, 157.

11. Clark Clifford, *Counsel to the President: A Memoir* (New York: Random House, 1991), 503.

12. David McCullough, *Truman* (New York: Simon and Schuster, 1992), 907.

13. The president recognized the need to make policy adjustments to mitigate the growing disenchantment with the war effort.

14. For example, Keynesian economics, the appointment of liberal judges, the institution of wage and price controls, exploration of affirmative action in the field of employment, the creation of the Department of Education, and the establishment of Earth Day.

15. Supporters of Henry "Scoop" Jackson, the longtime senator from Washington State.

16. Craig Shirley, *Reagan's Revolution: The Untold Story of the Campaign That Started It All* (New York: Nelson Current, 2005), 123.

17. James Baker, *Work Hard, Study, and Keep Out of Politics!* (New York: Putnam, 2006), 51.

18. Quoted in Douglas Brinkley, *Gerald R. Ford* (New York: Times Books, 2007), 138.

19. Ford even delayed abruptly a long-planned signing ceremony with the Soviet Union to limit the megatonnage of underground nuclear blasts, for fear it might be portrayed as a weakening of our defense effort. See Shirley, *Reagan's Revolution*, 214–215.

20. State Department efforts to move China policy along by facilitating expanded access in the U.S. textile market were short-circuited by Dick Cheney and Jim Baker, who for political reasons were eager to placate textile interests in key southern states where Reagan's challenge was particularly strong.

21. Shirley, *Reagan's Revolution*, 179.

22. Henry Kissinger, *Years of Renewal* (New York: Simon & Schuster, 1999), 764.

23. Ibid., 760.

24. Patrick Tyler, *A Great Wall: Six Presidents and China: An Investigative History* (New York: Public Affairs, 1999), 195–196.

25. Ford's decision to spurn a request for a meeting with Aleksandr Solzhenitsyn damaged him with conservatives, but he claimed in his memoirs that he "decided to subordinate political gains to foreign policy considerations" (*A Time to Heal: The Autobiography of Gerald R. Ford* [New York: Harper & Row, 1979], 298).

26. When Kissinger proposed to slow down an initiative toward Namibia lest it adversely affect the president's reelection chances, Ford admonished him to persevere: "I think if South Africa is involved in the solution, [and] if it is right, we should do it, and the political consequences will come out all right" (quoted in Kissinger, *Years of Renewal*, 983).

27. Hamilton Jordan, *Crisis: The Last Year of the Carter Presidency* (New York: Putnam, 1982), 301.

28. Kenneth M. Pollack has argued persuasively that Khomeini had no interest in a negotiated settlement with the United States until the fall of 1980 when the hostages had served Khomeini's purpose in mobilizing support for the revolutionaries; the attack by Iraq highlighted Iran's need for military spare parts; and Iran's position in the Muslim world was being eroded by its continued hostage-holding, in *The Persian Puzzle: The Conflict Between Iran and America* (New York: Random House, 2004), 130–172.

29. Jordan, *Crisis*, 100.

30. Jimmy Carter, *Keeping Faith: Memoirs of a President* (New York: Bantam Books, 1995), 466.

31. Richard Darman, *Who's in Control? Polar Politics and the Sensible Center* (New York: Simon & Schuster, 1996), 15.

32. When the president was forced to leave the dinner, looking pale but game, Barbara Bush remained to give his toast. She glanced at me with mock severity, and noted, "The president's illness was Ambassador Armacost's fault. He and the president played tennis with the Emperor and Crown Prince this afternoon. They lost. In fact they lost badly, and it just makes George sick to lose!" She then smiled broadly, and the crowd laughed. Unfortunately, the film clips shown on television that weekend ended before she smiled. A number of friends called subsequently to inquire whether my next posting would be to Mali, Madagascar, or Mongolia.

33. Zbigniew Brzezinski, *Second Chance: Three Presidents and the Crisis of American Superpower* (New York: Basic Books, 2007), 79.

34. To be sure, it did not bring the process to a successful conclusion. Negotiations quickly stalled. The Gulf War had not dissipated distrust between the parties nor had it overcome their reflexive reluctance to adopt a conciliatory approach to the bargaining.

35. Dennis Ross, *The Missing Peace: The Inside Story of the Fight for Middle East Peace* (New York: Farrar, Straus and Giroux, 2004), 85.

36. Townsend Hoopes, *The Devil and John Foster Dulles* (Boston: Little, Brown, 1973), 132.

37. Quoted in Dan Balz and Haynes Johnson, *The Battle for America: The Story of an Extraordinary Election* (New York: Viking, 2009), 21–22.

38. Brinkley, *Gerald Ford*, 53.

39. Ford readily acknowledged that he was not Nixon's first choice. Due to an amendment to the Constitution, his choice required Senate confirmation; Nelson Rockefeller was opposed by conservatives, Ronald Reagan by liberals, John Connally was involved at the time in a scandal, and Melvin Laird maneuvered skillfully to avoid the nod. Ford was the candidate who seemed most likely to sail

through the Senate unscathed. See Thomas M. DeFrank, *Write It When I'm Gone: Remarkable Off-the Record Conversations with Gerald R. Ford* (New York: Putnam, 2007), 204.

40. Robert Caro, *The Passage of Power*, vol. 4 of *The Years of Lyndon Johnson* (New York: Knopf, 2012), 115.

41. Shirley Anne Warshaw, *The Co-Presidency of Bush and Cheney* (Stanford, Calif.: Stanford University Press, 2009); Barton Gellman, *The Angler: The Cheney Vice Presidency* (New York: Penguin Press, 2008), 1–60.

42. There was one additional advantage; if Johnson became vice president, he would vacate the Senate majority leader's job, thus permitting Kennedy to install the more pliant and adaptable Mike Mansfield.

43. Quoted in Balz and Johnson, *Battle for America*, 315.

3. CAMPAIGNS

1. H. R. Haldeman, *The Haldeman Diaries: Inside the Nixon White House* (New York: Putnam, 1994), 298.

2. For detailed reconstructions of Truman's decision and the political and strategic considerations that shaped it, see David McCullough, *Truman* (New York: Simon & Schuster, 1993), 595–620; Michael Beschloss, *Presidential Courage: Brave Leaders and How They Changed America, 1789–1989* (New York: Simon & Schuster, 2007), 211–220; and Allis Radosh and Ronald Radosh, *A Safe Haven: Harry Truman and the Founding of Israel* (New York: HarperCollins, 2009).

3. Quoted in Robert Suettinger, *Beyond Tiananmen: The Politics of U.S.-China Relations, 1989–2000* (Washington, D.C.: Brookings Institution Press, 2003), 141.

4. Taylor Branch, *The Clinton Tapes: Wrestling History with the President* (New York: Simon & Schuster, 2009), 394.

5. Stephen Sestanovich, *Maximalist: America in the World from Truman to Obama* (New York: Knopf, 2014), 3–13.

6. Robert Caro, *The Passage of Power*, vol. 4 of *The Years of Lyndon Johnson* (New York: Knopf, 2012), 235.

7. Quoted in Clarke Thurston, *JFK's Last Hundred Days: The Transformation of a Man and the Emergence of a Great President* (New York: Penguin, 2013), 63.

8. Caro, *Passage of Power*, 402.

9. Ibid., 390.

10. Michael Beschloss, *Taking Charge: The Johnson White House Tapes, 1963–1964* (New York: Simon & Schuster, 1997), 362.

11. Gordon M. Goldstein, *Lessons in Disaster: McGeorge Bundy and the Path to War in Vietnam* (New York: Times Books, 2008), 97.

12. H. R. McMaster, *Dereliction of Duty: Lyndon Johnson, Robert McNamara, the Joint Chiefs of Staff, and the Lies that Led to Vietnam* (New York: Harper/Perennial, 1997), 78.

13. In July 1964, at General Taylor's request, Johnson increased the U.S. military advisory force in Vietnam from 16,000 to 22,000, but neither the public nor Congress was informed.

14. Caro, *Passage of Power*, 535.

15. Goldstein, *Lessons in Disaster*, 133.

16. Quoted in Stanley Karnow, *Vietnam: A History* (New York: Viking, 1983), 395.

17. Ibid.,133–134.

18. Quoted in Randall B. Woods, *LBJ: Architect of American Ambition* (New York: Free Press, 2006), 516.

19. Goldstein, *Lessons in Disaster*, 137–143.

20. Quoted in Robert Dallek, *Nixon and Kissinger: Partners in Power* (New York: HarperCollins, 2007), 266.

21. Ibid., 269.

22. Haldeman, *Haldeman Diaries*, 223.

23. Soviet military aid to Hanoi surged 30 percent in 1971.

24. Henry A. Kissinger, *White House Years* (Boston: Little, Brown, 1982), 1066.

25. Haldeman, *Haldeman Diaries*, 391.

26. Kissinger, *White House Years*, 1362.

27. For example, Saigon's political prisoners, arms replacement questions, and a cease-fire in Laos and Cambodia.

28. Theodore White, *The Making of the President, 1972* (New York: Atheneum, 1973), 116.

29. Quoted in John Harris, *The Survivor: Bill Clinton in the White House* (New York: Random House, 2005), 44.

30. Ibid., 51.

31. For ample evidence of this search, see Richard Sale, *Clinton's Secret Wars: The Evolution of a Commander in Chief* (New York: St. Martin's Press, 2009), 42–51.

32. Quoted in William Hyland, *Clinton's World: Remaking American Foreign Policy* (London: Praeger, 1999), 143.

33. Harris, *Survivor*, 197.

34. Ibid., 201.

35. Ivo H. Daalder, *Getting to Dayton: The Making of America's Bosnia Policy* (Washington, D.C.: Brookings Institution Press, 2000), esp. chap. 3 for an analysis of the Clinton administration's shift from a policy of containment to one of engagement.

36. Richard Holbrooke, *To End a War* (New York: Modern Library, 1998), esp. 231–315.

37. Ibid., 345.

38. Thus read the banner on an aircraft carrier onto which President George W. Bush flew in the spring of 2004 to hail the success of the military campaign in Iraq.

39. Bremer did not attribute the decision to political or electoral pressures, but he acknowledged their presence: "Although nobody spelled it out," he said, "I could figure it out." This accelerated timetable also furnished a convenient occasion to shuffle Ambassador Bremer offstage.

40. George Shultz, *Turmoil and Triumph: Diplomacy, Power, and the Victory of the American Deal* (New York: Simon & Schuster, 1993), 466.

41. Beth A. Fischer, *The Reagan Reversal: Foreign Policy and the End of the Cold War* (Columbia: University of Missouri Press, 1997), 36.

42. Shultz, *Turmoil and Triumph*, 467.

43. Ronald Reagan, *The Reagan Diaries*, ed. Douglas Brinkley (New York: Harper-Collins, 2007), 210.

44. Quoted in James Mann, *The Rebellion of Ronald Reagan: A History of the End of the Cold War* (New York: Viking, 2009), 79.

45. Henry Kissinger, *Years of Renewal* (New York: Simon & Schuster, 1999), 765–767.

46. Ibid., 989.

47. Ibid., 1015.

48. Walter Isaacson and Evan Thomas, *The Wise Men: Six Friends and the World They Made* (New York: Simon & Schuster, 1986), 461. Luce, a Republican from Connecticut, was elected to the House of Representatives in 1942; in 1952, President Eisenhower appointed her ambassador to Italy and in 1959 ambassador to Brazil.

49. McCullough, *Truman*, 631.

50. Ibid., 648.

51. Ibid., 648–649.

52. Isaacson and Thomas, *Wise Men*, 461–462.

53. Sestanovich, *Maximalist*, 77.

54. Quoted in Jean Edward Smith, *Eisenhower in War and Peace* (New York: Random House, 2012), 697.

55. Smith noted that "the agreement was largely hortatory," and "left the signatories considerable wiggle room" (ibid., 687).

56. Townsend Hoopes, *The Devil and John Foster Dulles* (Boston: Little, Brown, 1973), 373.

57. Smith, *Eisenhower in War and Peace*, 697.

58. James Hagerty, in Eisenhower Administration Project, part 4, 216–217, microfiche, Columbia Center for Oral History, Butler Library, Columbia University, New York.

59. Andrew Goodpaster, in Eisenhower Administration Project, part 4, 83, microfiche, Columbia Center for Oral History.

60. Hamilton Jordan, *Crisis: The Last Year of the Carter Presidency* (New York: Putnam, 1982), 19.

61. Ibid., 180.

62. Gary Sick, *October Surprise: America's Hostages in Iran and the Election of Ronald Reagan* (New York: Times Books, 1991), 101.

63. Jordan, *Crisis*, 55.

64. Sick, *October Surprise*, 159.

65. Warren Christopher, *Chances of a Lifetime* (New York: Simon & Schuster, 2001). Presidential papers that might illuminate this issue have not been opened to public scrutiny.

66. Kenneth M. Pollack, *The Persian Puzzle: The Conflict Between Iran and America* (New York: Random House, 2004), 171.

4. CAMPAIGNS

1. Ted Sorensen, *Kennedy: The Classic Biography* (New York: HarperCollins, 2009), 205; Arthur Schlesinger, *A Thousand Days: John F. Kennedy in the White House* (New York: Houghton Mifflin, 1965), 72.

2. John Prados, *Safe for Democracy: The Secret Wars of the CIA* (Chicago: Dee, 2006), 239.

3. Sorensen, *Kennedy*, 206.

4. For an analysis of this episode in covert action, see Stephen Kinzer, *The Brothers: John Foster Dulles, Allen Dulles, and Their Secret World War* (New York: Times Books, 2013), 147–160.

5. Andrew Bacevich, *Washington Rules: America's Path to Permanent War* (New York: Metropolitan Books, 2010), 63–64.

6. Quoted in Robert Dallek, *Nixon and Kissinger: Partners in Power* (New York: HarperCollins, 2007), 85.

7. Quoted in James Traub, *The Freedom Agenda: Why America Must Spread Democracy (Just Not the Way George Bush Did)* (New York: Farrar, Straus and Giroux, 2008), 3.

8. The phrase was George Stephanopoulos's in *All Too Human: A Political Education* (Boston: Little, Brown, 1999), 157.

9. Quoted in Sorensen, *Kennedy*, 157.

10. Quoted in John Heileman and Mark Halperin, *Game Change: Obama and the Clintons, McCain and Palin, and the Race of a Lifetime* (New York: Harper-Collins, 2010), 111.

11. Quoted in Herbert S. Parmet, *Eisenhower and the American Crusades* (New York: Macmillan, 1972), 143.

12. The CNN headline at trip's end, "Was Romney's trip a 'great success' or gaffe-filled disaster?" was not the result that Romney coveted. See John Sides and Lynn Vavreck, *The Gamble: Choice and Chance in the 2012 Presidential Election* (Princeton, N.J.: Princeton University Press, 2014), 116–117.

13. James Lilley and Jeffrey Lilley, *China Hands: Nine Decades of Adventure, Espionage, and Diplomacy in Asia* (New York: Public Affairs, 2004), 220.

14. Ibid.

15. Quoted in Bob Woodward, *State of Denial: Bush at War, Part III* (New York: Simon & Schuster, 2006), 11.

16. Ibid.

17. An outcome that Carter later dismissed as the "if Ford had won the election option."

18. John Harris, *The Survivor: Bill Clinton in the White House* (New York: Random House, 2005), 43.

19. Ibid., 44.

20. E. J. Dionne, "Obama's Bush Doctrine," *Washington Post*, November 28, 2008, A29.

21. David Sanger, *Confront and Conceal: Obama's Secret Wars and Surprising Use of American Power* (New York: Crown, 2012), 18.

22. James Mann, *Rise of the Vulcans: The History of Bush's War Cabinet* (New York: Viking, 2004), esp. 234–260.

5. PRESIDENTIAL TRANSITIONS

1. Jimmy Carter, *Keeping Faith: Memoirs of a President* (New York: Bantam Books, 1995), 230.

2. William P. Marshall and Jack M. Beermann, "The Law of Presidential Transitions," *North Carolina Law Review* 84, no. 4 (2005): 2.

3. Henry A. Kissinger, *White House Years* (Boston: Little, Brown, 1982), 18.

4. Quoted in Colin Powell, *My American Journey* (New York: Random House, 1995), 565.

5. For a case study of this intervention, see Jeane J. Kirkpatrick, *Making War to Keep Peace* (New York: HarperCollins, 2007), chap. 2.

6. William Hyland, *Clinton's World: Remaking American Foreign Policy* (London: Praeger, 1999), 53.

7. Ibid., 54.

8. Bartholomew Sparrow, *The Strategist: Brent Scowcroft and the Call of National Security* (New York: Public Affairs, 2015), 459.

9. Hyland, *Clinton's World*, 51.

10. Powell, *My American Journey*, 566.

11. Walter Bagehot, *The English Constitution* (London: William Clowes, 1867).

12. Recounted in John Prados, *Safe for Democracy: The Secret Wars of the CIA* (Chicago: Dee, 2006), 233, on the basis of Clark Clifford's notes on the Kennedy–Eisenhower meeting.

13. In this respect, Eisenhower perhaps helped box Kennedy in on an issue on which he was in any event risk-averse.

14. He resisted the advice of former president Eisenhower, who urged him to "solicit blanket resignations from all of his senior advisers—in essence to sweep the slate clean and handpick his own team . . . and reorganize the White House, particu-

larly the national security bureaucracy." For McGeorge Bundy's recollection of Eisenhower's advice to LBJ, see Gordon M. Goldstein, *Lessons in Disaster: McGeorge Bundy and the Path to War in Vietnam* (New York: Times Books, 2008), 101–102.

15. Herbert Parmet, *George Bush: The Life of a Lone Star Yankee* (New York: Scribner, 1997), 357.

16. Bill Clinton, *My Life* (New York: Knopf, 2004), 449.

17. Michael Gordon and General Bernard Trainor, *Cobra II: The Inside Story of the Invasion and Occupation of Iraq* (New York: Pantheon, 2006), 14. In 2002, the National Missile Defense (MMD) became the National Missile Agency (NMA) to differentiate the various other missile defense programs.

18. The Bush administration even put together some contingency plans for president-elect Obama in case he confronted crises in his early days in office— for example, a North Korean nuclear test, a cyber attack, or a terrorist strike. See Peter Baker, *Days of Fire: Bush and Cheney in the White House* (New York: Doubleday, 2013), 619.

19. For an elaboration of this theme, see David Rothkopf, *National Insecurity: American Leadership in an Age of Fear* (New York: Public Affairs, 2014), 84–112.

20. Jimmy Carter, *Keeping Faith: Memoirs of a President* (New York: Bantam Books, 1982), 559, 577–580.

21. Al Haig, *Caveat: Realism, Reagan, and Foreign Policy* (New York: Scribner, 1984), 175.

22. Ibid.

23. George Kennan, *Memoirs, 1950–1963* (Boston: Little, Brown, 1972), 170.

24. Richard Reeves, *President Kennedy: Profile of Power* (New York: Simon & Schuster, 1993), 31.

25. Robert Dallek, *An Unfinished Life: John F. Kennedy, 1917–1963* (Boston: Little, Brown, 2003), 304.

26. Reeves, *President Kennedy*, 31.

27. Dallek, *Unfinished Life*, 304.

28. Ibid., 344.

29. Prados, *Safe for Democracy*, 211.

30. Samuel Popkin, *The Candidate: What It Takes to Win—and Hold—the White House* (Oxford: Oxford University Press, 2012), 200.

31. Arthur Schlesinger, *A Thousand Days: John F. Kennedy in the White House* (New York: Houghton Mifflin, 1965), 233.

32. Prados, *Safe for Democracy*, 232.

33. For a detailed exposition of the CIA's evolving plan, see ibid., 204–235.

34. Quoted in David Rothkopf, *Running the World: The Inside Story of the National Security Council and the Architects of American Power* (New York: Public Affairs, 2005), 83.

35. Dwight D. Eisenhower, *White House Years: Waging Peace, 1956–1961* (New York: Doubleday, 2000), 238.

36. Prados, *Safe for Democracy*, 231.

37. Ibid., 232.

38. Clark Clifford, *Counsel to the President: A Memoir* (New York: Random House, 1991), 344.

39. Schlesinger, *Thousand Days*, 238.

40. Kissinger, *White House Years*, 53.

41. Ibid., 49.

42. Even some of LBJ's advisers were initially cool to the idea once the election was over. Clifford initially urged Johnson to start the SALT talks at a lower level, but LBJ was unwilling to commence such discussions "unless they began with a summit" (*Counsel to the President*, 599).

43. Powell, *My American Journey*, 390.

44. At the time, the outcome of the presidential election remained unresolved, tied up by political maneuvering and court action as a result of a dispute over the vote in Florida.

45. For an analysis of these talks, see Peter Beinart, *The Crisis of Zionism* (New York: Times Books, 2012).

46. Dennis Ross, *The Missing Peace: The Inside Story of the Fight for Middle East Peace* (New York: Farrar, Straus and Giroux, 2004), 769.

47. Quoted in Madeleine Albright, *Madame Secretary: A Memoir* (New York: Miramax, 2003), 459.

48. Ibid.

49. Ibid., 463.

50. Don Oberdorfer and Robert Carlin, *The Two Koreas: A Contemporary History* (New York: Basic Books, 1997), 438.

51. Ibid., 468.

52. Ibid., 468–469.

53. Ibid.

54. Ibid., 439.

55. Before president-elect George W. Bush's inauguration, senior Clinton administration officials briefed Colin Powell, the secretary of state–designate, about the state-of-play with Pyongyang. He regarded the possibilities of a deal on missiles as promising, but his conviction was not shared by the president, who made his reservations crystal clear when South Korean president Kim Dae-jung visited Washington in March 2001.

6. LAUNCHING A PRESIDENTIAL TERM

1. Samuel Popkin, *The Candidate: What It Takes to Win—and Hold—the White House* (Oxford: Oxford University Press, 2012), 272.

2. Presidents who are reelected certainly can and do revise their agendas and adapt their styles of governance during the early months of a second term—sometimes in highly consequential ways. But starting from scratch is a quite different enterprise.

3. Stephen Sestanovich, *Maximalist: America in the World from Truman to Obama* (New York: Knopf, 2014), 7.

4. Cyrus Vance, *Hard Choices: Critical Years in America's Foreign Policy* (New York: Simon & Schuster, 1983), 58.

5. Joe Klein, *The Natural: The Misunderstood Presidency of Bill Clinton* (New York: Doubleday, 2002), 81.

6. Harry Truman, Lyndon Johnson, and Gerald Ford inherited policy teams and policy-making procedures from predecessors who had been removed unexpectedly from office by death, assassination, and impeachment, respectively. Inevitably, they accorded initial priority to preserving continuity of personnel and policy. Only gradually did they make their foreign policy team their own and adjust its policy priorities accordingly.

7. Robert Dallek, *Camelot's Court: Inside the Kennedy White House* (New York: HarperCollins, 2013), 75–76.

8. Conrad Black, *Richard M. Nixon: A Life in Full* (New York: Public Affairs, 2007), 573.

9. Cecil V. Crabb and Kevin V. Mulcahy, *American National Security: A Presidential Perspective* (Pacific Grove, Calif.: Brooks/Cole, 1990), 256–257.

10. Dean Acheson, *Present at the Creation: My Years in the State Department* (New York: Norton, 1969), 250.

11. Richard Nixon, *RN: The Memoirs of Richard Nixon* (New York: Grosset and Dunlap, 1978), 952.

12. Quoted in Gordon M. Goldstein, *Lessons in Disaster: McGeorge Bundy and the Path to War in Vietnam* (New York: Times Books, 2008), 43.

13. Arthur M. Schlesinger Jr., *Journals, 1952–2000* (New York: Penguin Press, 2007), 90–91. Arthur Schlesinger Jr., one of Kennedy's close White House aides, acknowledged that his statements about Cuba in his debate with Nixon had been jingoistic. Two distinguished journalists—James Reston and Walter Lippmann—had described those comments as a major campaign blunder.

14. Quoted in Goldstein, *Lessons in Disaster*, 42.

15. Evan Thomas, *Ike's Bluff: President Eisenhower's Secret Battle to Save the World* (Boston: Little, Brown, 2012), 405.

16. Quoted in James Rasenberger, *The Brilliant Disaster: JFK, Castro, and America's Doomed Invasion of Cuba's Bay of Pigs* (New York: Scribner, 2011), 131.

17. Schlesinger, *Journals*, 110.

18. Rasenberger, *Brilliant Disaster*, 120.

19. Richard M. Bissell Jr. Papers, Dwight D. Eisenhower Library, Abilene, Kansas; Bissell, interview with Ed Edwin, June 1967, 32, Eisenhower Administration Project, part 4, Columbia Center for Oral History, Butler Library, Columbia University, New York.

20. Ibid.

21. Ted Sorensen, *Kennedy: The Classic Biography* (New York: HarperCollins, 2009), 305.

22. Rasenberger, *Brilliant Disaster*, 147.

23. McGeorge Bundy was sufficiently annoyed with Goodwin's opposition to the covert operation that he denied him entrée to many meetings in which the issue was to be discussed. See Goldstein, *Lessons in Disaster*, 37.

24. Rasenberger, *Brilliant Disaster*, 158.

25. Ibid., 51.

26. Ibid., 139.

27. Quoted in Frederick Kempe, *Berlin 1961: Kennedy, Khrushchev, and the Most Dangerous Place on Earth* (New York: Penguin, 2011), 174.

28. Sorensen, *Kennedy*, 303.

29. Ibid., 306.

30. Near the end of his life, Bundy came to believe that this is precisely what Bissell and his associates had done, and he regarded it as a form of "entrapment." See Goldstein, *Lessons in Disaster*, 42.

31. Ibid., 44.

32. Quoted in John Lewis Gaddis, *The Cold War: A New History* (New York: Penguin, 2005), 168.

33. When Kennedy took office, there were 700 U.S. military advisers in South Vietnam; by the time he was assassinated in 1963, there were 16,000.

34. Jeane J. Kirkpatrick, *Making War to Keep Peace* (New York: HarperCollins, 2007), 81.

35. Both General Colin Powell and Secretary of Defense Les Aspin were wary about the operation.

36. Kirkpatrick, *Making War to Keep Peace*, 84.

37. These events were recounted in the movie *Black Hawk Down* (2001).

38. Taylor Branch, *The Clinton Tapes: Conversations with a President, 1993–2001* (New York: Simon & Schuster, 2009), 4.

39. For an assessment of the work of the Scowcroft Commission, see Bartholomew Sparrow, *The Strategist: Brent Scowcroft and the Call of National Security* (New York: Public Affairs, 2015), 224–228.

40. Klein, *Natural*, 71.

41. Both wrote retrospective memoirs chiding their Bush administration colleagues for having paid too little heed to their dire warnings: Richard Clarke, *Against All Enemies: Inside America's War on Terror* (New York: Free Press, 2004); and George Tenet, *At the Center of the Storm: My Years at the CIA* (New York: HarperCollins, 2007).

42. James Mann, *Rise of the Vulcans: The History of Bush's War Cabinet* (New York: Viking, 2004), 246.

43. Condoleezza Rice, *No Higher Honor: A Memoir of My Years in Washington* (New York: Crown, 2011), 64.

44. William Gleysteen, *Massive Entanglement; Minimal Influence* (Washington, D.C.: Brookings Institution Press, 1999), 23.

45. Don Oberdorfer and Robert Carlin, *The Two Koreas: A Contemporary History* (New York: Basic Books, 1997), 88.

46. Ibid., 87.

47. Patrick Tyler, *A Great Wall: Six Presidents and China* (New York: Public Affairs, 1999), 386.

48. After the meeting, I asked Lake who the other folks in the Oval Office were. He avoided a direct answer but suggested that it would be clear in the morning newspapers. It was; the *Washington Post* reported allegations involving the president and Paula Jones.

49. David Halberstam, *War in a Time of Peace: Bush, Clinton, and the Generals* (New York: Scribner, 2001), 155.

50. Ibid., 229.

51. Lou Cannon, *President Reagan: The Role of a Lifetime* (New York: Public Affairs, 1991), 56.

52. Jimmy Carter, *Keeping Faith: Memoirs of a President* (New York: Bantam Books, 1995), 159.

53. According to Daniel J. Sargent, President Carter believed that the United States had "cheated the Panamanians out of the canal" (*A Superpower Transformed: The Remaking of American Foreign Relations in the 1970s* [New York: Oxford University Press, 2015], 255).

54. Carter, *Keeping Faith*, 156.

55. John Harris, *The Survivor: Bill Clinton in the White House* (New York: Random House, 2005), 95.

56. Ibid.

57. Branch, *Clinton Tapes*, 84.

58. Sherman Adams, *Firsthand Report: The Story of the Eisenhower Administration* (New York: Harper, 1961), 49.

59. U. Alexis Johnson, *The Right Hand of Power* (Englewood Cliffs, N.J.: Prentice Hall, 1984), 165.

60. David Halberstam, *The Coldest Winter: America and the Korean War* (New York: Hyperion, 2007), 627.

61. NSC-68 was a secret report, approved by President Truman, that outlined key features of what came to be known as the policy of containment that foreshadowed American's post–World War II rearmament.

62. For an analysis of the development of the "New Look" defense policy in 1953 and 1954, see Samuel Huntington, *Common Defense: Strategic Programs in National Politics* (New York: Columbia University Press, 1961), 64–88.

63. A thorough summary of the Solarium Exercise is found in Robert Bowie, *Waging Peace: How Eisenhower Shaped an Enduring Cold War Strategy* (Oxford: Oxford University Press, 2000), 123–146.

64. Ibid., 258.

65. David Rothkopf, *Running the World: The Inside Story of the National Security Council and the Architects of American Power* (New York: Public Affairs), 72.

66. George Kennan, *Memoirs, 1950–1962* (Boston: Little, Brown, 1972), 181–182.

67. H. R. Haldeman, *The Haldeman Diaries: Inside the Nixon White House* (New York: Putnam, 1994), 118; Walter Isaacson, *Kissinger: A Biography* (New York: Simon & Schuster, 1992), 165.

68. *The Reluctant Sheriff* was the title of a book published years later by Richard Haass while serving as vice president for foreign policy at the Brookings Institution in the late 1990s.

69. George H. W. Bush and Brent Scowcroft, *A World Transformed* (New York: Random House, 1999), 60.

70. For a detailed exposition of these political and diplomatic maneuvers, see James A. Baker, *The Politics of Diplomacy* (New York: Putnam, 1995).

CONCLUSION

1. In fact, President Obama doubled down in Afghanistan in early 2009 by authorizing substantial increases in U.S. deployments there before reconsidering the merits of that course a year later.

2. Dick Cheney, *In My Time: A Personal and Political Memoir* (New York: Threshold, 2011), 477.

3. President Bush wanted to allow some U.S. forces to remain until 2015; President Malicki wanted them out by the end of 2010; Obama had the end of 2011 as a target.

4. Stephen Sestanovich, *Maximalist: America in the World from Truman to Obama* (New York: Knopf, 2014), 326.

5. Ibid.

6. Gideon Rose, "Get Real" [op-ed], *New York Times*, August 18, 2005, A23.

7. These enduring truths were the essence of Walter Lippmann's advice to America's leaders during World War II, as in *Foreign Policy: Shield of the Republic* (Boston: Little, Brown, 1943).

8. Eisenhower also presciently warned against the dangers posed by a growing "military–industrial complex," though there is little evidence that his successors paid this much heed.

9. In the wake of the Arab oil embargo, Ford and Kissinger did assimilate into U.S. foreign policy the coordinated management of global interdependence and created the G-7 as an instrument for its pursuit. See Daniel J. Sargent, *A Superpower Transformed: The Remaking of American Foreign Relations in the 1970s* (New York: Oxford University Press, 2015), 165–197.

10. The Carter Doctrine claimed that any attempt by an outside power to gain control of the Persian Gulf region would be an assault on vital U.S. interests to be repelled "by any means necessary, including military force."

11. Clinton's retaliatory measures in responses to terrorist attacks against U.S. facilities in the Middle East and East Africa were dismissed by critics as "pounding sand."

12. Sestanovich, *Maximalist*, 146.

13. Obama also possessed an exalted sense of his ability to transform problems through the power of his rhetoric.

14. Alexis de Tocqueville, *Democracy in America*, ed. Phillips Bradley (New York: Knopf, 1945), 234–235.

15. Ironically, Kennan was a consistent critic of the shape Harry Truman and Dean Acheson, let alone Dwight Eisenhower and John Foster Dulles, gave to the containment policy he had designed. See George F. Kennan and Frank Costigliola, *The Kennan Diaries* (New York: Norton, 2014), esp. 197–276.

16. Britain, France, and Israel were exceptions to this general rule.

17. Andrew Bacevich, *Washington Rules: America's Path to Permanent War* (New York: Metropolitan Books, 2010). Bacevich maintains that the reflexes underpinning these "rules" include a gigantic defense budget and a behemoth military establishment, an incestuous network of special interests served by it, a covey of legislators who serve as "spokespersons" for the military–industrial–congressional complex, and a wide array of NGOs that labor to update its rationale and provide suggestions for its maintenance or expansion.

18. Peter Baker, *Time of Fire: Bush and Cheney in the White House* (New York: Doubleday, 2013), 644.

19. As we have seen, struggles for the nomination place a premium on mobilizing the support of "party regulars" whose national security views are less likely to be marked by an inclination to compromise.

20. There are at least two noteworthy exceptions: George H. W. Bush's choice of Dan Quayle in 1988 and Mitt Romney's selection of Paul Ryan in 2012. Bush possessed more than sufficient foreign policy experience himself; Romney evidently decided that the election would turn almost exclusively on domestic issues.

21. Quoted in William B. Quandt, *Camp David: Peacemaking and Politics* (Washington, D.C.: Brookings Institution Press, 1986), 14–15.

22. Only Jimmy Carter and George H. W. Bush were deprived of a second term, and they appear the exceptions that prove the rule.

23. Nixon felt that his first debate with Kennedy had gone badly in 1960. When facing reelection as an incumbent in 1972, he refused to debate George McGovern.

24. Kurt M. Campbell and James B. Steinberg, *Difficult Transitions: Foreign Policy Troubles at the Outset of Presidential Power* (Washington, D.C.: Brookings Institution Press, 2008).

INDEX